MW01291131

SOUTH KOREA
THE PRICE
OF EFFICIENCY AND SUCCESS

Dani,
Thank you for your
interest in our book.
Best regards,

3-3-30

DR. JOHN GONZALEZ AND YOUNG LEE

SOUTH KOREA: The Price of Efficiency and Success

Copyright © 2019 by John Gonzalez and Young Lee,
skoreaefficiency@gmail.com

All rights reserved. This book or any portion thereof may not be reproduced, stored in a retrieval system, or transmitted in any form or by any means, electronic, photocopy, recording, etc., or used in any manner whatsoever without the prior written permission of the publisher except for the use of brief quotations in a book review.

Independently published
Printed in the United States of America
First Printing, 2019

Cover by Enrique Arredondo (ArsDesigns)
Typesetting by Allan Ytac (Angelleigh)

ISBN: 978-1-67-423215-7

Table of Contents

For the victims of the Sewol ferry tragedy.

Introduction

My Journey to Korea

I began visiting Korea in the 1990s. Before stepping foot on Korean soil, I had made a few friends who told me how beautiful their country was, so I wanted to see it for myself. Some of those trips included meditation tours that enabled me to visit Buddhist temples in rural areas. When the tours had concluded, I would take the time to visit large cities, like Seoul and Busan, on my own to get a different perspective.

As I visited Korea for the first time, the country's technological advancements impressed me to no end. I recall how convenient it was for me, even way back then, to rent a cellular phone at the airport so I could be in touch with friends and family members both in the country and back home. I also recall how impressive it was to walk around in Seoul, where I saw many people using cell phones in the late 1990s. Back in the States, it seemed to me that a smaller percentage of people owned one. After thinking about it, I realized that it made total financial sense for a country, like Korea, which was undergoing a technological transformation, to skip the concept of expanding landlines and embrace the buildup of broadband and wireless technology. After all, it is more efficient.

On my first visit, the "talking elevators" in my hotel also impressed me. I was accustomed to "silent" elevators back home, where I pushed the button to summon it. While waiting for the elevator, especially if I was in a hurry, I would watch the light panel indicating where the elevator was so I could prepare myself to board. When these "silent" American elevators arrived, the doors would open and I would enter. I would push the button to choose the floor where I was going, and the doors closed. During the ride, I would keep an eye on the light panel to make sure that I did not miss my floor. When I arrived at the requested floor, the doors opened, and I walked out. That was the extent of my interaction with elevators.

In Korea, however, riding elevators was a different experience. I pushed the button to summon it. As it arrived, it announced itself by calling my floor number in an electronic voice coming from a speaker inside the elevator. Although I did not understand Korean, I assumed the next phrase I heard was: "The doors are opening." I walked in and chose the floor of my destination. The elevator called out loud the floor number I had selected. I later found out that in Korea I could "un-do" the floor number if I made a mistake, something I could not do in the United States. I recall that back home, the unavailability of this function was a source of frustration, particularly when I was in a hurry because if I made a mistake, the elevator had to make an undesired stop. In Korea, after I chose my destination, the elevator moved up or down. Just before arriving at the floor I had selected, it called the floor number out loud and indicated that the doors were opening. The doors opened; I got out. It was like taking a guided tour. I could imagine what an efficient experience it must have been to ride those elevators for people who understood Korean. They could engage in other activities while in the elevator, thus skipping the inefficiency of watching a lit-up floor indicator on the elevator panel. This "talking elevator" feature was and continues to be an excellent tool for individuals who may be physically challenged or visually impaired. Nowadays, in Korea, elevator riders can check their email or favorite social network account, check their makeup in the elevator mirrors or make sure that their complexion is glowing and every hair is in place while the "talking elevator" is guiding them to their destination.

The efficient use of technology continued to impress me even at restaurants, where I noticed inconspicuous buttons at the end of each table that customers used for summoning a server. While conducting research for this book, I found that these devices are known in the industry as "push-for-service systems." When customers pressed the button on their table, a bell sounded and a server immediately said something aloud to acknowledge the call. The server signaled to the client who had pressed the button that someone would be arriving any second to find out how they could be of service. Based on my personal observations alone, the use of this system appears to have expanded since I started visiting Korea. This use of technology, of course, is meant to enhance customer service, but the button was first and foremost efficiency-driven. The customer promptly gets a server's attention; the servers immediately know which table needs assistance; the customer's needs are promptly met, and they can get on with the business of consuming the meal. What a difference between this experience and one in the States where it may take a great deal of effort to flag a server in a busy restaurant! In most American restaurants, a server is assigned to specific tables, meaning that other servers may or may not be able to help you.

One technological apparatus that has found its way into restaurants in the U.S. is a gadget called a "table tracker." It is square with one side curved, about 3½ to 4 inches on each side. According to LRS, one of the makers of this device, table trackers increase productivity and efficiency and boost customer satisfaction.[1] The use of the technology eliminates the servers' responsibility of taking orders and the restaurant avoids the need to hire a host/ess who is normally responsible for showing customers to their table. Instead, menus are available at the entrance and a person is hired to take orders and issue table trackers to all customers. After the order is placed, customers proceed with tracker in hand to pay at the cashier, also located near the entrance. After paying for their meal, they move on to select a table. The system informs the cooks and servers what the customers ordered, and it notifies the servers where the customers are seated. Once the meals are prepared, the servers deliver the food to the customers and retrieve the trackers. When customers are done with their meal, the servers clear the tables. In essence, servers are relegated to delivering food to customers and busing tables. In this scenario, the servers perform the duties of both servers, except for taking orders, and busboys/busgirls, thus generating additional savings for the restaurant owner. In this example, the concepts of efficiency and automation are clearly evident.

Some U.S. restaurants which do not accept reservations and are located in and around shopping malls are now making use of a similar electronic instrument called "guest pager." Guest pagers are also square 3½ to 4 inches on each side with rounded corners. According to LRS, the guest pager is one of their guest management solutions.[2] The guest pager provides restaurant patrons in the type of environment described above, the opportunity to enhance their outing experience by going out for a stroll or window shopping while avoiding the grueling wait at a restaurant lobby after checking in. Similarly, restaurant owners avoid having a crowded lobby full of hungry customers waiting for their name to be called. I have used this system myself and I found it to be quite liberating when the customer stays within the signal range of the system.

In my personal experience, I have seen guest pagers used in Korean coffee shops for quite some time to inform the customer that their order is ready for pick up. In the U.S., even today, baristas are still calling out customers' names.

Based on my experience, I first noted the efficient use of this type of technology in Korean restaurants and coffee shops, years before it made its way into the United States. A characteristic that will become evident in this book is that Koreans are early adopters and trendsetters, especially when it comes to the efficient use of technology for the convenience it affords.

In addition to technology and cars, Korea exports its pop culture in the form of K-Pop, soap operas, and in-vogue trends. Three such trends are the extensive use of Botox and plastic surgery as well as the efficient use of technology. Even though Koreans did not invent Botox or plastic surgery, through their export of soap operas, they have been very successful at attracting people from other Asian countries to visit Korea to receive these types of treatments. Globalization has facilitated the spread of these

11

trends, especially when trends are congruent with a receptive culture.

As I continued to visit Korea for short intervals, I admired the glittering shopping centers, the tall skyscrapers, the efficient subway system in Seoul and Busan, the expansive national highways with long tunnels that significantly shorten travel time in a mountainous country, and of course, the high-speed trains, better known as KTX (Korea Train eXpress). In short, Korea epitomized every infrastructural and cultural attribute that one would expect in a developed country. Today, the extensive use of technology in Korea is even more pronounced than it was in the 1990s. A prime example of this increased technology is ubiquitous access to the internet. Broadband in Korea is accessible from practically anywhere in the country. Moreover, it is fast. In fact, it is faster than the bandwidth available in many parts of the United States. According to Fastmetrics, in the first quarter of 2017, Korea enjoyed the number one spot among the top 10 countries in the world with the fastest internet with a 28.6 average Mbps (megabits per second). The global average internet speed was 7.2 Mbps. The same quarter, the United States finally cracked the top 10 countries at number 10 with an average Mbps of 18.7. By comparison, Korea held the number one spot continuously since Fastmetrics first began documenting data in the fourth quarter of 2015.[3]

From the end of 2018 to April 2019, companies from Korea (KT) and the United States (AT&T and Verizon) raced neck-and-neck to the finish line in their effort to be the first company in the world to launch a 5-G network or fifth generation cellular technology. In the end, companies from both countries claimed to be first. Regardless, the point here is that Korea has developed cutting-edge technology capable of competing with the most technologically advanced countries.[4] This reality is a testimony to the remarkable technological transformation achieved since the end of the Korean War.

Another example of the effective use of technology is the universal use of dash-cam recorders, which are inconspicuously located next to the rear-view mirror of a vehicle. Koreans refer to this type of camera as a "black box." These instruments record everything that happens in front of the vehicle. Nowadays, some of these recorders have the capability of recording video and sound both in front of the car and inside the car. Consequently, if an accident occurs, there is no need to waste time arguing as to whose fault it is. It is all recorded. In Korea, insurance adjusters review the recording and can more efficiently assign fault. Although these cameras are readily available in the U.S. at stores such as Best Buy and Amazon and are reasonably priced below $200, some at less than $100, their use is still limited. When it comes to technology, my sense is that Koreans tend to be much more early adopters than Americans. One reason is that Koreans have a propensity for appreciating efficiency in general, but particularly the efficacy that technology affords.

Another convenient and smart innovation that impressed me in the more recent past was the proliferation of manual, but especially power-folding, side-view mirrors (or wing mirrors) on cars. Undoubtedly one of the reasons for the extensive use of this device is the fact that some of the streets in Korea, particularly in the older sections of many towns, are so narrow that the capability of folding the side mirrors gives drivers more room to navigate. Nowadays, this convenience is available on luxury cars in the United States.

My fascination with the aforementioned practices and other efficient uses of technology coupled with my interests in philosophy, religion, and teaching motivated me to consider a teaching assignment in Korea after my retirement in the United States.

During my American teaching and administration career, I had known a few teachers who had taught in foreign countries during their sabbaticals. Their sense of adventure impressed me, and I knew that one day I, too, would have the courage to go to a foreign country to practice the profession for which I have an enormous passion. I took early retirement and struggled for a year trying to adjust to my new lifestyle after having been extremely active and involved in education from the classroom to counseling and finally to administration. Since I had so much free time on my hands in retirement, I decided that it was time for me to experience a new environment. The attachment I had to Korea made the country an ideal place for me to explore. So, I decided to rent an apartment in Korea for one year. Having lived in large cities most of my life, I was looking for a less hectic environment. I settled in Jukjeon, a small town south of Seoul. It was close enough to the big city and convenient enough for travel purposes. Since I did not have

Korean residency at the time, I could only live in the country for 90-day intervals as a visiting tourist. I spent quite a bit of time traveling to nearby towns, trying different Korean dishes, attending yoga classes and visiting cafes.

The most valuable part of this experience was the contact I had with Koreans through my yoga classes. Through my observation and conversations with them, I learned a great deal about Korean culture. I did not own a car at the time; therefore, I used public transportation which limited my explorations of the country. I was particularly fond of visiting and walking around in Jukjeon café street (to Koreans, this street is known as Bojeong-Dong Café Street or 보정동카페거리). Even though the difficulty of relying solely on public transportation was somewhat limiting, it gave me the confidence that I could survive in a foreign country. It propelled me to a much more enriching experience in the ensuing four years.

The adjustment to retirement was not easy. Then, I recalled that practicing my profession outside of the U.S. had always intrigued me. Therefore, this was a perfect time for me to achieve that dream. After returning to the U.S. from my one-year sojourn in Korea, I applied for a few teaching positions in the late spring of 2012. I interviewed via Skype for a job at an accredited American high school that operated under the auspices of a university. The prospective job was a teaching/guidance counseling position which would provide me with the additional opportunity to teach an English class for the university. This job was tailor-made for me, given my professional experience. My dream had become a reality faster than I had imagined. Suddenly, I found myself in Korea ready to begin my new assignment in early August of 2012. This once-in-a-lifetime experience was feasible for me because I was single and had no children. Had this not been the case, I believe that the feasibility would have been quite challenging, perhaps even impossible.

As I started my assignment, I had no idea of the profound impact that my experience in Korea was going to have on my consciousness. I was about to learn what many expats grow to realize: Living in a foreign country is very different from visiting one as a tourist. As a resident, I was about to delve into the fabric of their society and learn the nuances of Korean human behavior, both subtle and otherwise. I was about to have the privilege of looking at the underbelly of the country from within it. Also, I was about to undergo a reality check related to my view of Korean society, one that would enable me to compare the Korea that I remembered from my initial visits as a tourist or as a member of a meditation tour group to present-day Korea as a "resident." In retrospect, I am grateful for the opportunity. I am thankful to the Korean people, those who embraced me with open arms, those who put aside their shyness and tried to speak English to me, as well as those who chose to keep their distance. Through their approach to social interaction with someone who looks, talks, and acts differently from them, I was able to immerse myself in their culture. Thank you!

I am grateful to have lived and worked in Korea. Thanks to this opportunity, I could witness and confirm the beauty of the country that my friends had relayed to me. I had the chance to travel throughout the country in the five years I lived there. On weekends in spring and fall, I particularly enjoyed visiting places I had not seen. This enabled me to witness the fantastic palette of Korea's natural colors and the inherent beauty of the country. One of the most impressive and stunning images that will remain forever engraved in my memory is the variety of flowers that form a colorful landscape in cities, highways, and mountains throughout spring, summer and fall. It seems as if the color of the landscape changes every two or three weeks, depending on the blooming flower. The kaleidoscope of colors appears to start every year with ubiquitous cherry blossom trees that bloom from late March to early April. The autumn season concludes with a spectacular shower of ginkgo biloba tree leaves and others that turn bright yellow, red, and brown. The changing leaves in fall are a sight to see, especially in the mountains and around Buddhist temples. Streams and falls are delightful and refreshing any time of the year, but particularly in the summer.

Located primarily in the mountains, Buddhist temples with streams or rivers running nearby are of particular attraction to Koreans and tourists alike. They provide a place to rest, meditate or pray before or after an invigorating hike in the nearby mountains. In the spring, summer or early fall, entire families enjoy a picnic by a river. In the summer, both adults and children relish playing and getting wet in a stream. The sound of children playing echo up and down streams and make the mountains even more vibrant. On the way to and from the mountains, hikers, from millennials to baby boomers, and Buddhist temple visitors can satisfy their hunger with *bibimbap*. The iconic blend of rice, mountain-grown vegetables, such as beansprouts, carrots, radish, cucumber, your choice of meat or no meat, a fried egg, and red pepper paste is served in a dish of your choice, either in a hot stone pot or a deep dish at room temperature. *Bibimbap* is garnished with numerous side dishes made from nutritious mountain-grown vegetables and is served at any number of restaurants leading into or out of the town. Some of those side dishes may include fermented sesame seed leaves, radish, seaweed, and the ubiquitous *kimchi* or fermented cabbage, which most Koreans eat with breakfast, lunch, and dinner.

A meal in a mountain town is not complete unless it includes the customary *soju*. For those who are not familiar with *soju*, the national drink of Korea, it is a neutral tasting, clear spirit. *Soju* was traditionally made from rice but nowadays it is mostly made from a blend of grains and starches such as wheat and sweet potatoes.[5] It is somewhat similar to vodka, but has half the alcohol. The alcohol content in *soju* is around 20 ABV (Alcohol by Volume), whereas vodka's is 40.[6] *Soju* is customarily consumed straight in small shot glasses but is also used in cocktails. One interesting cultural detail about drinking *soju* among Koreans is that consumers do not serve themselves. They serve each other. For instance, if I am having dinner with a Korean friend and we are both drinking *soju*, when our glasses are empty my friend refills my glass and I refill his. We toast, we down the *soju*, and we start over.

About Korea

South Korea ("Korea," hereafter) rose from the ashes after the Korean War (1950-1953). Korea's remarkable economic transformation is often referred to by observers and historians as the "Miracle on the Han River." According to the *World Atlas*:

> The phrase was introduced by South Korea's Prime Minister, Chang Myon, as part of his New Year address in 1961 in which he requested his fellow South Koreans to withstand the discomfort that came with change and be optimistic of economic growth. The phrase was derived from a similar phrase; 'Miracle on the Rhine,' coined in reference to the dramatic economic resurgence of West Germany soon after the Second World War.[7]

Since the 1950s, the country has shifted from being among the poorest countries in Africa and Asia to one of the top 20 economies in the world. The country's Gross Domestic Product (GDP) expansion since the 1960s has been nothing short of spectacular. According to The World Bank data, Korea's GDP grew from $2.417 billion in 1961 to $1.012 trillion in 2006, when it surpassed the one trillion-dollar mark for the first time.[8] According to the International Monetary Fund (IMF) and The World Bank, Korea's economy is the 4th largest in Asia and the 12th largest in the world based on its 2017 GDP of $1.531 trillion. The chart below shows Korea's GDP growth trajectory from 1960 to 2018 in trillion US$ (see fig. 1).

Figure 1: "GDP (Current Trillion US$)," graph from *World Bank national accounts data.* [9]

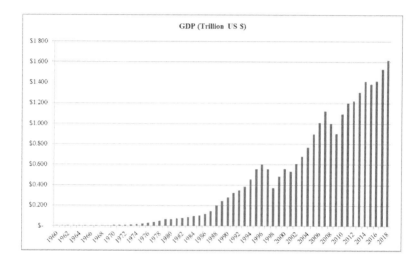

Another indicator of this amazing transformation is Gross National Income (GNI) per capita, formerly referenced as GDP per capita. Korea's GNI per capita experienced an astounding increase from 1962 to 2018 (see fig. 2). According to The World Bank, Korea's GNI per capita grew from $120 to $30,600 in that same period.

Figure 2: "GNI per capita, Atlas Method (Current US$)," graph from *World Bank national accounts data.*[10]

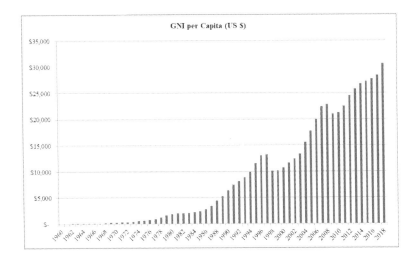

Today, Korea's economy is exports-based. As such, it follows that the historical trajectory of exports resembles the patterns established by GDP and GNI growth shown above: "South Korea's exports, which amounted to only USD 32.82 million in 1960, surpassed the USD 10 billion mark in 1977 and reached USD 495.4 billion in 2016."[11]

The country's five top export items are as follows: 1) semiconductors, 2) ships, offshore structures, and parts, 3) cars, 4) petroleum products, and 5) flat panel displays and sensors.[12]

Korea's economy is considered to be mixed. According to the *Business Dictionary*, a mixed economy is "An economic system in which both the private enterprise and a degree of state monopoly (usually in public services, defense, infrastructure, and basic industries) coexist. All modern economies are mixed where the means of production are shared between the private and public sectors. Also called dual economy."[13] It is well known that the Korean economy is dominated by family-owned conglomerates called *chaebols* that produce everything from cars to television monitors, laptops, cell phones, and more. They also own major supermarket chains, hotels, apartment buildings, and department stores such as Lotte Mart and Lotte Department Stores, as well as bakeries like Paris Baguette. As a result of the overwhelming influence that these *chaebols* have on the economy, both the country and the people of Korea depend heavily on the success of these corporations. Not surprisingly, from a very early age Koreans aspire to join one of these conglomerates as full-time employees after college graduation for economic security and to assure themselves of a successful life-long career.

As alluded to earlier, Korea produces some of the most advanced technology capable of competing with similar products assembled by major companies anywhere in the world. Koreans have accomplished this impressive achievement through efficiency in a highly competitive environment that permeates throughout the culture. These two themes—competitiveness and efficiency—will resonate time and again in the various aspects of my observations of Korean society. Efficiency, in particular, is pervasive from the lower echelons of society to the Blue House (the equivalent of the U.S. White House). The public expects a 3% GDP annual growth, and the effectiveness of every presidency is judged by whether it can achieve this target.

Companies like Hyundai Motors, Kia Motors, LG, Samsung Electronics and others successfully compete on the world stage against renowned corporations like Apple, Ford, GE, GM, Google, Honda, Intel, Kenmore, Toyota, and Whirlpool. However, there is a sense, even among Koreans, that for Korean conglomerates to maintain their competitive edge, they need to continue to promote growth, creativity, and innovation—but especially growth.

Technology, business, and industry have set the pace for the unprecedented trajectory reflected in the above charts. For example, in 2017, Korea ranked third among electronic circuit component exporting countries behind only Hong Kong and Taiwan.[14] According to *Investopedia*, as of April 18, 2017, Samsung Electronics was the second largest semiconductor company in the world with sales of $43.54 billion.[15] The number one semiconductor company was Intel with sales of $56.31 billion.

Korean people have many reasons to be proud of their country's achievements. Some of the nation's advancements have been showcased during international sporting events, commencing with the 1988 Seoul Summer Olympics. Korea also hosted the 2002 World Cup bi-nationally with Japan and more recently, the 2018 PyeongChang Winter Olympics. The 1988 Seoul Summer Olympics, though, had a special significance for Korea. Lee Charm, former head of the Korea National Tourism Agency referred to it as Korea's "coming-out party."[16] In today's parlance, it may be referred to as Korea's debut on the world stage.

Prior to this event, people around the world associated Korea almost exclusively with the Korean War. After the torch was extinguished, however, the country's powerful image was that of a nation where a rich tradition coexists with a vibrant, youthful, modern, and technologically advanced society. The infrastructure that was built for these events, an effort that continues to this day with the constant expansion of highways, tunnels, railways, high-speed trains and broadband accessibility, has enhanced mobility, communication, and entertainment.

Today, Korea exports much more than cars and technology. Korean food, beauty products and pop culture are becoming popular around the world. Thanks to the entrepreneurial nature of Koreans, people around the globe can enjoy Korean cuisine from Abu Dhabi to Beijing, London, Los Angeles, New York, Paris, and Siem Reap. Television dramas and K-Pop are in high demand all over Asia, making a dent even in the West. Korea is exporting K-Pop to the world. According to the Korea Creative Content Agency, in 2016, global sales related to K-Pop, including revenue from CDs, concert tickets, streaming music, and related merchandise and services, reached 5.3 trillion Korean won (KRW) (~$4.7 billion).[17] Those who had been living under a rock, so to speak, and were not familiar with K-Pop, experienced a taste of the infectious music during the closing ceremony of the 2018 PyeongChang Winter Olympics with the performance of the popular group EXO. Also, K-Beauty cosmetics have become a worldwide phenomenon.

These accomplishments did not happen by accident. Korean people have demonstrated that they are hardworking, entrepreneurial, goal-oriented, tenacious, and efficient. These qualities have contributed enormously to the nation's evolution from an underdeveloped state after the Korean War to one of the most technologically advanced countries in the world. Also, Koreans espouse fundamental values that account for the nation's high standard of living. These values include strong support for the national agenda. This collective effort is reflected by a uniform willingness to make the necessary individual, as well as collective, sacrifices for the good of the nation, a strong work ethic, emphasis on education, and efficiency. However, the emphasis on efficiency has taken its toll on some aspects of society as well as the psyche of the nation, hence the title of this book. In my analysis, I demonstrate how efficiency permeates throughout the society and moreover, the ways in which efficiency is the driving force behind the country's astonishing rise from the ashes since the end of the Korean War.

About this Book

This book is meant not as a criticism, but as an observation from an outsider's perspective about culture and the role it plays in the evolution of economic progress. The commentary is also meant to show how a country's policies and procedures, and their resulting attitudes, need to be revisited to ensure congruence with the pace of economic and technological progress. Finally, it is meant to place a mirror in front of the Korean people so they can judge for themselves whether their current state of affairs can be used as a springboard toward the successful evolution of the country's overall development. Or, do they need a thorough and systematic review of policies and procedures at various levels of government, business, and industry? Do these entities need to ensure that appropriate safety regulations are in place and rigorously followed, and enforced? Also, do they need to recognize that taking shortcuts with selfish motives are usually carried out at someone else's expense and are accompanied by unintended consequences and casualties of innocent bystanders? Meaningful, fundamental and profound change is up to the Korean people.

Also, this book provides a historical perspective only where one is needed to understand how a specific current situation developed. A significant number of books about Korea delve thoroughly into the historical perspective. Instead, the present work focuses primarily on describing the current state of affairs based on extensive research, the power of observation, and systematic analysis. A great many of the sources cited are from credible Korean newspapers or news outlets that offer an English version of their website. A handful of the citations are from news sources that either only publish or broadcast in Korean or the particular article or report was only published or broadcasted in Korean. In these cases, Young Lee, the co-author, translated the articles or news reports. These instances are noted in the endnotes at the end of each chapter. The remaining articles and reports are from English-speaking countries. I purposefully attempted to consult a variety of sources in an effort to triangulate the information and balance the sources.

Since this book focuses on Korea, I made a concerted effort to avoid passing judgment and making value-loaded comparisons to other cultures, societies, and economies. However, it is difficult, if not impossible, to be totally objective when the observer, in this case myself, is born and raised in a different culture, and the observer's perception of reality is affected by their own culture, socioeconomic background, level of education, religious background, and upbringing, to name but a few factors. In those instances where comparisons are made, it is to make a point about where Korea is in relation to other countries.

I decided to write this book to show my appreciation for Korea and the Korean people. It is my way of giving back to the country that opened its doors to me and enabled me to relish its long history and natural beauty. Social behaviors are examined, and I attempt to identify patterns that tend to repeat from one area of society to another, thus indicating that they are firmly ingrained in the fabric of the culture. I question the source of behavioral patterns and attempt to determine whether efficiency is the driving force, thus the title of the book. Recognizing that Korea has arrived on the world stage to join other economic powers in record time, I ask this question: What has been neglected in this evolution and what has been the human toll associated with individual and collective sacrifices? Therefore, the set of observations presented is for individuals, Korean or otherwise, who are open-minded and realistic enough to accept that, as in all societies including those in the West, there is work to be done to achieve real, long-lasting progress, and for this society to be more egalitarian and compassionate. Compassionate societies recognize that values need to be revisited and questioned to ensure their relevance, that attempting to get around a rule or regulation may give one person or a select group of entities an advantage, but places others at a distinct disadvantage and may endanger the safety of many.

It is both humbling and reassuring to recognize that societies often behave in ways that reflect nature, particularly in relation to the large spectrum of human progress. Economic and technological advancement seem to go hand-in-hand; however, consciousness-level development appears to happen independently of the first two, just like autumn leaves change colors at their own pace rather than in unison. This natural process gives me hope that Korea's consciousness level will not only equal but surpass its level of economic and technological progress in the near future.

John Gonzalez

Endnotes

1. "Homepage," *LRS Table Tracker*, accessed 25 June 2019, *lrus.com*.

2 Ibid.

3 "Internet Connection Speed by Country," *Fastmetrics*, accessed 25 June 2019, *fastmetrics.com*.

4. Roger Cheng, "The 5-G wireless revolution, explained," *c|net*, 27 October 2019, *cnet.com*.

5. Sam Dangremond, "Here's Everything You Need to Know About Soju, the National Drink of Korea," *Town and Country Magazine, 8 February 2018, townandcountrymag.com*.

6. Cat Wolinski, "The Differences Between Soju, Shochu, and Sake, Explained," *Vinepair, accessed 27 June 2019, vinepair.com*.

7. Joseph Kiprop, "What Was the Miracle on the Han River?", *World Atlas*, 6 February 2018, *worldatlas.com*.

8. "GDP (Current US$)," data file, *World Bank national accounts data, and OECD National Accounts Data Files, n.d., databank.worldbank.org*.

9. Ibid.

10. "GNI per capita, (Current US$)," graph, *World Bank national accounts data, and OECD National Accounts data files, accessed 26 November 2019, databank.worldbank.org*.

11. "The Korean Economy – Miracle on the Hangang River," *Korea.net*, accessed 27 June 2019, *korea.net*.

12. Ibid.

13. "Mixed Economy," *Business Dictionary*. Accessed 7 February 2019, *businessdictionary.com*.

14. Daniel Workman, "Electronic Circuit Component Exports

by Country," *World's Top Exports*, accessed 29 June 2018.

15. Justin Walton, "The World's Top 10 Semiconductor Companies," *Investopedia*, 11 December 11 2017.

16. Andrew Salmon, "A Sporting Host: how South Korea has continued to build on the legacy of the Seoul Olympics," *South China Morning Post*, 5 July 2015, *scmp.com*.

17. Soohee Kim, "The $4.7 Billion K-Pop Industry Chases Its 'Michael Jackson Moment,'" *Bloomberg*, accessed February 13, 2019.

Chapter One

Cultural and Behavioral Patterns

The Korean culture is imbued with a competitive environment. Within it exists cultural and behavioral patterns that lead to success for the country in terms of GDP and for individuals, in areas such as education. Eventually, this creates financial success for the country as measured by GNI per capita, and for corporations as determined by profits. The cultural and behavioral patterns which are the determinants of financial success are unity, harmony, sacrifice, consensus building, the *pali pali* culture and *gap* and *eul*. Overlaying these cultural and behavioral patterns is the pervasive concept of efficiency. The following chapter is an analysis of these cultural and behavioral patterns and their role within this paradigm of efficiency in a competitive environment.

Unity and Harmony

Racially, ethnically, culturally, and linguistically, Korea is still a largely homogeneous country. Unity and harmony are universal values for Koreans. These concepts are evidenced by national symbols and practices including the national flag called Taegukgi (or *Taegukki*). The white background represents the purity of the Korean people and their quest for peace. The inner circle, or *taeguk*, is divided equally and represents the harmony and balance between *yin* and *yang*, the two cosmic forces which oppose each other but achieve perfect balance. The bottom blue section represents *yin*, and the red upper area signifies *yang*. Examples of *yin* and *yang* include:

Figure 1: Examples of Yin and Yang

Yin	*Yang*
dark	bright
cold	hot
the moon	the sun
night	day
winter	summer
woman	man

The four black trigrams called *Kwae* surrounding the *taeguk* circle are composed of broken and unbroken bars. Individually, they represent the elements of heaven, earth, water, and fire. Together, they stand for the principle of movement and harmony of *yin* and *yang*.

Figure 2: Flag of South Korea[1]

Conformity and Differentiation

Despite the extremely competitive nature of the society, Koreans tend to conform to social norms. This conformity is congruent with the cultural concepts of unity and harmony. Culturally, Koreans avoid standing out and being perceived as different, which theoretically seems like a harmonious social pattern. However, the competitive nature of the culture compels Koreans to differentiate from one another in a number of contexts, one of which is when a socioeconomic distinction is involved. They can smoothly navigate this dichotomy of conformity and differentiation with ease.

Associated with this socioeconomic-status-conscious tendency is the question pertaining to the university from which an individual graduates, whether in Korea or abroad. Prospective employers, generally speaking, give special consideration to candidates possessing a degree from a reputable university abroad, particularly the United States, because of their anticipated linguistic and cultural contributions. Therefore, it follows that Koreans who have earned a degree from a reputable university abroad are held in high esteem.

As far as graduates from domestic universities are concerned, the media, and Koreans in general, consider someone with a degree from one of the top universities, including the top three that traditionally have been considered as the most prestigious in Korea, Seoul National University, Korea University, and Yonsei University, also referred to by the acronym SKY, as having their career and high socioeconomic status set for life. Indeed, for 2019, uniRank ranks these three as the top universities in Korea.[2] These rankings are backed by the fact that many prominent politicians, doctors, lawyers, engineers, professors, and journalists are graduates from SKY universities. More precisely, pertaining to the influence held by Seoul National University graduates:

> Half of the lawmakers in [the] current National Assembly of Korea are SNU [Seoul National University] alumni. Judges in the high court and Supreme [C]ourt are mostly from SNU, which is 88% of all. More than half of [the] cabinet members in the present ministry are also SNU alumni. [Fifty-five percent] of CEOs of [the] top 500 companies in Korea are SNU graduates.[3]

Nowadays, however, with the proliferation of university rankings, the use of different criteria in their development, and Korea's emphasis on technology, the panorama is more fluid. In reviewing the various university rankings available, the musical-chairs-esque movement becomes apparent. Therefore, the concept of the three top universities that compose SKY has become purely symbolic. They remain highly ranked, but not necessarily as number one, two, and three. For instance, for 2018-2019, *U.S. News & World Report* ranks the top five universities in Korea as follows:

1. Seoul National University
2. Sungkyunkwan University
3. Korea Advanced Institute of Science and Technology (KAIST)
4. Korea University
5. Yonsei University[4]

Times Higher Education: World University Rankings, which identifies Microsoft, Salesforce.org, Adobe, Huawei, and HSBC, among others, as their partners, lists the following universities as their top five:

1. Seoul National University
2. Sungkyunkwan University
3. Korea Advanced Institute of Science and Technology
4. Pohang University of Science and Technology (POSTECH)
5. Korea University[5]

And, finally, the Center for World University Rankings (CWUR), lists the following as the top five universities:

1. Seoul National University
2. University of Science and Technology, Korea
3. Sungkyunkwan University
4. Yonsei University
5. Korea University[6]

Based on these three rankings, the only three patterns that one can discern pertaining to the symbolic SKY acronym are as follows: they all place Seoul National University at the top, Korea University is among the top five on all three rankings, and Yonsei University appears on two out of the three rankings.

In addition to the university where a person graduates, Koreans consider other factors within the socioeconomic differentiation, including the type of car people drive, the type of job they have, their father's occupation, whether they wear designer clothes or carry designer-label accessories, and whether they rent or own their own home.

I realize that people in the West also use similar factors to judge the socioeconomic status of a person; however, once they feel comfortable with a person they just met, Koreans have a tendency to be inquisitive. In an effort to get to know the person better, they ask very direct, personal questions that would be considered inappropriate in the West. The questions may include such topics as the marital status of the person, their father's occupation, the type of car they drive, the number of children they have, and if the children are of college-attendance age, what universities they are attending. The question about the father's occupation will generate the most information regarding a person's socioeconomic background, because the answer will be an indicator of such variables as how much support the person received in terms of supplemental education while growing up, whether they live in an upscale neighborhood with the best *hagwons*—after-school academies or "cram schools"—and how much wealth they may inherit from the father. The questions also reflect the values of the present-day Korean culture. Even in this seemingly trivial social aspect, Koreans are very efficient. They find out as much information about another person in as little time as possible.

Another area where the differentiation is palpable, certainly much more pronounced than in the West, is age. Koreans are extremely conscious about age. They tend to associate with, date, and marry people their own, or very close to their own age. Age-mismatch associations are so rare that when someone associates with another person outside of their age group, it is considered more than a faux pas; people wonder if there is something wrong with that person.

Unity, Conformity, and Individuality

Examples of behavioral patterns exemplifying unity/conformity on one hand and individuality on the other will be discussed in the remaining sections of this chapter.

Children learn the concepts of unity and conformity at a very early age. They are teased by other children, and even bullied, if they stray from established norms. As a concrete example, because historically Korea has been racially homogeneous, Koreans can instinctively tell when someone is of a mixed marriage even if to a non-Korean the person looks and talks like a full-fledged Korean. Consequently, it is not uncommon for children of mixed racial backgrounds to be bullied.

Traditionally, children are expected to grow up following a conventional path. This path includes being studious and earning good grades in school and commensurate test scores to be able to gain admission to a top-tier university. Men are required to perform their military service, unless granted an exemption for medical reasons. Eventually, both men and women are expected to secure a white-collar job at a major corporation, get married, raise children, and sacrifice themselves for their children's education, the way their parents sacrificed for them, so they too can follow the time-tested path to economic stability and overall success. White-collar jobs exist at smaller companies; however, the initial goal is to secure the "dream job" or a white-collar job at a major corporation because of higher compensation, much better benefits, and job security associated with those jobs. When individuals are unsuccessful at securing the "dream job," then they have to settle for a white-collar job at a smaller company for much less compensation, benefits and job security.

The differentiation between university-bound students and those that are not begins before they enter high school. Students who demonstrate strong academic potential, attend regular high schools, unless their parents can afford tuition for a private or international school. Conversely, students whose grades and test scores show a lesser academic potential in elementary and middle school have the option of attending an occupational or technical high school. Students in regular high schools who are unable to earn good enough grades with matching test scores to enter university are relegated to blue-collar jobs. They can enroll in a university that specializes in career and technical education, or if they are fortunate enough to have parents who own a business, they may be incorporated into it. If they are entrepreneurial and their parents have enough money to support a business venture, they may start a business of their own. Another option is for them to complete any number of certificates to obtain the necessary skills for an entry-level position at a small company.

The old, well-traveled road to economic success appears to be less reliable for millennials than it once was for baby boomers. Two factors seem to contribute to this perception: the prohibitive costs of supplemental private education and test preparation, which are viewed as essential and are universally used in Korea to provide children with every possible advantage to prosper in a competitive university admission environment, and the view that the playing field is skewed toward those who are more affluent. In theory, this is true as well in other capitalist countries; however, it will become evident throughout this book that the difference is the degree of intensity. It appears that competition is more fierce in Korea than in other capitalist countries such as the United States.

Access to higher education is quite different in the West, specifically in the United States where the wealthy may also be perceived as having a distinct advantage in providing their children with the best preparation possible for university access and eventual career success. Children from middle-class and economically disadvantaged families in the U.S., however, have the opportunity to succeed as long as they demonstrate academic potential, successfully complete a college preparation curriculum, earn respectable scores on college admission tests, and can demonstrate through such measures as participation in extracurricular activities, community involvement, and leadership, that they have the potential to succeed and contribute to the diversity of the school.

The biggest difference is that in Korea, private supplemental education and test preparation, as reflected in the university admission test score, are determining factors in the university admission process. Conversely, in the U.S., private supplemental education is not universally used, primarily because the college admission process is more holistic. Therefore, the competitive aspect is not focused on test performance. Universities in the United States use multiple criteria much more widely to determine admission. They do so in order to assemble a diverse freshman class that reflects society as a whole and that will make a contribution to the institution and to society.

The fact of the matter is that the trend to make ACT (American College Test) and SAT (Scholastic Aptitude Test) scores optional for university admission purposes is growing in the United States.

This movement began in Winter 2004-2005 and has been gaining momentum ever since. As of June 10, 2019, there are 242 four-year colleges and universities that make these test scores optional.[7] According to Fair Test, "More than 1,000 four-year colleges and universities do not use the SAT or ACT to admit substantial numbers of bachelor-degree applicants."[8] On June 14, 2018, the University of Chicago announced that it would make the test scores optional. So far, the University of Chicago is the most prestigious university in the United States to join the movement. It was ranked third in the 2018 college rankings published by *U.S. News & World Report* at the time of the announcement and the acceptance rate for the freshman class of Fall 2018 was seven percent.[9] As to the reason for making the test scores optional, James G. Nondorf, vice president for enrollment at the University of Chicago, is quoted as saying in an email:

> It is about doing the RIGHT thing, which is helping students and families of all backgrounds better understand and navigate this process and about bringing students with intellectual promise (no matter their background) to UChicago (and making sure they succeed here too!)[10]

Other reasons for the under reliance on supplemental private education in the United States include the accessibility of quality higher education at different levels and the diverse paths that students can take.

For instance, community colleges in the U.S. with their multiple missions, including transfer preparation, represent an outstanding alternative for high school students who may not have an academic record worthy of university admission, thus these students may not have the sufficiently strong academic preparation or the social maturity to succeed at university. However, after they spend some time at community college and successfully complete their lower division requirements, these students generally perform very well once they transfer to a four-year public or private university. The difference is that after spending some time at the community college, students are more mature and have attained a solid academic foundation as well as strong study skills. It is also possible that some high school graduates who are university admissible may opt to attend a community college first for financial considerations. Their parents may lack the financial means to pay for university costs or they may simply wish to save money on tuition while they are completing their lower division requirements.

Another key societal difference between Korea and the United States, specifically as perceived by prospective employers, is concerned with a job applicant's college/university trajectory. In the U.S., it matters little where one begins university studies. What matters is where one graduates. For example, the fact that a job applicant attended a community college or a state university does not detract from the applicant's accomplishment of graduating from an Ivy League school or a top-level university. Conversely, in Korea, the institution where one begins higher education studies is of utmost importance. Generally speaking, only the top academic students gain admission into the elite universities. The overarching reason is the excruciatingly competitive nature of the university admission process. By gaining admission into a highly selective university, high school graduates show that they are academically and socially prepared to thrive in such an environment and are capable of succeeding in an academically demanding university program. Yet another reason is that the transfer phenomenon does not have the essential role that it does in the U.S. In summary, because of systemic differences, Korean students do not have the variety of options that American students have; therefore, the pressure to perform well in high school and on the Korean university admission test known as *Suneung* or the College Scholastic Ability Test (CSAT) is extremely high.

Some frustrated and disheartened young people are choosing not to follow the traditional path. They refer to Korea as "*Hell Joseon*" in reference to the historical *Joseon* Dynasty (1392-1910) to express their view of the struggle to live up to society's expectations especially for the economically disadvantaged. This trend is discussed in more detail in Chapter Eight.

The emphasis on wearing school uniforms in public and private schools is an example of this tendency to follow group norms. This is not to say that all schools require uniforms; however, many of the schools tend to espouse a uniform policy. A more widely observed example of this tendency to conform to group norms is a behavior that appears to apply almost exclusively to Koreans. As I traveled extensively throughout the country, particularly in areas that were frequented by Koreans from various parts of the nation either on weekends or during holidays, I noticed a very peculiar behavior as people eagerly posed for pictures.

In today's experiential age, when smartphones with cameras are ubiquitous, based on my own experience, it appears that young Koreans make extensive use of their cell phone camera and selfie sticks to take selfies and subsequently post them on social media. It is true that millennials particularly have universally embraced social media; however, Koreans, in typical Korean fashion when it comes to adopting new trends, have taken it to the next level. They seem to have a love affair with social media, specially the practice of taking pictures of food or selfies in restaurants they visit for the first time and posting them online to share with their friends. In short, the difference is the degree of intensity. I recall visiting some of the places frequented by Korean tourists holding cell phones and selfie sticks include traditional Korean villages, typical Korean restaurants in open markets and other places like the mural village (*Byukhwa Maul*) in Tongyeong. The unusual, but charming, behavior I noticed during these excursions was Koreans posing and making a victory or peace sign. In my travels throughout Europe, North America, parts of the Middle East and portions of Asia, I have not witnessed such universal fascination with the victory or peace sign as I saw in Korea.

One of the fundamental differences between Korean and Western societies is the emphasis on group conventionality in the former and individuality in the latter. It appears that the prominence of conformity, at least as far as Korea is concerned, has geographic as well as historical roots. A strategically located peninsula surrounded by historically powerful nations like China, Russia, and Japan, Korea has been susceptible to foreign aggression and in some instances invasion and eventual occupation. Consequently, Koreans have recognized the advantages of being a united people. Thus, united they have been able to repel aggressors and free themselves from the shackles of oppression by foreign countries. United, they were able to recover from the devastation of the Korean War and transform the country into the 12ᵗʰ largest economy in the world. Therefore, the concept of unity runs deep in the fabric of the society. This wide-spread commitment to integration is expressed in the slogan 뭉치면 살고 흩어지면 죽는다, which translates as "united we stand, divided we fall." However, the expression in Korean carries a much stronger connotation. It literally means "we live if united. if not, we die." Some administrations have used this slogan to rally the people behind initiatives that are considered beneficial to the entire nation. It is also emphasized in the armed services, in the workplace, in schools, and even within families.

The Korean national unity fervor was evident before and during the 1988 Seoul Summer Olympics as well as during the 2002 World Cup when the country, along with Japan, hosted the FIFA (in French: Fédération Internationale de Football Association; in English: International Federation of Association Football) event. At the date of this writing, it is perhaps too early to judge the impact of the unity fervor shown during the 2018 PyeongChang Winter Olympics, which was split between the heartwarming show of unity between the two Koreas during the opening ceremony and the unconditional support for athletes representing South Korea during specific events.

The 1988 Seoul Summer Olympics, including infrastructure buildup, cost Korea $8.2 billion in today's U.S. dollars.[11] The games served to showcase and change the image of the nation to the world. Before the 1988 Seoul Summer Olympics, Korea was best known for the Korean War. After the games, the world perceived Korea to be a highly industrialized, economically advanced country. The event provided a morale booster for the people. In retrospect, it appears that the money spent to organize the games and introduce modern Korea to the world was money well spent. The 1988 Seoul Summer Olympics catapulted Korea onto the world stage as a technologically and economically advanced nation.

According to *The Washington Post*, Korea spent $2 billion on stadiums, roads and related infrastructure in preparation for the 2002 World Cup.[12] Government and business leaders valued the intangible benefits of co-hosting the event. Kim Joo Hyun, vice president of Hyundai Research Institute in Seoul, is quoted as saying: "This is a total makeover of Korea's image to the world."[13]

Aside from the 1988 Seoul Summer Olympics, the 2002 World Cup, and the 2018 PyeongChang Winter Olympics, the country has hosted other important international sports events with a lesser unifying impact such as the Asian Games in 2002 and 2014, most likely because Koreans recognize the unparalleled potential intangible benefits of hosting an event of the magnitude of the

World Cup or an Olympiad. The unprecedented infrastructure build-up in preparation for the 1988 Seoul Summer Olympics and the 2002 World Cup, made Korea an ideal host for subsequent international sports events.

It is evident that the Korean people were proud of co-hosting the 2002 World Cup and showcasing their country to the rest of the world. The entire country rallied behind their team. People in Seoul, Busan and other cities in Korea, and even expatriates living in Los Angeles took to the streets by the thousands wearing the traditional red T-shirts and accompanying red bandanas to watch and root for the Korean national team whose games were shown on giant TV screens. This enthusiasm and energy undoubtedly contributed to the country's best showing in a World Cup event: Korea took fourth place.

History will judge the performance of Korea as the host country of the 2018 PyeongChang Winter Olympics, but based on first impressions, it appears that the highly polished image transmitted was that of a nation that is much more mature, self-assured, confident, and technologically advanced than the Korea presented in prior worldwide events. The 2018 PyeongChang Winter Olympics was no longer Korea's debut on the world stage, but more akin to an encore or a return engagement. The world was much more familiar with Korea as an economic power and a nation that exports quality products like smartphones, automobiles, cosmetics and yes, even K-Pop. The 2018 event was more of a reaffirmation that South Korea has a respectable place on the world stage, despite the tensions with its neighbor from the north.

Sacrifice

The concept of sacrifice runs deep in the collective psyche of the Korean people. Specifically, the idea of individual sacrifice for the benefit of the group or the larger society holds particular significance. This idea is evident throughout the culture. Individuals not only voluntarily sacrifice, but are expected to do so. For example, family members sacrifice their personal interests for those of the family; individual employees sacrifice for the benefit of the unit or even the entire company or corporation; students sacrifice for the good of the whole class; soldiers sacrifice for the good of the platoon. The concept is so ingrained in the culture that it even has a prominent place in the lexicon of Koreans. It is not uncommon to hear in everyday conversation the motto " 대를 위한 소의 희생," which means: "For the large, sacrifice the small." In other words, "individuals should act or sacrifice for the benefit of the group." This saying should not be confused with "all for one and one for all" since the latter implies a reciprocal benefit to both the individual and the group. The Korean slogan reflects the culture since it incorporates the concepts of unity, conformity, and harmony. More importantly, it accentuates the devaluation of the individual vis-à-vis the group, which is observed in a variety of contexts including the classroom, the armed services, and social gatherings.

All males, unless exempted for medical reasons, are required to complete their military service and sacrifice approximately two years of their life for the good of the nation. The length of service depends on the branch of the military; hence the variability in time served. Their sacrifice is viewed as a contribution toward repelling a possible invasion from their neighbor to the north.

In most Korean companies, entry-level employees are required to participate in company training, which often includes trust-building exercises and physical training; some drills may consist of army-style exercises with overtones associated with acculturation to the company values. This practice is meant to impress the importance of individual employee sacrifices for the good of the company.

At a more sublime level is the conviction on the part of the older generation, those who lived through poverty before, during and after the Korean War. Their strong belief is that individual citizens should sacrifice their happiness, if necessary, for the good of the country.

Following are concrete examples of notorious collective sacrifices:

Historically, Korea as a country has frequently been compelled to fight outside invaders, primarily due to its strategic geographic location between China and Japan. In its modern history, the country overcame the Japanese occupation that lasted from 1910 to 1945, and subsequently the Korean War from 1950 to 1953. The individuals who made the ultimate sacrifice by contributing to the liberation of the country from the Japanese have been immortalized as heroes. Their heroic deeds are still emphatically taught in schools.

A more recent example of a collective sacrifice took place during the Asian financial crisis that affected some East Asian countries beginning in July 1997. Korea was one of the countries that was affected the most intensely, alongside Thailand and Indonesia. Other countries were affected to a lesser extent. During the time leading to the crisis, Korea accumulated an increasing trade deficit. Conglomerates borrowed recklessly, jeopardizing the solvency of banks. The country practically depleted its foreign currency reserves, which led to sharp devaluations of its currency, the Korean won. Also, according to *Forbes*: "Foreign investors yanked nearly $18 billion out of the country. Hundreds of thousands lost their jobs."[14] The currency crisis is known among Koreans as the IMF (International Monetary Fund) Crisis. In exchange for a $55 billion bailout, the most massive IMF bailout up to that point, Korea reluctantly agreed to implement severe cuts in public spending, open its markets to foreign goods and investors, and reduce the ability of conglomerates to expand.

Realizing the individual and collective impact of the IMF conditions, about one-quarter of all Koreans, almost 3.5 million people participated in a national campaign to pay back the IMF loan as soon as possible by donating their gold jewelry, coins, trinkets, and medals. They showed a great sense of unity, collective sacrifice and nationalism vis-à-vis this problematic situation by standing in line outside donation centers to offer their gold for a national cause. According to *Forbes*, the campaign yielded 226 metric tons of scrap gold totaling $2.2 billion. The donations were melted into gold bars and delivered to the IMF as an initial payment on the loan. Even though the gold contributions made only a small dent into the total amount of the bailout, the campaign served as a national call-to-action and inspiration to pay off the loan before the end of 2001, almost three years ahead of schedule.

Consensus Building

In addition to the existing pressure to conform to social norms, Koreans have an innate desire to reach consensus, the underlying belief that the best decision is the one endorsed by most. In other words, other people's opinions are valued highly in the decision-making process. For example, when selecting a *hagwon* for their children, mothers of elementary, junior and senior high school students take into consideration the opinion of other mothers in their network whose children have gained admission to prestigious universities. Mothers utilize the same consultation process when choosing a private tutor or an international school for their children.

Consultation and consensus building is especially applicable to daily lives, even when Korean students are faced with very personal decisions such as submitting an essay for the U.S. university admission process or choosing a country for a job internship. Three fundamental motives in consensus building for Koreans are the desire to fulfill societal norms, to gain an advantage in a competitive environment, and to develop maximum efficiency. The latter signifies taking the road well-traveled as determined by the consultation process, thus minimizing mistakes and increasing the probability of success.

The intensified pressure to ensure their own, and their family's, future financial well-being forces students to behave obsessively. For example, most of the students I counseled asked two or three teachers, and in some instances university professors, to review their autobiographical essay before submitting it with their college admission application. On the one hand, students recognize the crucial role the essay plays in the university admission process. On the other hand, students have the core belief that procuring the opinion of several people on the essay structure and content provides them with the best possible chance to put their strongest foot forward.

Aside from the culture-driven behavioral patterns, ethical issues appear to be at stake when viewed through the lens of a Westerner. Directions for essay writing provided by university admission officers on admission applications are, generally speaking, explicit and specific enough for applicants to follow. These instructions are there to ensure a leveled playing field for all applicants. If essays are utilized by admission committees to determine the applicants' potential to succeed in a rigorous academic environment, are essays providing a false measure? The substantial input provided "by committee," by consensus, or by someone other than the applicant, can alter the quality and meaning of the essay significantly.

For students who apply for university admission abroad, the process of selecting a college or university from among several admission offers presents yet another example of the role that consensus building plays in Korean society. Being cognizant of the competitive nature of their culture, high school students recognize that the university selection process is of utmost importance to their financial security and therefore their future success. Without exception, the students I assisted with the non-Korean university application process engaged in lengthy consultation with relatives, friends, family friends, and respected members of the community, including teachers, pastors, and university professors, before finally arriving at a decision. It may take a while for a Western counselor who is used to dealing directly with the students and their parents regarding these crucial decisions to realize that when counseling Korean students additional players with significant influence on the decision-making are not sitting at the table; instead, they are standing in the background, and are only accessible to the students and their parents. Although the students were well-guided by an area expert, they were still compelled to go through this informal consultation process to reassure themselves of success and efficiency in decision-making. As an example, a senior I assisted with the college application process, who received acceptance letters from about ten institutions in the United States and a $25,000 scholarship from one university, consulted not only with his parents but several university professors and family friends who had attended university in the United States before making his final decision. The concern in cases like this is that students who have the opportunity to make a momentous decision that may have profound personal and professional repercussions for the rest of their lives and who ask non-experts such as relatives, friends, family friends, university professors, and other respected members of the community for their opinion prior to making such decisions, may be receiving incomplete information or perhaps even disinformation or biased opinions that may not be in the best interest of the students.

A similar example, but at a different level, is one of a university student I met. He consulted extensively not only with relatives, but also with friends, professors and former supervisors before finally deciding to choose Singapore over Australia for a job internship in hotel management. After he returned to Korea from his internship in Singapore, I had the opportunity ask him about the usefulness of the consultation/consensus building process in relation to his choice between Singapore and Australia. Below is his answer in his own words:

> I consulted professors, friends, and parents about my problems. In fact, at that time, I wanted to go to Australia rather than Singapore. However, I went to Singapore because I had to consider various factors such as [my financial] conditions and my career. People around me said Singapore would help me more in terms of my introverted personality, career and [financial condition]. People around me have recommended a way to help me from a more objective point of view. Among them, the [financial] question [was] the biggest [factor] in determining which country to go to.

The language training [in] Australia was very expensive, but in Singapore I was able to earn money and be self-sufficient. So I chose Singapore.

It's hard to say that I didn't regret my choice after going to Singapore. When I heard about my friends who planned to go to Australia together, I thought I would like to live in Australia. But as a result, I don't regret the year I spent in Singapore. If I [had gone] to Australia [instead], I could have made another memory, but life in Singapore helped me a lot and made many unforgettable memories.[15]

Even though this case study is anecdotal in nature, it provides a glimpse into the reasons that Koreans engage in similar consultation/consensus building processes when faced with a critical decision and the benefits they perceive from the engagement.

This consultation process appears to be the rule rather than the exception. Assuming that this rule is generally and essentially accurate, it reflects the value that Koreans place on consensus building and opting for the road well-traveled, since it is the one that has produced positive results for others. By taking the established path, the probability that they, too, will experience success is therefore enhanced. The rationale is that there is no need to "re-invent the wheel" and take unnecessary risks by making an independent decision. The concept of efficiency also comes into play in these types of decision-making situations. Students avoid wasted effort and disappointments by consulting with those who know them and their circumstances well and have had successful experiences in similar circumstances.

Consensus-building patterns of behavior are evident outside of education as well. An example of the consultation process that takes place and leads to consensus building is palpable in the real estate industry. When faced with the prospect of purchasing real estate, Koreans usually take into consideration the opinion of family members, relatives, and friends. Before making a commitment, they consult extensively with others who have had successful experiences in this area. This consultation process and consensus building is a way of conducting an informal survey of the people within the influence circle of Koreans whose opinion they trust. The results of such an inquiry makes Koreans feel confident that they are making a decision that will benefit them in the long run. It is in essence an efficient way to ensure success, and it is applied in any number of areas, aside from those already mentioned, including doctor and hospital selection for medical treatment, stock selection for investment purposes, fashion trends, restaurant selection, and acquisition of goods and services.

Competition and Efficiency

As discussed previously, an intensely competitive environment is embedded deeply in the fabric of the Korean culture. The preferred method of dealing with the brutal competition that is so pervasive throughout the society, from the higher levels to the lower echelons, is via efficiency. To this end, quantitative measures represented by numerical values and ranking systems are widely used. Generally speaking, efficiency is achievable for educational entities, government agencies, business and industry, as well as the general public, by implementing a ranking system that assigns numerical values to a set of criteria. Boiling down simple variables to a numerical value is undoubtedly efficient. The added value of using these rankings is the perceived fairness by the general public. Fairness is highly valued by Koreans especially because of the extremely competitive environment. Koreans do not mind or shy away from competition as long as there is a perception of fairness in the evaluation process.

The challenge, however, is that factors such as personality traits, potential, motivation, and the internalization of values, are more difficult to quantify. Even though complex factors can be assigned a numerical value, a qualitative method, even though is more complex and time-consuming to interpret, is often more effective at analyzing empirical data such as human behavior, motivation, and personality characteristics than purely quantitative metrics. The effectiveness and fairness aspect of qualitative measures is enhanced when a carefully designed rubric is employed.

As aforementioned, institutions of higher learning in the United States are leading the way in establishing a new paradigm that in essence reverses the practice of utilizing standardized test scores for admission purposes that began in the 20th century:

> [These practices have] the idealistic goals of rewarding academic merit, breaking social class barriers and

giving all students a chance to prove they belong in college. But studies have found a strong link between scores and economic background. Privileged students, with wider access to books, museums, tutors and other forms of cultural or academic enrichment, tend to get higher marks.[16]

If a correlation between test scores and economic background is found to have statistical validity in the United States, perhaps the same conditions are true in Korea. If so, that correlation discredits the belief that utilizing standardized test scores is a more fair way of determining university admission. To provide wider access, some universities in the United States are relying less frequently on test scores as predictors of success in an academic environment. This new trend shows that admission officers are beginning to recognize the fallacy of relying on standardized test scores for making admission decisions, and the propensity to exclude students with intellectual potential. They have begun to assign more weight to qualitative information about the applicant.

On the subject of fairness, *The Chronicle of Higher Education* reported that James G. Nondorf, University of Chicago's vice president for enrollment, had "heard lingering concerns about what some people described as enduring barriers to access: One of those was Chicago's testing requirement." Mr. Nondorf was quoted as saying:

It was time that we looked at the application process and made sure it was fair for everyone. High-school counselors will tell you about a kid who would be a perfect fit for Chicago, who's not a good tester but who's talented in other ways, but who chose not to apply. You have enough of those interactions, and it tells you that the requirement is holding some students back, that it's scaring them away.[17]

This new paradigm will most likely take time to reach Korea primarily because of the brutally competitive environment and the trust the society has placed on objective criteria or quantitative measures for the sake of fairness. The irony is that the very same test-based process that is perceived as enabling a degree of fairness may be doing exactly the opposite by excluding students with intellectual potential.

Examples of Efficiency

Student Rankings

Admission to university in Korea is a very long and extremely competitive process, one that begins as early as junior high school. School officials infuse efficiency into the process by assigning rankings to students. These rankings are called 내신 (pronounced "*naesin*"). Beginning in junior high and continuing through high school, student rankings are derived from a combination of locally developed and national tests. Student rankings become an integral part of the students' lives and their psyche from a very early age. Students often refer to the rankings when talking among themselves. They are aware that through these rankings they are building their case toward university acceptance, the first step toward a dream job, and eventual financial success. Universities take these rankings into consideration, along with other factors, when making admission decisions. In my role as the guidance counselor, I recall reviewing transcripts of incoming students from Korean schools and noting the ranking system. The only time I reviewed these rankings was when I transcribed an incoming student's transcript because they gave me an indication of where the student was in relation to his class at the Korean school. However, once the student began earning grades at the American school, the rankings became irrelevant since the grades earned at the American school were a more realistic indicator of the student's potential in a second language environment.

Hagwons and Private Tutoring

The concept of after-school academies, or "cram schools" known as *hagwons*, and private tutoring are examples of the pervasive emphasis on efficiency that permeates the Korean culture. *Hagwons* and private tutoring are discussed more in detail in Chapter Three, but for this chapter, the discussion will focus exclusively on their function. Also, unless otherwise specified, in this chapter only the reference to *hawgon* indicates both *hagwons* and private tutoring. Even though *hagwons* which specialize in meeting the academic needs of adults do exist, the fundamental role of *hagwons* is to provide elementary, junior and senior high school students with academic support in areas that are considered to be crucial for success in the university admission process. However, there are *hagwons* that specialize in other areas, including the arts. Generally speaking, Koreans view the academic support that *hagwons* provide as above and beyond the education delivered by elementary, junior and senior high schools. As stated earlier, these academies emphasize areas such as English education (e.g., conversation), mathematics, science, and performing arts. In addition, they provide support in preparation for the *Suneung*. This test includes an English section. Other tests required for international university admission include the SAT (Scholastic Aptitude Test), the ACT (American College Testing), the TOEFL (Test of English as a Foreign Language), and the TOEIC (Test of English for International Communication). The TOEFL is mainly applicable for students planning to attend university abroad, and the TOEIC is used to assess English proficiency for the workplace. Parents perceive the training provided by *hagwons* in the area of test preparation for the *Suneung* as a way to level the playing field in a highly competitive university admission process. *Hagwons* provide their children with test-taking strategies as well as test practice. Therefore, if a *hagwon* can significantly increase a student's score on the *Suneung* in a relatively short period of time through efficient test-taking strategies, the cost of attending the cram school will be worth every Korean won spent on it. Because of the highly competitive process for Korean university admission, a student's enrollment in *hagwon* for test preparation purposes is not an option, but a necessity. The challenge for students from families with limited financial resources is that their family's particular situation may prevent them from accessing the better quality *hagwons* that children from wealthier families can afford, or it may even prevent them from participating at all, thus placing them at a disadvantage.

Naver and Trending Topics

Naver, one of the most popular internet portals in Korea today, was founded on June 2, 1999.[18] It includes widely used services such as search engine capabilities, news, email, community services, including blogs, cafes, and rankings of real-time trending topics. In 2018, Naver came in at no. 34 on *Forbes'* Top 100 Digital Companies list.[19] In addition, the same year, it was ranked number nine on *Forbes'* World's Most Innovative Companies list.[20] Conflicting information renders inconclusive the question about whether Naver or Google is the most popular search engine in Korea. Some search engine result pages rank Google higher, others rank Naver as the go-to search engine for Koreans. The Egg, a company specializing in search and digital marketing, conducted research to determine the search engine market share in Korea. After reviewing data provided by search engine result pages, comparing search volumes of a sample of key words, and comparing keyword trends in Google, Naver, and Daum, another Korean search engine, The Egg concluded that the best source of Korean search engine market share data is KoreanClick (2016), which "shows that the dominant search engine in Korea is still Naver (74%), followed by another local search engine Daum (16%), and finally Google (10%)."[21] However, The Egg also acknowledges that Google has been gaining shares rapidly over the years, while both Naver and Daum have been trending downward.[22]

Naver's real-time trending topics service has become a phenomenon that is unique to the Korean culture. In addition to providing the general trending topics, Naver presents trending topics by age category. The phenomenon underscores the emphasis on efficiency. It is not uncommon for Koreans to ask each other, "What is the number one trending topic?" When people pose this question, Koreans know exactly that the question refers to Naver's number one real-time trending topic. In other words, Koreans identify the number one trending topic by visiting the Naver website. The top topic then becomes the "topic du jour" thanks to the use of technology, thus "cutting to the chase" efficiently and eliminating any wasted effort and time. The real-time nature of the trending topics reflects the ephemeral quality of issues that are in vogue as well as the fickle nature, and the tendency to gravitate toward fads. By contrast, United States websites do not breakdown the trending topics by age category, and people do not ask, "What is the number one trending topic?" and expect others to know what they are talking about.

Pali Pali **Culture**

One cultural characteristic that is very specific to Korea is the tendency to do everything quickly. This characteristic is commonly referred to as "*pali pali*" or "hurry, hurry." I will examine in detail instances throughout the book that reflect this tendency. Therefore, this section will serve as an introduction of this peculiarity. Koreans are keenly aware of this culturual concept which they view as a tool for success. They inculcate it on children from a very early age. Schools, *hagwons,* and private tutors promote the adoption of the "*pali pali*" characteristic by teaching students to solve problems quickly because how fast they solve problems determines their academic success. When eating in a restaurant, unless they are enjoying drinks, Koreans like to eat fast, pay for their meal, and go. Restauranteurs and servers expect no less. Whether eating out or in, Koreans prefer their food delivered fast. Fast food delivery is readily and universally available. It is also considered an acceptable alternative, particularly since restauranteurs commit to fast delivery. As discussed in the Introduction, Korea's internet speed has held the number one spot in the world for as long as these data sets have been documented from the fourth quarter in 2015 to the first quarter in 2017. Koreans also enjoy their fast internet access. They also erect structures fast. Examples and issues surrounding buildings erected in record time will be discussed in Chapter Six. The infatuation with a fast-paced lifestyle is attributed to the rapid economic expansion of the country that took place in record time after the Korean War.[23]

My Experience with the Medical Profession

While in Korea, I had the opportunity to visit some hospitals and clinics to attend to my personal needs. The affordability of the services was astonishing. As an example, as of this writing, the cost of a liver ultrasound test in Korea is less than $100 without medical insurance. By comparison, in the U.S., a similar test costs $390 on average according to New Choice Health, Inc. [24]

One of the major hospitals I visited most frequently was associated with a national university. As such, it was a research hospital consisting of approximately 40 departments. Each time I visited the hospital, I was amazed by the number of patients not only in one unit, but throughout the hospital. Every time I walked into a specific department, I saw several dozen patients in the waiting room. There were two receptionists, one at each end of the floor. Even though there was always a long wait, doctors saw patients in an orderly fashion. Once a patient checked in with the receptionist, they would wait for their name to appear on a screen in front of the doctor's office. Instead of being escorted to an examination room, each patient would see the doctor for a few minutes in the doctor's individual office. The doctor did not need to walk around to different examination rooms. They simply stayed in their offices, seeing patient after patient. The emphasis on efficiency was evident. Even though the number of patients appeared to be overwhelming, the use of technology enabled the staff to process everyone efficiently. Equally efficient was the process that I, as a patient, went through. In a three-hour period, I underwent blood tests, an ultrasound test and a visit with the doctor. By the time I stepped into the doctor's office, the test results were already in the system; thus the doctor was able to reference them during my interview/examination.

I visited other hospitals and clinics and found that they made use of technology in a very similar fashion to provide patients with a very seamless and efficient process. Therefore, I believe that my experience with this hospital was typical practice and not an aberration.

On March 2, 2018, during a news telecast on KBS, one of Korea's largest broadcasting companies, a story related to the country's emphasis on efficiency was televised. The story directly relates to my personal observations described in the section above. The segment focused on the concern over the number of patients assigned to nurses in Korea. The School of Nursing at Seoul National University provided the statistics presented during the broadcast. According to the statistics quoted during this segment, nurses in Korea are assigned 43.6 patients on average, eight times more than in the U.S. where the average is 5.3 patients and five times more than in the United Kingdom at 8.6 patients. The news segment also reported that a joint study between Chonbuk National University and Ulsan University indicate that the insufficient number of nurses is responsible for approximately 9.2% of total medical complications. These complications might have been avoided if nurses had a smaller number of patients assigned to them.[25] However, efficient utilization of medical professionals and facilities contributes to keeping medical costs significantly affordable to the public.

Match-making Clubs

Competitiveness and efficiency coexist as a complementing pair, even in the social aspect of Korean society. There are many match-making clubs which interested men and women can access to find their ideal mate. The operators of these clubs happily accept applications from clients who provide very detailed personal and family information. This information is corroborated through an interview with the candidate. The data are converted to numerical values, which are used to efficiently and quickly generate a ranking system. This ranking enables match-making club operators to identify potential candidates for an individual. Below are sample lists of the type of information collected from clients. It is worth noting that although the data for men and women are similar, there is a subtle difference between the two.

Sample Information Collected from Male Clients

- » Profession and education
- » Income and property ownership
- » Family wealth, responsibilities, and socioeconomic status
- » Appearance (i.e., looks, height, and weight)
- » Age and marriage history

Sample Information Collected from Female Clients

- » Appearance (i.e., looks, height, and weight)
- » Age and marriage history
- » Profession and education
- » Family background (e.g., father's occupation)

It is worth pointing out the materialistic nature of the information collected from clients. These questionnaires reflect cultural aspects that have been embedded in Korean society for many years. It is evident that the data sets obtained from male clients have a financial bias. Property ownership, for example, is undoubtedly an indication of financial stability and wealth. On the one hand, family wealth is an essential factor for male clients, specifically. Historically in Korean society, males have inherited the majority of the family assets. On the other hand, family background, such as a father's occupation, indicates financial status or family prestige and reputation attributed to a female client.

Based on the queries, Korean matchmakers are clearly more direct and pose questions that go beyond the questions asked by dating services in the United States, such as questions about family background and father's occupation. Korean matchmakers use these data to evaluate and rank or categorize the client. This system is more thorough than dating systems in the United States. American dating systems generally show the facts about potential candidates that match the criteria identified by the client. The client then selects the potential candidates for dating. This is a trial-and-error system which could be lengthy, and therefore, possibly inefficient.

Conversely, Korean matchmakers themselves determine who the client is allowed to contact based on the candidates' evaluation and rank or category. This system is more efficient because the trial-and-error period is significantly reduced, if not eliminated, since the match-maker has already pre-screened both the client and the potential candidate, and has determined the viability of the match based on their rank or category. In other words, the match-maker will introduce a potential candidate and a client if their respective ranks match. A matchmaker will not introduce a client to a potential candidate from a higher or lower tier because that would be opening the door to a mismatch, thus a waste of time.

Adopting New Trends

As stated earlier, the tendency to conform and the desire to differentiate from one another as a result of the competitive nature of Korean society represents a dichotomy that Koreans seem to be able to navigate successfully. The competitive environment, particularly when it comes to differentiating the socioeconomic status of an individual from the rest of the society, may explain why when a new trend surfaces in society, whether in the economy, in fashion, or in social media, the trendsetters or early adopters seem to gravitate in the same direction at least until the latest trend has been generally adopted. When a new pattern is in vogue, the urge to stand out, to be different, to be better than others, including family and friends becomes the driving force of individual, and subsequently of group behavior.

Because the fundamental tendency to conform promotes homogeneity and harmony but discourages individuality, people tend to differentiate themselves from the pack by acquiring material possessions. They include such items as a more expensive car or apartment, more stylish clothing; eating in a more costly or fashionable restaurant, or shopping/hanging out in a newer or more prestigious mall in a more upscale neighborhood. However, once that trend is more generally adopted, people switch and find a new material possession, interest, place or activity that sets them apart from the rest. Restaurants, in particular, seem to fall victim to their success. Some new specialty restaurants that engage in an effective promotional campaign have the potential to attract a sufficiently large clientele to generate initial success, but once the novelty effect wears off, the large crowds can fade rapidly.

The popularity of and subsequent blasé attitude toward fusion Korean-Mexican food provides an interesting example of this pattern of early adopters establishing a new trend to distinguish themselves from the masses, and then moving to a new area of interest once the novelty wears off or the fad is adopted more universally. In 2011, three Korean-Americans decided to open a fusion Korean-Mexican restaurant called Vatos Urban Tacos in Itaewon, a multicultural, foreign-friendly area of Seoul where 20,000 foreigners reside. In 1997, Itaewon was designated as a special tourist zone.[26] "Travelers [and Korean residents] can taste authentic cuisine and experience culture from around the globe on the World Food Street where there are 40 restaurants operated by foreigners."[27] In addition, to international food, visitors as well as locals can enjoy shops, bars, and clubs that are foreigner-friendly. On weekends, Itaewon is particularly crowded with foreigners, locals and American servicemen and women who gather in this diverse environment to shop, eat, and party.

The restaurant was a huge success due primarily because of its location and the target audience—foreigners who were familiar with and enjoyed Korean and Mexican cuisine, and Koreans who had savored Mexican food in the United States. The Korean early adopters were those who had traveled or studied in the US; therefore, their socioeconomic status is assumed to be commensurate to those who could afford travel or study abroad. Other Koreans who had never been to the United States and had never tried Mexican food, saw this as an opportunity to be perceived as having a higher socioeconomic status, so they visited the restaurant to try the food. In a similar situation, early adopters in the U.S. would not necessarily be considered of a higher socioeconomic status.

Eventually, the owners opened at least three other restaurants in very strategic districts of Seoul: Yongsan-gu, the fashionable Sinsa-dong district, and Songpa-gu. In addition, a multitude of Korean entrepreneurs who were impressed with the success of Vatos Urban Tacos tried to duplicate the experience. Mexican restaurants in Seoul became commonplace. Once the trend became mundane, fusion Korean-Mexican food lost the perception of "special" quality and the novelty. The food was no longer considered trendy, so it lost its attractiveness outside of Vatos Urban Tacos. No other Mexican restaurant in Seoul has been able to match the success of Vatos Urban Tacos, CNN reports that the "waits can take up to three hours on weekends."[28]

To complete the story, ultimately, the owners of Vatos Urban Tacos brought the experience to market internationally. They opened a restaurant in Singapore and another in the Philippines.

A Korean friend of mine explained the dichotomy of wanting to conform to social norms and simultaneously taking action that accentuates difference, which in essence shows the competitive aspect of the culture, by saying: "We all look the same. We all have black hair and slanted eyes. Therefore, we want to be better than or at least look different, and more trendy than, everyone else. Aside from fashion, that is one reason why the young dye their hair of a different color, women are attracted to super expensive (*myung-poom*) items such as cosmetics, jewelry, and luxury handbags by Louis Vuitton, Hermès, and Chanel, and men gravitate toward expensive cars."[29] My friend continued on to say that these expensive handbags are such a vital status symbol

71

for Korean women that some will purchase the bags even though their salary is not commensurate with the cost of the expensive items. The difference between Korea and the United States is the degree or intensity of this practice. Specifically, it is common for Korean women to acquire expertise in the area of designer bags to such a degree that they are able to identify the specifications associated with an item, such as the price, whether it is a new or classic design, and how rare the item is. In addition, one of the most popular topics among women is precisely luxury designer bags.

News 1 published eye-opening statistics regarding 2017 worldwide luxury bag sales which indicate that Korea held the number four postion behind much more populous countries: the United States, China, and Japan.

Figure 3: 2017 Luxury Handbag Market
* Excludes Duty Free Shop and Black Market Sales[30]

Rank	Country	Sales in Trillion Korean Won*
1	United States	16.9
2	China	6.3
3	Japan	6.2
4	Korea	3.2
5	France	3.0

News 1 claims that spending in Korea on luxury handbags for 2017 would be number two in the world if duty free shop sales were included.[31] This point becomes even more emphatic given the population difference between Korea and the United States. In 2017, at 50 million, the Korean population was one-sixth of that of the United States at 326 million.[32]

The Shake Shack Phenomenon

An example of the propensity to differentiate from others on a superficial level is a recent phenomenon: the craze over Shake Shack burgers. On July 22, 2016, in the midst of high anticipation, the high-end burger chain, through an exclusive contract with SPC Group, the nation's largest bakery company, opened its first restaurant in the affluent Gangnam district in the south end of Seoul. On the opening day of the Shake Shack location, people lined up for hours in the sweltering summer heat. Some reported waiting for an entire night to ensure that they were among the first to savor the taste of the burgers, fries, and shakes. *The Korea Times* reported that approximately 1,500 people waited between two and three hours to get a taste of the American premium burger. The Korean reaction to this franchise exemplifies their desire to differentiate themselves from the crowd, the fascination with novelty, and the longing to emphasize or emulate a higher socioeconomic status. On the surface, the attitude vis-à-vis the opening of the first Shake Shack restaurant in Seoul would be no more than a typical reaction to novelty. However, when analyzed through a social lens, the behavioral patterns become evident.

First, generally speaking, Koreans do not like to wait in line, especially for food. Throughout the country, high-quality food is readily available, a result of the oversaturation of restaurants that not only prepare foods of all kinds, but emphasize efficiency. American fast food, specifically pizza, and hamburgers, is readily available thanks to the proliferation of American fast food chains such as Pizza Hut, Papa John's, McDonald's and Burger King. However, these restaurants established a foothold in Korea so long ago that they are no longer considered a novelty. According to *Modern Seoul*, McDonald's opened its first restaurant in Seoul in 1988.[33]

Second, in today's experiential culture, young Koreans, in their 20s and 30s in particular, have vigorously embraced social media just as millennials throughout the world have done. One of the activities that increases their visibility is the practice of food photo sharing. Consequently, the opportunity to be a part of a new trend that includes enduring a two- or three-hour wait in the blistering summer heat, to taste a quality prime burger, which only a select group will be able to experience, boosts the photographer's prestige enormously. Consequently, the long wait itself becomes a social event. Given these conditions, social media contributes enormously to the Shake Shack novelty phenomenon. Thanks to social media, these trendsetters post and share food photos and upload pictures of themselves and friends on their web pages. For some of them, it is an opportunity to inform or remind their friends and acquaintances that the taste of Shake Shack burgers brings back memories of the first time they experienced them back in New York. In their minds, traveling in the U.S. makes them "unique."

Third, the prices charged by the more traditional burger chains range within the amount of money that Koreans usually spend on lunch, which is around 8,000-10,000 Korean won (~$6.80-$8.50). By comparison, a no-frills outing at a Shake Shack restaurant in Gangnam would include possibly a basic single Shack burger for 6,900 Korean won, basic fries for 3,900 Korean won, a regular fountain soda for 2,700 Korean won, and a basic shake for 5,900 Korean won, which would add up to 19,400 Korean won (~$16.50). By paying two or three times the amount that they often spend for lunch, customers feel that they are set apart from the crowd. It is a status symbol they underscore through their selfies. The long delay in the heat and humidity of the middle of summer is an additional benefit in showcasing the experience. It shows that the burgers are not only worth the price but the wait. It is fashionable. It is expensive for Korean standards. Therefore, it is trendy. The Shake Shack phenomenon has expanded to other parts of Seoul, and it will eventually open in other cities in Korea since, according to NPR (National Public Radio), the SPC Group plans to open as many as 25 Shake Shack restaurants in Korea by 2025.[34] The novelty eventually will wear out, other trendy, expensive restaurants will pop up, and the early adopters will be the first to move on while the rest will continue to try to catch up.

The North Face Fad

The recent intense popularity of The North Face activewear among young people is another excellent example of this tendency toward finding something physical to differentiate oneself from the masses. Not long ago, wearing The North Face apparel became popular among the well-to-do, especially their children who would do anything to convince their parents to purchase clothing items, particularly jackets, with the logo of this particular manufacturer. The popularity of this brand name spread like wildfire. It became the latest craze among the masses who go hiking on weekends and holidays, and even among individuals of lower socioeconomic status. When this fad spread to the middle-class, wearing the attire lost its glamour. Consequently, people at the upper echelons of the socioeconomic ladder, and eventually those below, moved on to wearing other brands. This is not to say that the brand name is unpopular. On the contrary: It remains a status symbol, but it has undoubtedly lost some of the appeal it had when it first became popular.

After the 2018 winter season, the most popular brand of bench coats, or "long padding coats," as they are often called in Korea, was Discovery Expedition's Leicester model. Discovery Expedition is the brand name of a Korean clothing company, which sold 200,000 Leicester model bench coats in winter 2018. The Exploring model of bench coats by North Face came in second with an estimated 100,000 units sold:[35]

Bench coats are thick and stuffed with materials like down feathers from ducks and other birds. The term "long padding" became widely-used in Korea only after the "PyeongChang long padding" – a bench coat sold as official merchandise of the PyeongChang Winter Games – attracted great media attention after people lined up for hours outside department stores to purchase one of these limited-edition coats.[36]

Figure 4: North Face's Exploring and Discovery Expedition's "Leicester" Bench Coat[37]

The long-padding coat became the latest winter fashion among middle and high school students in fall 2016. With temperatures dropping in November, one could spot these trendy coats on the streets. They became even more popular in fall 2017 as the fad continued to spread among teenagers. Koreans in general, but especially teenagers, have a tendency to gravitate toward new trends at a high degree of intensity. This tendency is magnified particularly with clothing as a result of the social pressure, even from one's own family, to wear the latest styles. It is common for a person's relatives to point out in a very direct fashion, that the clothes they are wearing are out of style. In the case of long-padding coats, teenagers, who did not want to stand out in their school or among their friends, pressured their parents to purchase these coats that ranged in price between 50,000 Korean won (KRW) (~$47) and one million KRW (~ $935); however, apparently only those that cost above 200,000 KRW (~ $187) could satisfy the fashion-conscious youth. This fashion consciousness undoubtedly places a burden on parents who already have financial pressures associated with private education costs. Generally speaking, Korean parents assume the full financial responsibility for raising their children, and normally they prefer that their children not work so they can focus on their studies. However, if a child happens to desire an expensive item that the parents cannot afford, in some instances the teenager will take the initiative to obtain a temporary part-time job to enable them to purchase the item.

Teenagers around the world tend to be fashion-conscious; however, among Korean teenagers, there is the added cultural pressure and desire to blend in or conform to group norms. Because of their uniformity, these long-padding coats appear to have social significance for Koreans who find "comfort in uniformity rather than individuality."[38] It is not surprising then that the official 2018 PyeongChang Winter Olympics long-padding coats, which were released on October 26, 2017, flew off the shelves. They came only in three colors—black, white and gray and cost 149,000 Korean Won (KRW) (~$137 U.S. dollars). They were sold out within two weeks of their release. People camped out the night before outside the stores that advertised the PyeongChang padded coats to ensure they were able to purchase one.

Gap and *Eul*

Another code profoundly ingrained in the fabric of society is the *gap* and *eul* relationship. These terms are used to differentiate between two parties:one with authority or power and another without it. In English, one might use antonyms big and little, large and small, strong and weak, or perhaps even top dog and bottom dog. Many relationships are based in these two concepts.

An example of the *gap* and *eul* relationship is the "nut rage" incident aboard a Korean Airlines flight. One of the passengers, who happened to be the vice president and daughter of the current company owner and president, was served macadamia nuts in a bag instead of a bowl. She ordered the flight to abort the takeoff and return to the gate in order that the flight attendant who had served her the nuts could be escorted off the plane. She was later charged with, among other things, violating aviation security as well as employing violence against a flight crew member. Clearly, in this example, the company vice president felt that she had power and the flight attendant did not. Therefore, in the vice president's judgment, she felt justified to take the action that she did.

The relationship between major corporations and subcontractors is related to *gap* and *eul* as well as the concept of efficiency. Corporations outsource jobs that they prefer not to oversee in order to reduce costs. They utilize the bidding process to award contracts to subcontractors. The subcontractors first submit bids to the corporations, which usually assign the deal to the lowest bidder for efficiency and financial gain. Subcontractors recognize the need to present low proposals to have a chance of being awarded contracts. Therefore, once a corporation assigns the deal, the subcontractor has no choice but to cut corners for the project to be profitable. One option is to pay low wages, and another is to eliminate or minimize any training such as safety and risk management training. In this environment, subcontractor employees take risks to maximize their earning power. The result is a lack of emphasis on safety procedures for efficiency sake and short-term financial gains by both the subcontractors and their employees. As a result of this relationship between corporations and subcontractors, the former can avoid liability while the latter absorbs it. The subcontractors or smaller companies ultimately bear the financial responsibility. Korean subcontractors in areas such as construction, are willing to take on a greater degree of risk because of the high degree of competition in the industry.

The incentives behind the relationship between corporations, their subcontractors, and the general public appear to be the following:

Major Corporations

Major corporations are all powerful, primarily government-owned or family-owned *chaebols*. They need subcontractors for these reasons:

» avoid the monopoly syndrome
» maintain good public relations—they avoid being accused of destroying the competition, including mom-and-pop enterprises
» circumvent or minimize work that may not be within the scope of the company or that may not be profitable for them
» avoid or reduce training and supervision costs in the area/s being subcontracted
» elude insurance costs
» avert financial responsibility when accidents occur
» sidestep moral responsibility

Subcontractors

Subcontractors in many instances are small to mid-sized companies, or even mom-and-pop owned businesses, that cannot possibly compete with the major corporations either financially or in the scope of projects that they can complete. They benefit from the relationship with major corporations for the following reasons:

» generate business and maintain a steady revenue to stay afloat
» keep their employees working, or add employees to their payroll, who would otherwise be unemployed or hired by the major corporations

» provide a service that major corporations would prefer not be involved in

» keep costs low for the general public

The General Public

In this relationship, the public benefits primarily and most importantly in the following manner:

» pay lower prices for goods and services provided by major corporations in partnership with subcontractors

The three major players in the Korean economy are the government, major corporations, and the general public. These three entities, with their divergent interests, have an interdependent relationship with each other that is very difficult to change. The interdependence between these three key players appears in the chart below.

Figure 5: Interdependence of Major Economic Players

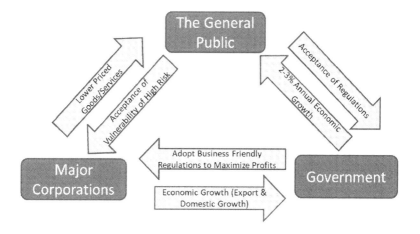

As depicted by the above flowchart, corporations like Samsung Electronics, Seoul Metro, and POSCO have an augmented capability to conduct business efficiently. As a result, they are able to deliver lower-priced goods and services to the general public. Government-adopted regulations favor this system, providing even more benefits, ultimately, for the general public. By doing so, the corporations can contribute to the 2%-3% annual economic growth sought by the government and expected by the general public. In return, the public accepts both the government-adopted regulations that favor corporations and the inherent vulnerability of high risk and an accident-prone environment. The interdependence between these three entities is so robust that in spite of the number of fatal accidents that have taken place as a result, the status quo is difficult to change. Given that the desires and objectives of each entity are met consistently through this environment, it would require a conscious effort by each and all of the parties to adopt a climate in which all parties win, and no one loses. It seems that in the existing relationship, public safety is sacrificed in favor of short-term financial gains.

Accidents have taken place in the process of subcontractors performing jobs for major corporations. When accidents occur, it is not unusual for safety violations to surface as the primary cause. However, the irony here is that subcontractors are often not required to provide safety training for their employees, especially to temporary employees as was the case in the April 16, 2014 *Sewol* ferry accident which is discussed in detail in Chapter Six. Temporary employees are frequently hired for financial efficiency. Because subcontracting companies perform the work, they are held legally and financially accountable for accidents. By contrast, only *some* key officials of the contracting corporation (e.g., on-site safety managers) are held responsible. In this relationship, as we saw earlier, corporations avoid liability for accidents by utilizing the subcontracting mechanism, which is allowed by law.

If subcontractors placed more emphasis on safety and were required to uphold safety regulations, their costs would increase. Those costs would be passed on to the major corporations and they, in turn, would pass them on to the public, which would likely be poorly received. The public's reaction when accidents occur is outrage toward the head of the subcontracting company and the major corporation involved. However, if the public is genuinely interested in minimizing the number of accidents, they must pressure subcontractors to assign equal emphasis to safety and profits. Consequently, the general public must be willing to bear the brunt of the cost increases.

The typical reaction of the general public, when accidents do occur involving a major corporation and subcontractor, is to identify the head of the subcontracting company and the key official/s of the corporation who oversee/s the project (e.g., on-site safety manager/s), fire them, prosecute them, and move on. However, focusing on individuals alone does not go far enough to avoid similar future accidents. The government, general public, and major corporations must also recognize their role in this interdependent relationship and live up to their responsibility.

This interdependent relationship indicates what appears to be a separation consciousness, which calls for each entity to have different motivations, goals, and objectives. In essence, with only a few exceptions, each body works toward its own goals and objectives, which may not be in line with the goals and objectives of the other two bodies. What is needed for all three entities to work effectively in concert is the adoption of a unity consciousness. This would create an environment where success is not only measured by corporate profits, but also strict adherence to safety measures that will reduce safety-related accidents, and generate stiff penalties for those who choose to disobey safety regulations. Adhering to these criteria may also mean that short-term profits will be impacted. Thus, a temporary adjustment to the expected 2%-3% GDP increase per annum may have to be accepted by the government and the general public. Furthermore, higher prices of goods and services may have to be endured by the genral public. Despite the short-term economic impact, this new environment would engender a collaborative attitude toward common goals, objectives, and problem-solving. In the long run, if the three entities could collaborate harmoniously toward the benefit of all, the needs of all three would be met. Adopting a genuine unity consciousness would take Korea back to its roots as a nation united for the good of all.

Another example of the *gap* and *eul* relationship is evident in the link between delivery men, who are extensively utilized, food vendors, and their clients. In this triad, consumers of delivery food remain at the top of the hierarchy. Their privileged position as consumers who have the income to pay for the food they order, which includes delivery costs, results in a socially respected position. Next, food vendors do retain some power as a result of their ability to hire/fire and pay the salary of delivery men. However, the food vendors have less power than clients, because they provide a service in exchange for the money clients are willing to pay for it. Delivery men are consequently at the bottom tier of this chain.

In such a position, they recieve pressure from both clients and food vendors, but they are not able to apply pressure on either of the other two parties. Given their position in the triad, clients can and do demand that their food be delivered hot and on time. They expect the food delivery service provider, as well as the delivery person, to be efficient. They are capable of applying pressure on the food vendors, and in turn vendors pressure delivery men to deliver the food as fast as possible regardless of how many traffic rules they have to break or whether they risk their own lives or the lives of others, in order to get the job done in a timely manner and efficiently. The issue of accidents involving food delivery men is discussed in more detail in Chapter Two. Once again, the concept of efficiency is clearly present in the triad composed of delivery men, food vendors, and clients.

Based on the discussion above, it is evident that in the *gap* and *eul* relationship, the pressure flows in the same direction as the flow of money. Therefore, it is safe to assume that in these examples, money determines who is on top and who is at the bottom of a *gap* and *eul* relationship. Even though the *gap* and *eul* relationship pattern very much resembles similar situations in other capitalist countries, the difference is in the higher degree of intensity that appears to exist in Korean society. This higher level of intensity may very well be related to the ubiquitous fierce competition. In the "nut rage" case, for example, the flight attendant had to excel in a brutally competitive environment to attain his job, whereas the Korean Airlines owner's daughter gained her high-level position by virtue of her relationship to the owner of the company—her father. It is safe to assume that she did not have to compete with others for her title. Her priviledged position with the company will continue even after the company owner dies, since it is common practice for the ownership of a *chaebol* or any company, privately- or publicly-owned regardless of its size, to be transferred to the next generation along with the corresponding socioeconomic status.

The remaining pages will show the pervasive nature of the cultural and behavioral patterns discussed in this chapter.

Endnotes

1. "Flag of South Korea," *Wikipedia*, accessed 14 November 2019, *en.wikipedia.org*

2. "Top Universities in Korea," *UniRank*, accessed 30 June 2019, *4icu.org./kr/.*

3. "Three Most Prestigious Universities in South Korea,"*Your University Guide*, accessed 1 July 2019, *youruniversityguide.wordpress.com*.

4. "Best Global Universities in South Korea," *U.S. News & World Report*, accessed 6 July 2019, *usnews.com*.

5. "Best Universities in South Korea 2019," *Times Higher Education*, accessed 6 July 2019, *timeshighereducation.com*.

6. "South Korea: CWUR World University Rankings 2018-2019," *Center for World University Rankings*, accessed 6 July 2019, *cwur.org*.

7. "Homepage," *Fair Test: The National Center for Fair and Open Testing*," accessed 13 November 2019, *fairtest.org*.

8. Ibid.

9. Eric Hoover, "An Ultra-Selective University Just Dropped the ACT/SAT. So What?", *The Chronicle of Higher Education*, 14 June 2018, *chronicle.com*.

10. *The Washington Post* reports James G. Nondorf's title as "Dean of Admissions and Financial Aid," whereas *The Chronicle of Higher Education* titles Nondorf "Vice President for Enrollment." Nick Anderson, "A shake-up in elite admissions: U-Chicago drops SAT/ACT testing requirement," *The Washington Post*, 14 June 2018, *washingtonpost.com*.

11. Kari Huus, "The Cost of the Olympics from the 1940s to today," 15 August 2018, *msn.com*.

12. Doug Struck, "Hosts Left to Foot the World Cup Bill," *The Washington Post*, 29 June 2006, *washingtonpost.com*.

13. Ibid.

14. Frank Holmes, " How Gold Rode to the Rescue of South Korea," *Forbes*, 27 September 2016, *forbes.com*.

15. A university student's retrospective look at his decision to select Singapore over Australia for an internship in hotel management, and the consultation process that helped him arrive at his decision. Anonymous, personal interview by John Gonzalez, text interview, 12-13 July 2019.

16. Anderson, "A shake-up"

17. Hoover, "An Ultra-Selective University."

18. "#1442 Naver," *Forbes*, accessed 8 July 2019, *forbes.com*.

19. Ibid.

20. Ibid.

21. "Debunking the Korean Search Market Share in 2017," *The Egg*, accessed 8 July 2019, *theegg.com*.

22. Ibid.

23. "Ppalli Ppalli Culture," *Korea Daily*, accessed 3 July 2019, *koreadailyus.com*.

24. *New Choice Health*, accessed 7 July 2019, *newchoicehealth.com*.

25. KBS," *Naver*, accessed 7 July 2019, *naver.me*.

26. "Destinations by Region," *Official Korea Tourism Organization*, accessed 9 July 2019, *english.visitkorea.or.kr*.

27. Ibid.

28. "Top Things to Do and See: Seoul," *CNN*, accessed 9 July 2019, *cnn.com*.

29. Anonymous, personal interview by John Gonzalez, in-person, 19 June 2018.

30. Hemin Jung, "Korean's love for luxury handbags has surpassed the French... Now, the 4th biggest market in the world," trans. Young Lee, *News 1*, 1 October 2018, *naver. me/GDvyOwGg*.

31. Ibid.

32. "The World Factbook," *Central Intelligence Agency*, accessed 8 July 2018, *cia.gov.*

33. "McDonalds in South Korea, *Modern Seoul*, 16 February 2013, *modernseoul.org.*

34. Sangyoub Park, "What's Behind South Korea's Shake Shack Fever?" *NPR*, 6 September 2016, *npr.org.*

35. "Discovery is no. 1 As Bench Coat Season Ends," *Korea Joongang Daily*, accessed 10 July 2019, *koreajoongangdaily.com.*

36. Ibid.

37. Ibid.

38. Sun-young Lee, "[Weekender] One coat that conquered street fashion in South Korea," *The Korea Herald*, 1 December 2017, *koreaherald.com.*

Chapter Two

Everyday Life

It is important to note that although I visited cities such as Seoul, Busan, Daejeon, Incheon, Yeosu, Mokpo, Pohang, Suwon, Jeju City, and Tongyeong on many occasions during the five years I resided in the country, I spent a large portion of that time in two rather small cities: Jukjeon and Jeonju. I lived in Jukjeon, a comparatively new city located just south of Seoul in Gyeonggi Province, for one year. Jeonju is the capital of Jeollabuk-do in North Jeolla Province, a relatively small city of 663,000 residents located in the Southwest area of the country.[1] This city is dwarfed by urban centers such as Seoul, which is home to 10 million, Busan, over three million, and Incheon and Daegu with over two million people each. Consequently, Jeonju is regarded by many Koreans living in the big cities as provincial. I recall a Korean friend who lived in one of the large cities asking me if there was a Paris Baguette shop in Jeonju. Paris Baguette is a popular chain of ubiquitous bakery stores. The answer was: "Of course there is." This rather innocent, but telling, question reveals the attitude that people living in the big cities have toward smaller cities. In fact, Jeonju attracts thousands of Korean tourists from as far away as Incheon and Seoul on weekends, holidays and in the summer to its primary tourist attraction, Hanok Village

(Traditional Korean Village). Regardless, the city is considered rural. This attitude remains, even in spite of the city's nomination to UNESCO's Creative Cities Network for Gastronomy in 2012. To a large extent, the perceptions from the big-city citizens are accurate, since Jeonju's two most dominant industries are tourism/ hospitality and agriculture.

Confirming UNESCO's designation, Jeonju is viewed by many as a gastronomical center for its home-style cooking that has been handed down from generation to generation. At the time that I lived there, the city of Jeonju also had the reputation as a rural town in part due to the limited public transportation. Routes to and from Jeonju, and particularly between Jeonju and Seoul, were challenging. Only a handful of KTX (Korea Train eXpress) trains per week passed through Jeonju. By contrast, as of this writing, four KTX trains travel daily from Seoul to Jeonju and four return back to the capital. Consisting of high-speed trains traveling at speeds of 300 kilometers (186.4 miles) per hour, KTX is considered the most comfortable, convenient, efficient and fastest way to get around in Korea.[2]

The official KORAIL (Korea Rail Road Corporation) website describes KTX as follows:

> High-speed rail service has not only reduced the travel time to anywhere in South Korea to less than 3 hours, causing a dramatic change in people's lifestyle, but also had a significant social, economic and cultural impact. High-speed rail is emerging as

a new transport means for the future equipped with state-of-the-art technologies that ensure a fast, safe, comfortable and environment-friendly ride.[3]

Because of my extensive experience in Jeonju, my observations of everyday life have a Jeonju flavor. This does not mean that these observations are not applicable to other parts of the country. What it does mean is that some of these experiences may have been more or less pronounced in Jeonju than if I had resided and worked in other parts of the country.

To balance my observations of the culture and people, I traveled extensively. As far as my own transportation was concerned, I had access to a car while working in Korea not only to facilitate going to and from work five days per week, but also to simplify my travels throughout the country. For example, on weekends I traveled to large and medium-sized cities such as Busan, Gunsan, Gwangju, Iksan, Incheon, Mokpo, Pohang, Pyeongchang, Seoul, Suwon, Tongyeong, and Yeosu. In addition, I traveled to small cities and towns, including Gimje, Gochang, Im Sil, Jinan, Jumunjin, Namhae, Namwon, Nonsan, Seocheon, Sunchang, and Suncheon, as well as the mountains to visit Buddhist temples. I also visited Jeju Island on several occasions and attended education conferences in Seoul and Incheon.

Throughout my travels, I continued to observe people's behavior. Invariably, two constant qualities that permeate throughout my observations are the emphasis on efficiency for efficiency's sake or constant questing for ways to go around an established rule, policy or law for the sake of convenience or in order to achieve quick financial returns. Below are some behavioral patterns I observed in everyday life. Some of these observations may appear trivial to the casual observer; however, they are representative of, and a microcosm of, pervasive behavioral patterns in the society at large.

The Eating Experience

Having had over 3,000 meals in public (i.e., in restaurants or at the university cafeteria) during my stay in Korea, I had the opportunity to make valuable observations about the eating habits of Koreans, particularly when eating in groups. This observation exercise also enabled me to reflect on the eating habits of Westerners so that I might compare and contrast the two. This process facilitated the identification of Korean eating habits that appear to be cultural in nature. The most obvious observation is that, generally speaking, in Korean cuisine an array of side dishes complements the main course. These side dishes are usually served before the main course or at the same time as the main course. Among other items, they consist of small layers of plain scrambled eggs, assorted vegetables fried in batter in the shape of a pizza, and a large variety of marinated vegetables with spices including garlic, red pepper, green onions, sesame oil and/or seeds, rice vinegar, ginger, and fish oil. These side dishes are like a painter's palette that adds to the variety of colors, but most importantly the rainbow of flavors that partakers are free to sample in the sequence or combination of their choice. To say that Koreans genuinely enjoy their food is an understatement. They eat with gusto and savor the variety of flavors as well as the consistency of each component. They innately know what side dish to choose and how much of it to mix with a small portion of the main course to maximize their experience.

It is important to point out that Koreans view lunch and dinner very differently. Generally speaking, Koreans approach lunch with a more efficient attitude. Therefore, when eating out, every facet, from traveling to and from the restaurant to ordering the food, being served, and paying the check, is approached with this mindset. Even if eating out with co-workers, the expectation is to return to work promptly within an hour. Even though a similar attitude toward the lunch hour may exist in other capitalist countries, the main difference is the apparent degree of intensity of this attitude. Everyone is cognizant and respectful of the time constraint. Lunch is a short break from work with the purpose of recharging the body with some nourishment to make it to the end of a long workday. A minimal amount of socializing is possible. This tradition of utilizing one's time efficiently during the lunch hour appears to have originated during the economic expansion period between the 1960s and 1980s, which seems to coincide with the beginning of the *pali pali* culture as well: "A great many Koreans had to work hard and long hours to attain the goal of high growth, shortening their lunch and dinner break."[4]

An example of efficient use of time during meals, but particularly at lunch, is the practice of calling the restaurant ahead of time and placing the order over the phone for the people in the group. Doing so ensures not only that the table is reserved and set ahead of time, but the food is prepared and served either just before the party arrives or as the party is arriving in the restaurant. This guarantees that the members of the party can start consuming their meal as soon as they arrive in the restaurant. Clearly, no time is wasted in this custom.

However, whether with family and friends or co-workers, dinner is viewed as an opportunity to socialize, unwind and truly enjoy a meal and possibly some drinks, such as beer and *soju*. Without the time constraints of lunch, dinner enables participants to drop the efficiency mindset. Thus, the ambiance is more relaxed. It is common practice for these dinners to last two or three hours. Because socializing occasionally with co-workers at the end of the day is expected to maintain good morale and interpersonal relations in the unit or company, some employees feel imposed upon. Despite this feeling, they participate regardless, out of concern of being ostracized if they do not. The feeling of being imposed upon is not unfounded, for Koreans put in some of the longest hours of work in the world as evidenced by OECD (Organization for Economic Cooperation and Development) data discussed in more detail in Chapter Six. Tagging a couple of hours for a social dinner to an already long workday does feel to many of them like an imposition on their personal time. This tradition is less of a concern now than it used to be because in 2018 a law was passed limiting the work week to 52 hours. It is true that working people in other capitalist countries such as the United States also have dinner occasionally with co-workers. However, the difference is that the degree of frequency and degree of pressure to participate is higher in Korea.

Sharing of food amongst Koreans as a charming, humanistic activity is an undeniable fact. Food sharing has a deeper meaning than the mere act of eating together; it represents communal solidarity, which in essence supports the concepts of unity, conformity, and harmony. These cultural attributes were discussed in Chapter One. Whether eating in pairs or as a group, the main course or courses, as well as the accompanying side dishes, are shared among the people at the table. Participants dig in with zest, enjoying every bite while being careful not to appear to be too eager, selfish or eating faster or larger quantities than the rest of the group members as a sign of consideration for the others. When family members, friends or very close individuals are present, it is common practice for people to use their chopsticks to grab a piece of food from either the main course or the side dishes and place it in another person's plate or even offer to put it in the other person's mouth as a sign of affection. The receiver accepts the gesture and they may reciprocate.

When eating out as a group in the West, the individualistic qualities of the culture are unmistakable because individuals do what they usually do: They give their order to the server often with precise indications as to how they want their food prepared. It is not surprising to hear individuals in the West declare that they are following a special diet or are vegetarian and therefore require very different food from the rest of their party. Americans, for example, believe that individuals are exercising their intrinsic right to be different when they point out their dietary needs in a social situation. The idea of reaching consensus on what food to order for everyone in the group is sometimes unimaginable, depending on the group you are dining with.

This scenario is very different in Korean society. The concepts of conformity and efficiency, are evident when small or large groups of people go out to eat together. The group may have a brief discussion about the menu options, but individuals will be agreeable about what to order as a group and yield to the wishes of the group or defer to one participant. This participant might be the senior member, or one who is most familiar with the menu choices offered by the restaurant. Individuals cannot imagine ordering something unique or different from the rest of the group.

Although the concept of following a vegetarian diet is not unheard of in Korea, when going out in a group the collective wishes take precedent. Furthermore, Korean food typically contains a wide array of vegetables, particularly among the side dishes. Therefore, it would be easy for a vegetarian to satisfy their hunger and adhere to a vegetarian diet in a group outing without much fanfare. In the five years I lived in Korea, I only came across one Korean who had chosen to follow a vegan diet.

In the scenario described above, the idea of conformity is clearly present. The concept of efficiency is easily explained by the fact that group consensus facilitates placing, taking, preparing, and serving the order. Therefore, it is smooth sailing for the leader of the group placing the order, the server taking it, the cook or chef preparing it, and the server serving it.

The situation is notably similar in instances during which food is ordered, whether at home or the office, and whether ordering one or several dishes. The concept of sharing remains prominent, and individuality is nonexistent. The advantage with Korean food is that ordinarily, the main course is garnished with side dishes that complement or enhance the flavor of the main course. People decide which side dishes to enjoy.

When it comes to food, the concepts of uniformity, conformity and efficiency are learned at an early age. When eating at home, families share meals: Everyone eats the same dishes. In other words, the concept of preparing different dishes for individuals does not exist. In America, for example, the idea of preparing somewhat different dishes for specific family members on account of diet or preference is not unheard of. In Korea, individual family members would not dream of requesting unique dishes specially prepared for them. This pattern of sharing continues through preschool, elementary school, the army, and the workplace. If the school provides lunch, the menu options are limited. If students bring their lunch from home, they share the side dishes with their friends. I observed student behavior at the high school where I worked that exhibited similar patterns. For example, if a group of students ordered food to be delivered to the school, they all ordered the same item from the menu. Also, whenever the school administration scheduled a student meeting during lunch, the food was catered. Moreover, whether the group was large or small, the students' absolute preference was to ensure that everyone ate the same dish, even when given the choice of two. During overnight field trips, whether dining in a restaurant or having a cookout, the uniformity, conformity, and efficiency concepts ruled the day in this respect, as well.

One of the teachers at the school where I worked followed a strict vegan diet. She encountered no difficulty when dining in restaurants alone, or in the university cafeteria, or dining out with other Westerners; she could select whatever she wanted. However, when food was provided by the school administration to facilitate an on-campus meeting during business hours, she experienced challenges in having the administrative staff remember to order a vegan meal for her. Doing so would mean that a special (read: different) meal had to be ordered for her. This would represent a departure from the norm. It is much more efficient to place a lunch order for a group if everyone is eating the same dish, so is taking the order and preparing it. Therefore, whenever the school administration provided lunch, the probability of her having to skip a meal was very high. Even though the administration was aware of her dietary needs, most of the time they still went ahead and ordered the same lunch for her that they ordered for everyone else. It appears that the concept of uniformity was ingrained in the minds of the administrative staff; therefore, it was difficult for them to remember that one faculty member had special needs.

Fast Food Delivery

Koreans have embraced the concept of "fast food." It is safe to say that it is part of the culture. In Korea, "fast food" is indeed fast, especially the delivery aspect. For the efficiency-minded Koreans, the delivery of fast food is pervasive and has been for many years.

Food delivery in this country was in vogue many years before Domino's Pizza, Uber Eats, and Grubhub became popular in the U.S. In Korea, even McDonald's delivers! While conducting research for this segment of the book, I came across a number of fascinating stories related to fast food delivery. All of the sources I consulted indicate that this concept was first introduced during the Joseon Dynasty (1392-1910). According to Korean Culture and Information Service (KOCIS):

> The earliest Korean delivery of food on record is *naengmyun* cold buckwheat noodles in soup in the Joseon [E]ra (1392-1910). In his book, the scholar Hwang Yun-seok (1729-1791) mentions that he ordered *naengmyun* for lunch with his colleagues on the day after the state examination. This was in July 1768. It appears that *naengmyun*, a delicacy enjoyed in the royal court, had gained popularity among noblemen, leading to the introduction of a delivery service. In Lee Yu-won's book, it is recorded that King Sunjo (r. 1800-1834) of Joseon ordered his servants to buy cold noodles and bring it back to the palace while moon-watching with his officials in the early years of his reign. In later times, food delivery expanded to various soups and noodles in the 1930s, and delivery became a common thing.[5]

The port of Incheon, located approximately 34 kilometers or 21 miles west south west of Seoul, officially opened in 1883.[6] The opening of the port attracted Chinese immigrants particularly to the city of Incheon until approximately 1910 when Korea came under Japanese rule. During this period, the Chinese population increased from approximately 200 in 1883 to 12,000 in 1910.[7] Because of a multicultural ambiance, the food culture underwent a kind of renaissance. Two of the dishes that surfaced as favorites were *jajangmyun*, a Korean-style Chinese noodle dish with black bean paste, and *naengmyun*, buckwheat noodles in a chilled broth. By mid-century, *jajangmyun* had become "one of the most popular foods among the general public."[8]

One of the most interesting stories I ran into about food delivery comes from the latter part of the Joseon Era. It revolves around a dish called *hyojonggaeng*. The story depicts not only Korean's art of cooking and their love for food, but also priceless cultural details that identify a nation:

> Korea's earliest known record on commercial food delivery service is one about *hyojonggaeng*, meaning 'soup eaten to chase away a hangover at daybreak when the bell announces the lifting of curfew.' [The modern-day version of this soup is *haejangkook* (해장국).] In the book Haedong jukji ('Bamboo Branch Lyrics of Korea') published in 1925, Choe Yeongneon, a scholar and calligrapher during the later years of the Joseon Dynasty, wrote about this hearty soup: 'People in Gwangju (a county south of Seoul, in Gyeonggi Province) are known to be good at cooking hyojonggaeng. They put cabbage hearts, bean sprouts, pine mushrooms,

shiitake mushrooms, beef ribs, sea cucumbers, and abalones into water mixed with thick soybean paste, and boil them all day. At night they wrap up the soup pots in padded blankets so they could be transported to Seoul. There the soup pots are delivered to the residences of senior government officials around the time when the morning bell rings. Pots would still be warm and the soup was highly prized as a hangover cure."[9]

It was not until the 1990s that the food delivery business became commercialized and expanded widely as a result of the proliferation of fried chicken restaurants and pizza franchises: "The food delivery market grew exponentially from this point."[10] As of 2019, "the volume of the food delivery market… is estimated at around KRW 15 trillion (about USD 13 million) per year."[11]

Contributing factors to the astronomical growth of the fast food delivery business include extreme weather conditions particularly in the summer and Korean's appreciation for convenience. Why bother to walk or drive in the pouring rain or in sweltering heat when you can have the food delivered to your home, school or place of employment? Another factor was the economic expansion that took place between the 1960s and 1980s along with the pali pali culture that made it possible.[12] Indeed, "food delivery was able to firmly take root thanks to the existence of many densely populated urbanized areas and the age-old custom of enjoying late-night snacks."[13]

In the 1990s when fast food delivery was beginning to take off, customers placed their orders by phone. That method was already considered convenient. Nowadays, however, mobile apps make the process even more convenient by providing customers with "various complimentary services, like providing user feedback, along with payment functions and offers of special discounts":[14]

> Currently, 30 to 40 delivery apps are engaged in fierce competition. The combined number of downloads of the top three delivery apps—Baedal Minjok, Yogiyo, and Baedaltong—has reportedly exceeded 40 million. To stay ahead of the pack, the Baedal Minjok app allows customers to use its 'all-in-one' location-based services, skipping the process of entering user information.[15]

In summary, today, food delivery service in Korea is efficient, convenient, and reasonably-priced. When you are in a hurry and do not have time to cook, or you do not particularly feel like taking the time to prepare a meal, or if you have done the math and have figured that fixing a home-cooked meal in Korea is probably more expensive than ordering fast food, you will save the time, effort and the aggravation of cooking by ordering from the comfort of your home, school or office. Why cook at home when you can have fried chicken, pasta, salad, Big Macs, Whoppers, hamburgers from Lotteria (a Korean fast food chain), Domino's Pizza, Chinese or Korean food delivered fast to your door for the same price as you would pay in a restaurant? You do not even have to tip the delivery person since tipping is not customary in Korea.

Food delivery services will even pick up the dishes after you are done with your meal. Some food delivery services operate 24/7, 365 days a year, including holidays, so if someone gets hungry in the middle of the night, no problem! Delivery men on motorcycles will do whatever it takes to get the food to the customer as quickly as possible. Pedestrians know this, so they stay away from the bicycle/motorcycle-designated section of the sidewalk. Yes, these delivery men do their job fast because restauranteurs expect it, and so do the customers. In fact, they demand that the food be delivered quickly. It's part of the fabric of the Korean culture to be efficient. The question is, "At what cost?"

In attempting to establish where Korea is in terms of fast food delivery, it is important to emphasize that there are two concepts embedded in this discussion: the concept of fast food delivery, and the idea of incorporating the use of technology into the process. There is no doubt in my mind that the fast food delivery concept and its commercialization has been around and embedded into the culture longer than in the West, for example. Without a doubt, technology is being utilized in other countries as well to simplify and make the fast food ordering process more convenient. However, given how long the fast food delivery concept has been around in Korea, how long technology has been infused into the process, how widely utilized, and how convenient it is in Korea, other countries, particularly in the West, are just beginning to catch up.

The Driving Experience

Based on my observation, police officers' responsibilities include traffic control at intersections, particularly during rush hour, at festivals in various cities throughout the country, and for crowd control during demonstrations. Those are the three scenarios in which a uniformed police presence was definitely visible during my stay. During the five years I lived in the country, I only saw one police officer issuing a traffic citation to a driver who had gone through a red light at an intersection. Maximum speed laws are efficiently enforced, mainly with cameras that are strategically located at intersections and various intervals on highways. These cameras have a dual function: They both act as radars and capture the image of the car, its license plate, and the face of drivers who break the speed limit law.

In my extensive travels on city streets and highways, I did not see a single patrol car enforcing speed limits. Whether the speed limit is 60, 70, 80, 90, 100, 110 or 120 kilometers per hour (kph), this information is readily visible on the GPS (Global Positioning System) available on nearly all cars on the road. Still another efficiency-driven advantage of the Korean GPS is that the system also warns drivers of an impending speed-enforcement camera, thus alerting them to maintain the posted speed limit at least while the car is within the camera's viewfinder. Korean drivers have learned to game the speed monitoring system, however.

As I drove on city streets, but particularly on highways, I noticed that it was common for the efficiency-minded drivers to slow down just in time for their vehicle to go through the camera range where their speed was calibrated. However, as soon as they cleared the camera, their speed appeared to reach 20-40 kph higher than the posted limit. Another less common practice for impatient drivers to avoid speeding citations is to pass slower traffic at high speeds on the far right or shoulder side of the road. These opportunistic drivers pass on the right, instead of the lane on the far left, whether there is a legal lane or not, thus avoiding being detected by the infamous speed enforcement cameras. This blatant disregard for laws that are meant to maintain order and promote traffic safety is an indication of the emphasis on efficiency, the importance of gaining an advantage over law-abiding and safety conscious citizens, and the underlying belief that rules are meant to be broken. It also appears that the penalty for speeding is not harsh enough to deter drivers from disobeying posted speed limits.

Concerned citizens and government officials are evidently cognizant that the existing national system of enforcing speed limits is broken. The government has begun to utilize a system commonly referred to in Korean as 구간단속, loosely translated as "Speed Control System for a Stretch of Road," that, in addition to monitoring speeds at designated spots, has the capability of averaging speeds over stretches of road. This system calculates the distance traveled by individual drivers by tracking license plate numbers, the elapsed time, and speed average on a given stretch of road. If a driver averages a speed above the limit, a traffic citation is issued and mailed to the driver's home. This new system appears to be more effective at controlling speed limits than the one that is currently in place throughout the country, which checks for speeds at designated intervals only without tracking speeds for a stretch of road. In 2015, I noticed this new and improved system employed on expressways near and around Seoul. The government has also vowed to deploy new police officers for traffic enforcement duties. The officers will focus primarily on enforcing speed limits. As of this writing, it is not known how many police or highway patrol officers have been or will be designated under the new initiative. Both of these initiatives are long overdue and send a message loud and clear to the Korean people indicating that the government is serious about improving road safety.

Koreans maximize technology for efficiency's sake via speed-enforcement cameras, GPS systems on cars that alert drivers where speed-enforcement cameras are, and dash-cam recorders for evidence purposes in case of accidents. Automation and its impact on the economy are discussed further in Chapter Eight.

As aforementioned, a large percentage of Korean drivers equip their car with a dash-cam recorder. Most drivers also rely on a GPS, one that comes with the car, one they purchase and install as an accessory, or one accessible via a cell phone. I felt fortunate that the car I drove had both a GPS and a dash-cam recorder. I definitely needed help with directions, and since I did not speak Korean, I certainly wanted to have concrete evidence that I could rely on in case I was involved in an accident. I heard horror stories from my colleagues who had witnessed drivers scream at each other and beat each other up over an accident. I also carried an international driver's license to ensure that my driving in Korea was legal.

Some of the most blatant traffic violations I witnessed would be considered rude at the very least, if not outright dangerous maneuvers when they are done in the West. This does not mean that drivers in the West do not break traffic laws, they do. Once again, efficiency seemed to be the motivator behind these driving patterns. For example, on a two-lane road where drivers in the far right lane have either the option of going straight or making a right turn at an intersection, they are expected to either make a right turn or speed up to go straight, thus avoiding causing a delay. If any driver obstructs the far right lane when drivers wanting to make a right turn are present, those in that lane will make use of their horn to ensure that the message, "You are blocking my way!" comes across loud and clear.

During the time I lived in Jeonju, I witnessed some truly outrageous maneuvers by impatient drivers. The one that takes the cake took place at an intersection, similar to the one depicted in the image below, where traffic was stopped for a red light. The driver in front of the far right lane decided that they needed to make a U-turn from that position. They timed the signal change perfectly, and just before the light turned green, the driver performed the maneuver at normal speed. The move is depicted by the arrow in the image below. I did not anticipate this daring move, so it surprised me. It happened so smoothly and without fuss that I did not have time to be scared. Fortunately, no one was hurt, and all went about their business without a single honk. The nonchalant attitude of other drivers who witnessed this maneuver was amazing. Their reaction is in total contrast with the response by the impatient drivers described in the previous paragraph who are not shy about letting other motorists know that they are impeding their progress. The point here is not that an unlawful traffic maneuver took place, since they happen even in countries that have strict traffic rules, but the fact that no one honked and everyone went on as if nothing had happened. To this writer, this is an indication that this type of extreme maneuver is not all that uncommon and that there is a high level of tolerance for this type of behavior, especially in cases where efficiency seems to have precedence over courtesy and public safety.

Figure 1: Image Depicting Illegal U-Turn[16]

Some of the most daring drivers are food delivery employees. These delivery people ride a motorcycle and carry the merchandise in a box attached to the back of the vehicle. A research study published in 2014 by Chung, Song and Yoon explains the reason for motorcycles to be the preferred method for food delivery, as opposed to the U.S. where the favored mode is a car:

> The quick service delivery requires high speeds on congested roads and easy accessibility on narrow ones. Accordingly, the use of motorcycles for delivery purpose is perceived by the industry to be the best mode of transportation, particularly because of their relatively easy accessibility and low cost of travel, especially in the Seoul metropolitan area with its highly congested roadways as well as a comparatively high portion of narrow alleys.[17]

The article goes on to describe the driving patterns of some food delivery drivers as follows:

> …motorcyclists in the delivery industry often commit traffic violations during delivery such as improperly weaving through traffic, crossing the centerline, driving over the speed limit, violating traffic signals…[18]

Also, it is a widely accepted practice for delivery people to drive on sidewalks and crosswalks or break numerous other traffic laws. As a result, it is not uncommon for these drivers to be implicated in serious accidents where injuries are involved. Consequently, they place their own lives and the lives of others at risk more often than the average driver. The research article mentioned above provides some statistics that may give the reader a more concrete idea of the seriousness of the problem:

> …the fatality rate for motorcycle crashes is about 12% of the fatality rate for road traffic crashes, which is considered to be high, although motorcycle crashes account for only 5% of road traffic crashes in South Korea.[19]

It is important to note, however, that some non-fatal road traffic crashes involving motorcycles go unreported. Therefore, the latter statistic quoted above may be artificially low and the problem with traffic accidents involving delivery men may be more serious than the statistics show. In some cases, to save money, food delivery business owners hire temporary workers to make food deliveries. In such cases, the business' liability insurance may not cover temporary workers' accidents. The delivery men may choose to use their own insurance coverage instead. If they use their own insurance, food delivery accidents may not be reported as such; therefore, they are not accounted for in food delivery accidents statistics. In some cases, delivery drivers may not want to involve their insurance company for fear that their insurance premiums will increase. In other instances, delivery men may not have insurance at all. It is not uncommon for drivers involved in an accident to settle the incident in cash whether the drivers have insurance or not. This practice also distorts the accident statistics.

For some years now, Korean society has been wrestling with this potentially dangerous situation without much success. How many accidents and casualties must take place for Koreans to finally realize that the efficiency they demand and take for granted comes at a very high price? As indicated earlier, customers expect efficiency and restauranteurs want to please customers; therefore, they both pressure the delivery staff to deliver the food fast. The truth of the matter is that these fast food delivery accidents are not the fault of one group of individuals; all three groups have a part in it. To eradicate this potentially dangerous situation, a change in the cultural mindset must take place: Efficiency for efficiency's sake or the sake of convenience or short-term financial gains must be balanced with safety.

Now that the Korean driving experience has been described, perhaps the issue of accidents associated with fast food delivery can be viewed in the context of the overall driving conditions.

Love Motels

"Love motels" are quite ubiquitous throughout Korea. They are motels where guests can rent a room for three to four hours during the day or in the evening for a romantic rendezvous or for sleeping during the night. My Korean friends assumed correctly that I was not aware about the concept of love motels when I first started visiting Korea. Therefore, they wanted to alert me about it, so I would not accidentally find myself in a situation in which I would feel uncomfortable.

Travelers in Korea need to know whether a motel they are considering for booking is for travelers or for a romantic rendezvous. Fortunately, love motels do not usually come up when doing a search for motels on the internet. Therefore, the concern for foreigners should not be as acute unless they do not have reservations and they resort to finding a place to stay on the go. For locals, this is not an issue since they are familiar with the concept and they can tell the difference between a love motel and a motel for travelers. Generally speaking, love motels are relatively less expensive than motels for travelers. Also, in many instances, love motels specify that the check-in time for the evening is after 8:00 or 9:00 p.m. or later. Finally, guest reviews are usually very explicit and alert the reader if the facility they are reviewing is a love motel. When renting a room for a few hours during the day, a guest pays the day rate, which is lower than the night rate. Usually, guests checking in after about 8:00 p.m., or those who are planning to stay overnight, must pay the night rate.

The business model used by love motel management is an example of the emphasis on efficiency found in most facets of the Korean culture. This business model is financially efficient for both motel management and guests. For motel owners and managers, this is an economically effective way of maximizing room availability. They can rent the same room to several guests in one day, thus maximizing revenue per room. It is economical for guests because they only pay for the time they use the room.

Construction

As a result of my extended stay in Jeonju, most of my Korean friends were Jeonju-born residents. I learned through them that the city had undergone a significant transformation in the last ten years. This transformation was fueled by a conversion of farms into apartment buildings, officetels (word combining "office" + "hotel," indicating efficiency or convenience apartments), villas, and the accompanying shopping areas and restaurant rows which facilitated the sprouting of new neighborhoods such as Shin-shi-ga-ji (New Town) and Hyuk-shin-do-si (Innovation City). Even during the time I lived in the city, the rapid pace of expansion continued.

Since I am an avid walker, I had the opportunity to walk through some neighborhoods. One of the activities that caught my eye during my daily walks was in and around construction sites. I noticed that projects were completed relatively quickly. Furthermore, I noticed that many, if not most, construction sites were in operation seven days per week, including Saturdays and Sundays, and even in late evenings. I noted this as peculiar. There is no way for me to know whether the workers were working longer shifts or they were being paid overtime. It could very well be that workers were on a rotating schedule and the site was covered by overlapping shifts. In the West, I was accustomed to seeing construction workers begin their eight-hour shift early in the morning, complete their shift in the early afternoon, and taking Saturday and Sunday off. Not so in Korea.

I had learned that Koreans have the distinction of being among the leaders in the world in terms of the number of hours worked.[20] However, when I made these observations, I was specifically thinking about the potential propensity for making mistakes or having accidents as a result of the apparent tight schedules, long hours and working seven days per week with no rest, if indeed that was the case. It is common knowledge that the body and brain need to rest to function at optimum condition. This observation is a prelude to the discussion about man-made accidents in Chapter Six.

In the West, it is not uncommon for construction companies and project owners or developers to agree to an incentive paid to the construction company and shared with the workers if the project is completed on time or early. I am not aware whether this tradition is common practice in construction contracts in Korea. If this incentive is indeed customary, it would partially explain the long hours and emphasis on efficiency. However, even this financial incentive, if indeed it exists in Korean construction contracts, should not preclude construction workers from taking Sundays off.

Swing Doors

A subtle and mundane exchange between strangers happens when two individuals approach a swing door either from opposite directions or in the same direction. In the West, if two individuals approach the door in the same direction, one behind the other, and if the person in front is aware that someone behind them has the intention of going through the same door, out of courtesy, they will hold the door and not let go until the person behind them grabs the handle to facilitate their entry as well. During my stay in Korea, I found that people generally reacted differently to a similar situation. On many occasions, I anticipated that people walking through a swing door in front of me would hold the door long enough for me to grab the handle to secure my own safe passage through the door. Instead, I ended up with a swing door practically hitting me on the face. However, if I happened to open a door and someone walking in the opposite direction noticed, they quickly accelerated the pace and went through the door before I did to take advantage of the fact that the door was being held open for a brief moment. Some may view the latter example as a matter related to lack of courtesy or rudeness; however, in my opinion, it is more related to efficiency. Thus, the underlying value of efficiency appears to be omnipresent even in the most common facets of daily life, including this seemingly insignificant encounter between two people.

Respect for Other People's Property

Coming from a country in the West where, generally speaking, people have to be on guard to ensure that their personal belongings are safe whether on the street, utilizing public transportation, in public places such as train stations and airports, or even at home, it was a breath of fresh air to live in a country where people show honesty and respect for other people's property. Some of my colleagues and I, and many of the students at the school where I taught, used public transportation, either local or inter-city buses, taxis, and occasionally trains. It was not unusual for students to forget some of their belongings, for example their cell phone, wallet, a textbook or their backpack in a taxi or a bus. Occasionally, this would happen to teachers as well. When these unfortunate instances happened, the school staff would intercede on their behalf and call either the bus or taxi company to inquire about the objects left behind. Every single time this happened, the items were returned or the owner was directed where to retrieve them. On occasion, a taxi driver would make a trip back to the school to return the items. Even wallets would be returned with the money still in them.

A Sense of Personal Safety at School

While working in Korea, I experienced a sense of personal safety and security that was less common in all the years that I worked in education in the United States. This was perhaps because guns are not allowed in Korea and school shootings are associated with schools in the U.S., but not in Korea. This does not mean that the school where I taught did not have discipline cases; however, the few cases that we did have were mild in comparison to those in the U.S. A colleague of mine, who taught at the same American school for approximately seven years and eventually went to work in another country in Asia, recently wrote me an email where she reminisced about "the innocent, kind Korean students"[21] at the school where we both had taught. This comment is a reflection of the high regard that Koreans have for the teaching profession as opposed to some Western countries where respect for teachers is, generally speaking, a thing of the past.

The common thread among most of the observations in this chapter is the concept of efficiency in everyday life in Korea. The reason for including them is to show the pervasiveness of efficiency. The remaining chapters will show that the concept has a positive and a negative impact on society and the economy. The non-efficiency related observations herein are to demonstrate that not everything is about efficiency in everyday life, particularly where a humanistic aspect is the driving force.

Endnotes

1. "Jeonju, South Korea Population," *Population Stat*, accessed 7 August 2019, *populationstat.com*.

2. "About KTX," *Life in Korea*, accessed 7 August 2019, *lifeinkorea.com*.

3. "KTX Overview," *Korail*, accessed 7 August 2019, *info. korail.com*.

4. Jeon Sung-Won, "Food Delivery Gets Its Apps," *Koreana*, accessed 7 August 2019, *koreana.or.kr*.

5. Jeon So-Young, "Food Delivery Paradise," *Korean Culture and Information Service*, accessed 7 August 2019, *kocis.go.kr*.

6. "Incheon Port: The Door to Economic Vitality," *Port of Incheon*, accessed 7 August 2019, *icpa.or.kr*.

7. Louise Do Rosario, "Seoul's Invisible Chinese Rise Up," *The Straits Times*, 22 October 2000.

8. Jeon So-Young, "Food Delivery Paradise."

9. Jeon Sung-Won, "Food Delivery Gets Its Apps."

10. Jeon So-Young, "Food Delivery Paradise."

11. Ibid.

12. Jeon Sung-Won, "Food Delivery Gets Its Apps."

13. Ibid.

14. Ibid.

15. Ibid.

16. Vlad Vasnetsov, "Untitled," *Pixabay*, accessed 14 November 2019, *pixabay.com*.

17. Younshik Chung, Tai-Jin Song, Byoung-Jo Yoon, "Injury severity in delivery-motorcycle to vehicle crashes in the Seoul metropolitan area," *Accident Analysis and*

Prevention, no. 62, 2014, p. 79-86.

18. Ibid.
19. Ibid.
20. See Chapter Six.
21. Anonymous, personal interview by John Gonzalez, email, 10 June 2019

Chapter Three

Education

As in other countries, education in Korea plays a crucial role in determining both success on the job market and eventual financial security and wealth. In Korea, which has a population of about 51 million people, the path that leads to financial success includes the best education from elementary through high school which then leads to prestigious universities and eventually to top-level jobs in major corporations.[1] For example, semiconductor manufacturing, the biggest income generator in Korea, requires a solid academic foundation in highly advanced sciences such as chemistry, physics, engineering, and computer science. The academic preparation for these fields requires extensive hard work, sacrifice, and a long-term commitment. However, the path is very well delineated. The trail is sprinkled with very clearly identified markers and directional signs that point students in the direction of job security and financial success.

A Road Well-Traveled

The trajectory to financial stability is a well-traveled path. Those students with the most robust support network have the best chance of succeeding and attaining the coveted financial rewards that can ensure a repeat of the cycle for the next generation. Korean parents have proven that they are willing to sacrifice everything for their children's education. The parents themselves are the essential elements of the students' support network. To ensure that their children can compete for a spot at a top-tier university, they are willing to make any number of drastic decisions, including spending a large portion of the family income, depleting the family savings and even borrowing money. Relatives, family friends, and acquaintances who have navigated the path successfully or studied abroad can provide advice or act as sounding boards when students need to make critical decisions. Families that have the financial means can avail themselves of *hagwons* and private tutors; the latter represents the most expensive option. *Hagwon* instructors and private tutors have the subject matter expertise and test preparation skillset to share with students. Then, the students can stand a chance in the brutally competitive university admission process. To be considered a "good mother," mothers usually consult with their networks for a recommendation on the best possible private education providers for their children.

Education as the Path to Financial Success

Following the Korean War, Koreans viewed education as a means to maintain the status quo by those who were in the upper echelons of the socioeconomic ladder. For those at the lower levels of the economic strata, education was a means to escape poverty. However, since the latter part of the 20th century, individuals from the less privileged socioeconomic ranks have struggled with the well-traveled path that people used to rely on for access to top-notch universities and eventually, hugely desirable lifetime jobs in major corporations. That path is simply not as reliable as it once was for previous generations. This unfortunate outcome repeats time and again, in spite of years of dedication and hard work at school and long hours of private education after school, as well as financial sacrifices by the family. This new reality is one of the unintended consequences of the highly successful push for the democratization of higher education, which began in the mid-1980s and continues in the present. This national effort has taken an existing competitive environment to a higher level. The democratization of higher education is discussed in detail in Chapter Eight.

The Education and Socioeconomic Cycle

Below is a flowchart depicting a Korean education and socioeconomic cycle from elementary school to eventual wealth and parenthood for those at the top of the pyramid. For those who find themselves in the bottom portion of the pyramid from the start, it is challenging, if not impossible, to break into the top section. Of course, there are exceptions. For example, those who have creative talent or extraordinary academic ability, or an exceptional entrepreneurial spirit, can transcend this traditional flow. Following the chart is the narrative describing the realities, conditions, and consequences in each of the stages of the cycle.

Figure 1: Flow Chart depicting the education and socioeconomic cycle in Korea.

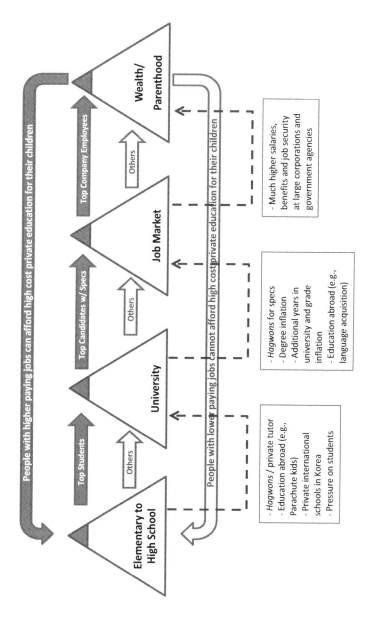

The Role of Private Education

A discussion about Korean education would be incomplete without mentioning the role that private education plays in the Korean culture in the form of enrichment, supplemental education, and test preparation through *hagwons* and private tutoring. As explained in Chapter One, *hagwons* are after-school academies or "cram schools" that families utilize extensively to provide their children with the aforementioned needs. Private tutors may be university students, university professors, *hagwon* instructors or professional tutors who are generally hired at a premium salary to provide language, artistic/musical training, and primarily subject tutoring and test preparation for the national university entrance examination. Tutoring sessions may be one-on-one. Alternatively, one tutor may work with a small group of students. Students begin utilizing these services at an early age and continue through high school. Therefore, tutees come from all levels of education—elementary, middle and high school. Middle and high school students are heavy users of subject matter tutoring. As might be expected, high school students frequently utilize private tutoring for test preparation purposes. Generally speaking, and depending on the student needs and parental economic resources, a student may receive subject matter tutoring in one, two, three or more courses.

As stated earlier, Korean parents are willing to sacrifice everything for their children, and particularly for their children's education. They willingly spend a significant portion of the family's income on these private education providers, including *hagwons* and private tutors. Government entities conduct surveys and maintain statistics on the estimated cost of private education for the entire country, the cost of private education as a percentage of household income, the per capita expenditures, and the participation rate at each stratum in education.

However, critics argue that statistics on private education costs as well as participation rates are extremely conservative. Some published statistics are presented here to give the reader an idea of the significance of private education in the Korean culture. However, the reader is cautioned to view the cited figures with an open mind. Furthermore, consider the critics' argument, as well. This may tip the balance in favor of critics who are skeptical of the published statistics and who insist that they are incredibly conservative.

The Cost of Private Education

A realistic expenditure figure on private supplemental education in Korea must include expenses derived from both *hagwon* and private tutoring. Government statistics reported by *The Chosun Ilbo* on March 27, 2017, indicate that "spending on private crammers reached W18 trillion [~ $16 Billion] last year [2016], up 1.3 percent compared to 2015. The total rose even though student numbers dwindled from 6.08 million to 5.88 million amid the shrinking birthrate."[2] However, the total expenditures on private crammers are significantly higher if the cost of private tutors is included. The article goes on to specify: "The state-run Korea Development Institute estimates that parents spend more than W30 trillion [~ $26.7 billion] a year on extracurricular tuition if private tutoring and overseas language courses are included."[3]

Based on the article cited above, it is clear that expenditure figures on private education beyond money spent on *hagwons* are only estimates whose accuracy is questionable. As far as estimates on the portion of household income spent on private education are concerned, *The Independent* reported in an article published on July 18, 2015, that Korean "parents… spend around 22% of their household income on education and educational service… It is one of the highest proportions of household spend on education among developed nations."[4] However, the article fails to specify its source and whether this figure represents either expenditures on *hagwons* or private tutoring or both. Therefore, critics who claim that estimates on private education expenditures are underestimated may question this number as well.

The perception that private education through *hagwons* and private tutors is the most efficient and effective way to prepare students for the grueling Korean university admission process forms part of the fabric of the culture. As expected, given the figures quoted above, the per capita expenditures on private education have increased significantly at least since 2007, the first year that Korean Statistical Information Service (KOSIS) collected, tabulated, and published the results of the annual survey on private education spending.[5] On March 17, 2018, *The Korea Herald* reported that monthly expenditures on private education increased by 33% in the ten years from 2007 to 2017. The article asserts that "households spent a monthly average of 384,000 won [US $359.38] per child on private tutoring in 2017, up from 288,000 won [~ $268] in 2007, according to a survey by South Korea's statistics agency and the education ministry."[6]

Absent concrete data on private education expenditures prior to 2007, other factors should be considered as possible indicators that the per capita expenditure increases began before 2007. One of those factors is the development of Gangnam, possibly the most affluent area in Seoul, which eventually attracted some of the best and most costly private schools and *hagwons* in all of Korea. Gangnam remained underdeveloped until the early 1980s.[7] Since then, however, the area's development trajectory parallels the country's economic expansion. In addition, the unprecedented growth in GDP and GNI per capita also began in the mid-1980s. Furthermore, the infrastructure build-up in preparation for the Summer 1988 Olympics contributed to the economic expansion and most likely to GDP and GNI per capita, which would have made it feasible for parents to increase spending on private education for their children. Finally, the astounding 70% attainment of any postsecondary degree for the 25 to 34 age group born from 1983 to 1992 could be considered the most direct indicator of increased spending on private education including test preparation.[8] In conclusion, Young Lee and I agree that given the indicators discussed, it is very likely that the increased spending on private education began in the mid-1980s.

It follows that the per capita spending on private education increases at the higher levels of education as students approach the university admission process. The above-cited article breaks down the average cost of private education by level:

Monthly expenditures on private education reached 515,000 won [~ $466] per high school student in 2017, up 43.5 percent from 2007.

Corresponding data per middle school students rose 39.5 percent to 438,000 won [~ $396] over a decade and that for elementary school students rose 19.9 percent to 307,000 won [~ $278].[9]

Young Lee and I reiterate that the figures quoted above are averages. Therefore, some families spend more and others less. The location of a specific *hagwon* is critical in determining the cost. A family whose child attends a *hagwon* in Gangnam should expect to pay much more than the average price estimate, since it is the district with the highest cost of living in Korea and it is where some of the most expensive *hagwons* are. Some families purposely move to Gangam, despite the expense, to provide their children with the best private education possible.

Critics who claim that the published statistics on private education spending in Korea are extremely conservative appear to have a strong case. They state that private tutors are required to register for income tax purposes. Therefore, critics claim that many, if not most tutors do not register. Thus, they argue that the number of actual tutors and their earnings are unknown. Assuming these arguments are accurate, then participation rates and private tutoring cost estimates are generally unreliable. Critics point not only to the fact that most, if not all, private tutor transactions are conducted in the form of cash. The cash flow is difficult, if not impossible, to track. *Hagwons* are required to register as businesses, whereas private tutors are not, and therefore this very expensive education alternative remains opaque.

Another issue is the cost of private tutoring. This cost is determined by several factors, such as:

> » Location: For example, if the tutoring takes place in an exclusive area like Gangnam, the cost is much higher.

> » The students-to-tutor ratio: A one-on-one tutoring situation is more expensive than small group tutoring.

> » The tutor's experience, level of preparedness and reputation: A professional tutor charges higher fees than a non-professional; university professors charge more than university students. There are part-time and full-time professional tutors. Full-time professional tutors are notorious for charging higher fees.

At the time of publication, the going monthly rate for subject matter private tutoring ranged between the equivalent of $300 and $1,000. As an example, the monthly cost of two-times-per-week private tutoring for a math class by a non-professional tutor is approximately the equivalent of $600 and $1,200 by a professional tutor. Therefore, if a high school student requires tutoring in three subject areas, which is entirely conceivable, the total monthly cost of private tutoring would be approximately the equivalent of $1,800 by a non-professional tutor and $3,600 by a professional. These high private tutoring costs, together with the common practice of paying for these services in cash, give credence to the critics' argument that the published participation rates and private education costs are not in line with reality because cash payments for tutoring are most likely not reported. The reality is that parents are willing to spend as much money as necessary to give their children an edge in the highly competitive university admission process, and taking into account only the amounts being reported paints a rather incomplete picture.

Private Education Viewed as an Efficient Investment or a Way to Get an Edge

A critical question is: "Why are Korean families willing to spend so much money on after-school supplemental, enrichment education, and test preparation?" The driving forces behind *hagwon* education and private tutoring are the highly competitive university admission process, concern for the children's future, and desire for financial success and social status.

First, jobs at major corporations in Korea are hard to come by. Only those candidates who graduate from one of the top-tier universities are usually considered. Therefore, high school students are under a great deal of pressure from parents, and themselves, to be admitted to one of the best universities in the country. As discussed in Chapter One, three of the top universities in Korea are Seoul National University, Korea University, and Yonsei University. The trio is commonly known by the acronym SKY.

The well-known obsession with and struggle for obtaining a degree from a top-level university was recently reflected in the popular

Korean drama produced by JTBC cable network titled *SKY Castle* (스카이 캐슬), so named after the acronym symbolizing three of the top universities. JTBC broadcasted the show weekly on Fridays and Saturdays from November 2018 until February 2019. The plot developed around wealthy parents who use every trick in the book to make sure that their children are accepted into the School of Medicine at Seoul National University:

> Director Jo Hyun-tak did not shy away from showing the dark side of the country's education hype on the show. During a press conference [in November 2018], he said viewers might experience different emotions as they see people trying all methods and pulling every string to send their children off to the best universities.[10]

The show gained such popularity that from December 10 to 16, 2018, it became the most talked about drama in social media.[11] Furthermore, "ahead of the series finale, … its most popular episode had been watched by 23 percent of South Korea's entire subscription television audience, the highest such rating ever achieved by a drama."[12]

The show gained unprecedented popularity primarily because Koreans identify with some of the plotlines, including expensive supplemental private education, grueling student schedules, and strategies used by parents to give their children an advantage in a highly competitive university admission process. Some of the plotlines "are inspired by real-life events, including a high school teacher's arrest [in 2018] on charges of stealing exam papers for his own daughters."[13]

Other plotlines include the "hiring [of] illegal help from a law professor to write an application cover letter to a college entrance coordinator that costs over 100 million won [~$86,349] a year to hire."[14] A "college entrance coordinator" is a consultant or "coach" who is contracted by parents to ensure that their child gains admission to the best university possible by taking the correct steps in preparation for a brutally competitive admission application process. The correct steps include making certain that the student follows an academically challenging schedule, receives top grades, and earns the necessary high scores on the *Suneung* test. For the student to achieve the highest possible grades and university entrance exam scores, the college entrance coordinator ascertains that the student attends the best *hagwons* and receives tutoring from some of the best tutors.

Second, Korean families lack the confidence that the Korean education system alone will provide their students with the necessary high-level preparation needed for them to be competitive when it comes to applying to top-tier universities. Often, it is the *hagwon* education and private tutoring that make the difference in university acceptance rates. In other words, private education costs are an efficient investment in the children's future. Students who are not accepted by top-tier universities and end up graduating from less selective institutions have a lower probability of successfully competing for jobs at the country's conglomerates. Their chances of being hired by major corporations like Samsung, LG, Hyundai, and POSTCO are reduced significantly. As of this writing, university students are finding it progressively more difficult to procure employment after graduation even from top-tier universities, even though they usually get priority consideration by major corporations.

Some graduates recognize that a B.A./B.S. degree not only does not guarantee employment, but neither does the degree necessarily provide them with the needed career entry-level skills. Some are enrolling in career and technical education programs while attending university or after completing a B.A./B.S. degree program. Thus, they may add technical skills or licenses to their resume, such as a computer operation license, CPA (Certified Public Accountant) license, Korean stenographer certificate, barista license, culinary license, and even foreign language training. These add-on certificates are commonly referred to as "specs" (specifications) on their resume. The purpose of this practice is to stand out from their peers in the job-hunting process. They do this out of desperation and to become more competitive in the job market, not necessarily with the intention to perform these jobs and utilize those skills.

The relevance of these added "specs" on an individual's resume is highly questionable. If, on the one hand, prospective employers are taking these additional, and superfluous "specs" into consideration when making hiring decisions, then the bar on job-filling decisions is being raised artificially and with no rhyme or reason. If, on the other hand, prospective employers are disregarding these "specs," then the whole exercise of taking classes and completing certificate/license requirements to add these skills sets to a resume is wasted effort, time and money. This additional exercise to pad one's credentials is a result of the brutal competition for jobs and the pervasive degree inflation that the democratization of higher education, or the push for everyone to have a four-year degree, engenders. Moreover, the economy cannot possibly absorb all the graduates that receive a bachelor's degree on a yearly basis. The economic impact and unintended consequences of the democratization of higher education, as well as degree inflation, are discussed in Chapter Eight.

Third, Korean parents view their children's private education as a necessity rather than a luxury. They consider the cost as an investment in their children's future, as well as their own. Consequently, parents are willing to spend the family savings on their children's private education costs. As aforementioned, when the savings are insufficient, parents are even willing to borrow money to afford the high cost of private education for their children.

The Gap Between the Haves and Have-nots

Despite this zeal for private education, the gap in participation between children from low-income and high-income families has widened significantly in the last ten years. The article in *The Korea Herald* quoted above identifies that private education participation rates among children from low-income families (defined here as families with a monthly income of 2-3 million Korean won [~ $1,809-$2,714]) fell sharply over the 10-year period between 2007 and 2017.[15] This trend is of particular concern since the possibility of a crossover between the top and bottom portions of the pyramid in the Education and Socioeconomic Cycle flowchart is minimal to nonexistent as it stands. This sharp decline is likely to make matters worse for students from lower socioeconomic backgrounds. The downward trend in the participation rate in private education by children from low-income families ensures that the status quo is maintained by favoring top students from elementary through high school, university and eventually the job market. Children from high-income families appear to be at a definite advantage given this survival-of-the-fittest system because their parents' ability to afford expensive *hagwons* and private tutors. *The Korea Herald* cites the following participation rate statistics for 2017 compared to 2007:

Figure 2: Private Education Participation Rates – 2007 and 2017

Children from Low-Income Families vs. Children from High-Income Families*[16]

	2007	2017
Children from high-income Families[1]	92.7%	80.8%
Children from Low-Income Families[2]	77%	58.3%

*Note:

1. High-income families: monthly income = 6-7 million Korean won [~$5,427 - $6,332].

2. Low-income families: monthly income = 2-3 million Korean won [~ $1,809 - $2,714].

The Good Mother Role

Every Korean child learns the folk tale about Han Seok Bong, a well-known calligrapher from the Joseon era (1392-1910) whose mother sold rice cakes for a living. She is viewed as the model of an ideal mother, because she sacrificed for her son and raised him well. The fact that she sold rice cakes for a living is an indication that she was not a typical full-time homemaker, in that she needed to work in order to support her son. Despite her limited means, she sent him to a Buddhist temple to study calligraphy with the masters so he could become as proficient as possible. Initially, his studies were supposed to last ten years, but he came back home after three years, believing that he had nothing more to learn from the masters. His mother knew better and wanted to teach him a lesson on humility, so she challenged him to a contest in which he would write letters, and she would cut rice cake. He agreed. As they went about their respective tasks, she blew out the candle, and they were left to continue the contest in the dark. When finished, they reviewed each other's performance and found that his letters were crooked, the sizes did not match and were difficult to discern, whereas the rice cake pieces that she had cut were the same size.

Realizing his error in judgment and understanding the lesson on humility, Han Seok Bong returned to the temple to study for seven more years. Subsequently, he returned to his hometown to his mother. Eventually, his reputation as a calligrapher became widely known throughout the land, even as far away as China.

Following the example set by Han Seok Bong's mother, traditionally, it is the mother in her role of "good mother" who is expected to do everything within her power for her children's success.

For example, many mothers sacrifice their retirement money to cover their children's private education costs. Also, it is not uncommon for some middle-aged mothers to procure employment to afford their children's *hagwon* and private tutor costs. Similarly, it is the mother who researches the *hagwons* and private tutors searching for those with the best reputation for her children. As discussed earlier, it is customary for mothers to inquire with their extensive network of friends about the best possible *hagwon* and private tutor alternatives. If a given *hagwon* or private tutor is held in high esteem by the mother's friends, it is more likely that institute or private tutor will receive the nod from the family. Since social pressure plays a significant role in decision-making at this level, these decisions are usually arrived at by consensus as outlined in Chapter One.

If a mother is wealthy, assertive and influential enough, she may be allowed to join the informal network of mothers at her child's school. If she is aggressive enough, she may be considered a *chima baram* (skirt wind), a term used to refer to an assertive mother who is looking after her children's wellbeing and using her influence to tip the scales on her children's behalf. In English, the term "helicopter mom" may be considered the closest equivalent to *chima baram*. The reason this function is considered a mother's role is because traditionally, women did not have access to the workplace. Therefore, they stayed at home to take care of the family, and specifically the children, both within the home and without home by ensuring that the future success of the children had a solid foundation. Today, some of the *chima baram's* responsibilities include ensuring that her children attend the best *hagwon* and that the parents hire the best private tutors to increase the likelihood of admission to one of the top universities. The *chima baram's* network enables its usually wealthy members to have exclusive access to valuable information. Also, it is instrumental in screening both cram schools and private tutors.

The *chima baram* identifies an informal leader called *dwagee-o-ma* [Korean: 돼지엄마] (mother pig followed by her baby pigs) who happens to be the most influential group member. This individual has the authority to determine who can join the group. Because of the competitive nature of the university admission process, mothers' network groups remain purposely small to share invaluable information only with a small and exclusive group of mothers. Mothers' networks are particularly prevalent in Gangnam, possibly the wealthiest area in all South Korea. Gangnam was made world-famous by Psy with his 2012 hit single and video "Gangnam Style." In his song and video, Psy pokes fun at the posh district for its emphasis on high-status lifestyle, which includes high rents and expectations.

Teaching-to-the-Test Environments and Their Profound Impact on Student Learning and Behavior

Private education providers, from *hagwon* instructors to private tutors, have infused the element of efficiency into private education. *Hagwons* that specialize in test preparation, be it the *Suneung*, SAT, ACT, TOEFL, TOEIC, or other tests, use the most efficient approach possible. They teach to the test by giving students extensive test practice through strategically selected items from previously published test forms, projecting the types of questions that will be on a given test, teaching students shortcuts to answer questions quickly and efficiently. They also provide pointers on how students may best manage their test time. Time-saving techniques include identifying the best answer choice by utilizing a process of elimination, thus avoiding having to work out the solution to a math problem. Instead, the student decides when it is advantageous to guess the answer. The emphasis is on efficiency through rote memorization, repetition, and test practice, not on creativity, critical thinking or self-expression. An article published by the BBC titled "South Korea's schools: Long days, high results," asserts that the "relentless focus on education has resulted in formidable exam performers."[17]

It is true that test preparation providers in other countries use similar techniques; however, two fundamental differences are the extent to which these services are utilized and the degree to which these strategies are applied to other circumstances.

This extensive exposure to test preparation, or the teaching-to-the-test approach, appears to have a profound impact on student learning processes and behavior. As discussed in Chapter Four, in the authors' experience, Korean students show the tendency to excel at multiple choice tests, but seem to have trouble when demonstrating the step-by-step process for arriving at the correct answer. Also, they appear to be more comfortable in a teacher-centered environment, or one that requires little student interaction or independent thinking, than a student-centered situation, or one that does require student participation. These observed behavioral and learning patterns appear to be rooted in the approach used by *hagwon* instructors and private tutors who focus on test preparation. Unfortunately, these learned behavioral patterns, and this approach to learning, are difficult to eradicate. Unless the student participates in an environment that promotes creativity, critical thinking, independent thinking and student participation through self-expression and inquiry, the learning and behavioral patterns will persist beyond the classroom. Private education is viewed as the key to elevate, or at the very least maintain, the socioeconomic status of the masses. Sadly, the element in the culture that has given students an advantage in a highly competitive university admissions environment has had some undesirable unintended consequences. Strategies espoused by test-preparation providers perpetuate a mentality that relies heavily on efficiency. These strategies appear to have become deeply ingrained in everyday life.

The purpose of these *hagwons* is to prepare students for tests by focusing on answering questions quickly and efficiently. Instructors are experts in this regard. Being avid users of ranking or rating systems for efficiency's sake, Koreans often refer to their star *hagwon* instructors and private tutors as "tweezer" teachers (족집게 선생님) to identify those who have the best test preparation strategies. In other words, they can coach students the most efficient way to select the correct answers on multiple-choice questions. They are particularly skilled at anticipating the types of questions that will appear on specific tests such as the *Suneung*. On a reading comprehension section, for example, the instructors are able to anticipate the questions that will be asked about a passage on the test. In other words, they pinpoint the questions that students should study for the test. Effective tweezer teachers conduct an item analysis of past *Suneung* tests. Through this item analysis, they screen not only for concepts that have been tested previously, but also how frequently a vocabulary word, mathematical problem or concept is included on the test. After conducting this item analysis, tweezer teachers make a determination as to whether they think a specific vocabulary word, mathematical problem or concept will be on the next test. Based on this item analysis, they advise the students whether to study a specific item or concept.

These "tweezer teachers" have reached almost celebrity status in the test preparation world. *Hagwons* that have this specialty use their star teachers' image on billboards and advertising campaigns.

Hagwons Specializing in English Instruction

It is true that participation in some *hagwons* provides students with a more individually tailored supplemental, enrichment or test preparation program. Therefore, I cannot emphasize enough that not all *hagwons* are created equal nor do they all share the same purpose; consequently, they do not employ the same strategies. Performance-oriented *hagwons*, those that teach art and music, are in a separate category. In the previous section, the discussion centers on *hagwons* that provide test preparation. In this section, the focus will be on *hagwons* that specialize in English instruction, which includes such skills as English conversation and grammar or a combination thereof.

English instruction begins in elementary school. Since Korean parents want their children to be proficient in English, students begin attending English instruction *hagwons* early on. The emphasis on English learning persists through middle and senior high school and throughout university. Eventually, this emphasis even continues in the workplace because of the globalization that has been spearheaded by the multinational corporations which are the backbone of the Korean economy. Consequently, in addition to the established English courses, Chinese language instruction is also rapidly gaining in popularity.

The range of reasons why individuals wish to improve their English proficiency is as wide as their diverse backgrounds. Some of the reasons are as follows:

» To prepare for a test
» To strengthen conversational skills for professional purposes

» To enhance conversational skills to fulfill a personal interest

» To gain a more solid grammar foundation and vocabulary expansion

Before they joined the American school where I worked, some of my colleagues had been employed as English conversation instructors in *hagwons* where instructors used a "cookie-cutter" approach with all classes. One curriculum is established for each proficiency level, a textbook is chosen, and the instructor is told to take the lead on the rest of the course. Because the demand for English instruction is so high, *hagwon* directors do not have the luxury of selecting the most prepared or qualified instructors. Also, they cannot possibly fill all the teaching positions with native English speakers. Therefore, in many instances, they hire Korean instructors whose command of the English language is questionable, particularly when it comes to their oral communication. It would also be unrealistic for these *hagwons* to attract only certificated/credentialed teachers from English speaking countries, precisely because *hagwons* commonly issue one-year contracts. These are temporary positions which would not be attractive to certificated/credentialed teachers because their preference is to obtain a tenure-track position.

Also, teachers who are already tenured in their home country would not find these positions compelling enough to leave their tenured position. The exception to this likelihood would be young, fresh-out-of-college certificated/credentialed teachers (i.e., recent graduates from teacher education programs with no teaching experience) who have an adventurous spirit or who, for one reason or another, are unable to land a teaching job in their home country, and most likely are paying off student loans. Other primary candidates would be recent baccalaureate recipients in similar situations who are adventurous and welcome the idea of working and traveling at the same time. This is not to say that there are no mature foreign teachers in Korea. They certainly exist. In fact, there are many who start their teaching career in Korea, fall in love with the country, and remain there for many years.

Although the situation seems to be improving, initially the preferred qualification for hiring was exclusively to be a native speaker of English from a country where the official language is English. Candidates from a country with historical ties to the United Kingdom (e.g., the United States, Australia, Canada, Ireland, and South Africa) received priority consideration for linguistic reasons regardless of the applicant's college major. More and more often, a bachelor's degree is required. However, in most instances, a teaching certificate or credential is not, but it helps. Consequently, the clear majority of candidates that are flocking to these positions are young college graduates with a bachelor's degree but no teacher education preparation and no teaching experience. Thus, most of these teaching recruits lack the necessary pedagogical knowledge to implement an effective teaching methodology based on the educational needs of the students. They are also deficient in classroom management skills, which is essential to a conducive learning environment. Classes in *hagwons* vary in size depending on a number of factors, including subject matter, grade level, and location. However, for the most part, these classes are smaller than regular classes in the United States.

Some of my colleagues who had worked in *hagwons* complained that the students were disrespectful and unruly. This disruptiveness calls for effective classroom management, a skill some *hagwon* instructors lack due to their lack of training. In some cases, they protested, their role was reduced to that of a babysitter. Another complaint from former *hagwon* instructors was the lack of support from administration in disciplinary matters. They found that administration sided with the students and parents instead of backing the instructors on discipline-related issues. By valuing the student perspective at the expense of the teacher's authority, the *hagwons* maintained (and still maintain) high enrollment. This attitude rendered the instructors powerless with little to no authority and an inability to implement high academic standards and enforce proper behavior. Fights between students were commonplace, especially among middle school (7th, 8th, and 9th grade) children. Regarding fighting between students, the administration took the attitude that fights represent differences between individuals and the students themselves should resolve the issue. Finally, former *hagwon* instructors complained that there were some issues receiving payment on time.

Because of these poor working conditions, the teachers who were certificated/credentialed did not last long in these *hagwons*. They soon applied for and successfully moved to international schools. Again, Young Lee and I want to emphasize that not all *hagwons* are created equal; therefore, the complaints described above do not apply to all *hagwons*. The situation in Gangnam, where the quality of supplemental enrichment education and test preparation is considered the best, is the exception to the rule. The school where I was employed enrolled some students who had had the fortune of attending outstanding *hagwons* that specialized in providing training in the performing arts. These students' talents were undoubtedly nurtured and developed to a high degree of proficiency.

Long Hours, Sleep Deprivation and Stress

Frequently, *hagwons* continue class until 10:00p.m., 11:00p.m. or even midnight, Monday through Friday. Some even operate on Saturday, depending on the school level (e.g., elementary, middle or senior high school) and location. Per the BBC, in 2008, a 10:00 p.m. curfew was established for *hagwons* in Seoul, but there is no uniformity among cities in this regard; they apply different restrictions.[18] Some cities allow *hagwons* to go on as late as midnight for high school students.

After attending *hagwons*, students go home and do their homework for their day classes, which forces them to stay awake until the wee hours of the morning. Consequently, these very same students are understandably exhausted and sleep-deprived. It is not surprising, given the high levels of competition, sleep deprivation as well as high levels of stress among students, that "intentional harm" (suicide) was the leading cause of death among youth 9 to 24 years of age from 2007 to 2017 according to Statistics Korea.[19] Young Lee and I recognize that a cause-and-effect relationship

149

between a high suicide rate and any specific factors need to be extensively studied before establishing such connection and said research is beyond the scope of this book. However, the conditions above do exist and appear to be contributing factors, even if the extant evidence is not enough to prove direct cause.

Alternatives to *Hagwons* and Private Tutors

An alternative option available to high-income parents is the option of enrolling their children in an international school. This option is indeed one that exposes students to a Western style of education. It is particularly beneficial for students who intend to apply for admission to Western universities to facilitate their academic and social adjustment, which is critical to student success.

Moreover, in this environment, students can associate with others who have attended either middle or high school abroad and thus possess a relatively good command of the English language. English fluency is a critical skill for students who need to compete against native speakers of English in an academic environment. Technically, a student who wishes to attend an international school must have attended school abroad previously. Korean parents recognize the long-term benefits for children who can attend and graduate from an international school.

However, the zeal to capitalize on these benefits, regardless of cost and means, drives some families to procure forged documents indicating that the students have attended school outside of

Korea. These forged documents, they hope, will enable their children to attend one of these highly sought after international schools. These fraud cases have surfaced in the media from time to time in major cities where these schools are usually located. The media attention that international schools have received is one reason why they have been a source of controversy. Critics portray the international schools as providing children of high-income families with an unfair advantage. The question of fairness and equal treatment is a source of consternation in the Korean society, primarily because of the competitive environment.

Parachute Kids

Sending children to study in the United States or other English-speaking countries is yet another popular, albeit expensive, choice for parents who have wealth significant enough to be able to afford thousands of dollars in expenses each month. These expenses include travel, tuition, boarding and other incidentals. The motivating factor to pay these fees is to enable their children to qualify for admission into a university abroad, primarily in an English speaking country, such as the U.S., Canada, Australia, or the United Kingdom. These "international students" are commonly known as "parachute kids." They attend international schools at all grade levels, from elementary to high school. As far as the latter is concerned, Korea is not funneling the most international students to the United States. China is the country with the largest delegation. According to a report titled *Globally Mobile Youth—Trends in International Secondary Students in the United States, 2013-2016* published by IIE (Institute of International

Education), in Fall 2016 there were a total of 81,981 international students enrolled in U.S. high schools.[20] The top six countries that sent children to the United States were China, South Korea, Vietnam, Mexico, Japan and Canada in that order. The fact that Korea with a population of just over 51 million people in 2018 is among these much larger countries in terms of the number of students enrolled in the United States speaks volumes about the emphasis that Korean parents place on the value of education in general. Particularly, the statistics reveal the perceived importance of acquiring a high school education and eventual baccalaureate completion from a university in the United States.[21] Based on estimates by the United Nations Department of Economic and Social Affairs, the population for the other countries in this category is as follows; China: over 1.415 billion, Vietnam: over 96.491 million, Mexico: over 130.759 million, and Japan: over 127.185 million.[22] Korean parents know full well that utilizing this strategy will give their children an edge in the university admission application process and eventually in the job market.

Sending students to study high school in the U.S. is feasible for Korean parents, especially if the family has relatives living there who are willing to host their son or daughter. However, not having relatives in the U.S. is not an obstacle, especially for wealthy parents. It is not uncommon for families that send their children to study in the U.S. to place them with a Korean or even non-Korean family willing to provide room and board and varying levels of supervision for a substantial fee.

However, for those who do not have relatives already living in the U.S., it is not unusual for Korean mothers to accompany the student while they study abroad. As stated earlier, this is a costly proposition in that splitting the family requires sufficient income not only to pay the student's tuition, travel and living expenses for both the child and the mother but also to provide for living expenses for two homes, one in Korea and another abroad. These families are commonly referred to as "wild geese families" in reference to the migration quality of wild geese and the long distances that these families must travel. In this type of arrangement, the father stays behind in Korea working to generate enough money to make this strategy possible. These fathers are commonly referred to in Korean as *gireogi appa* (Korean: 기러기 아빠, "goose dad"). Even though the U.S. is the destination of choice, Korean families also flock to other English-speaking countries such as Australia, Canada, New Zealand, the UK and the Philippines. I recall at least four of the students in the school where I taught had attended school in either Australia or the Philippines. At least three of those four students returned to Korea speaking English more fluently with either an Australian or Filipino accent after only one year. This observation is made only to show how impressionable children are and how quickly they adapt to their environment, not to judge whether speaking English with an accent is good or bad. Their experience in an English-speaking country contributed enormously to their improved performance on their return to the American school in Korea. These observations speak volumes in favor of an immersion environment where, based on the circumstances, a student is required to listen to and speak the target language not only in class but outside of class as well. It is safe to presume that these students' improved academic performance was due to their experience in an English-speaking country as opposed to having spent the same amount of time in the American school in Korea where they were exposed to English only during class time and they reverted back to Korean outside of class and throughout the remaining hours of the day. Also, living outside of Korea for a year appears to give these students more self-confidence socially and academically. Although these examples are purely anecdotal and the number of students involved is rather small, they seem to indicate that there are linguistic, academic, and self-esteem advantages to sending students to another country where the target language is the official language as well as the language of instruction. According to an article that appeared in the ABC (Australian Broadcasting Corporation) on June 17, 2015, "...an estimated 20,000 families...leave South Korea each year to go and live in an English-speaking country" to enable their children to acquire an English-language education.[23]

Once they attend school in an English-speaking country, depending on whether they graduate from high school, parachute kids have three tremendously advantageous options. These options are only possible if they compile a respectable academic record which includes the appropriate academic courses, a high grade point average, the required SAT or ACT scores and possibly the TOEFL test. The first option is to enroll in a prestigious private international high school in Korea, which will provide the student with a leg up in the brutally competitive university admission process. Alternatively, the student could apply for admission to a university in the U.S. or another English-speaking country. Finally, they could apply for admission to a prestigious university in Korea with the understanding that acceptance is not guaranteed. A common belief is that completing high school in the U.S. gives students an edge in the admission process for American universities. For Korean students who graduate from high school in the U.S., the third option, which is to apply to a prestigious university in Korea, is less viable. The estrangement with Korean education limits their exposure to an academic environment in the Korean language. Accordingly, linguistic deficiencies often develop even if students make a deliberate attempt to maintain a high level of exposure to the Korean language in their own private lives while living outside of Korea.

The option of sending children to study abroad, even when accompanied by their mother, presents an array of challenges for all parties concerned, including separation anxiety, stress, loneliness, depression, and inadequate nutrition. The issues become more severe if the children are not academically, socially or psychologically prepared to facilitate their adjustment to the new environment.

A Rude Awakening

One of the motivations for Korean students is to land one of the highly coveted jobs in a major corporation, which will provide them with inherent financial security and prestige. These jobs are viewed as compensation for all the time, effort, money, and sacrifices made by students and parents alike from the time the student enters elementary school until they graduate from university. The fierce competition for jobs, resulting from the democratization of higher education, has caused an awakening of sorts. The reality is that the job openings in large corporations are limited, and these corporations cannot possibly accommodate all the university graduates on an annual basis. Not even students from top-tier universities have a clear path to one of those jobs. Many are having trouble securing a position in the nation's conglomerates. Disenchanted students are beginning to recognize the fallacy that a bachelor's degree will ensure a place in the job market, and thus guarantee financial security. Some young people who are unable to compile the appropriate academic record or the desired admission test scores are beginning to realize that career and technical education, also known as vocational education, may be a viable alternative for acquiring practical skills and eventually securing a job. Recognizing that graduating from university with a bachelor's degree does not guarantee employment, in the recent past more high school students were opting to attend vocational schools. While conducting research for this book, I found that the idea was gaining in popularity at such a fast pace that the demand surpassed the number of slots available. Indeed, the job placement rate for vocational school graduates was on the rise. According to an article that appeared in the *Korea JoongAng Daily* on January 23, 2017: "The employment rate of vocational school graduates rose for the seventh consecutive year, the Ministry of Education said, from 16.7 percent in 2009 to 47.2 percent last year [2016]. The government's target rate by 2022 is 65 percent."[24]

The government recognized that it needed to be proactive to address the high youth unemployment rate. As such, the Korean government created a new type of state-run school in 2009. These schools are called Meister High Schools and, according to the article cited above, they teach "specific technologies related to the ten fastest emerging sectors, including semiconductors and robots [robotics]."[25] The government funds the schools and their number "rose from 20 in 2009 to 48 as of 2016."[26]

The best aspect of these Meister High Schools is that program development decisions appear to be based on research. Apparently, the schools utilize environmental scans to identify the ten fastest emerging sectors, thus meeting the needs of business and industry and maximizing employment possibilities for graduates. The *Korea JoongAng Daily* goes on to report that "Meister school graduates' employment rate has remained above 90 percent since 2013."[27]

More current data is needed as a result of the persistently high youth unemployment to determine the long-term effectiveness of this initiative. Although the impact of Meister High Schools is relatively small, given the number of sites, this new trend appears to be promising in terms of providing some young people employable skills. This type of training may not land them the "dream job" that many students may have hoped for, but at the very least, it provides them with marketable skills. It has become painfully apparent that the alternative option, which prepares students for higher education and corporate career tracks, does not always succeed in doing so.[28]

Update: By the date of this book's publication, this initiative appears to be losing traction as a result of high youth unemployment and the realization by young people that choosing to attend a high school that specializes in career and technical education sentences them to a socioeconomic status that is not appealing to them or their family. Such a life includes wages and benefits that are much lower than those offered by conglomerates, working conditions that are much harsher than they had hoped for, and job security that is not very reliable or consistent. In essence, these conditions are the antithesis of Koreans' culture- and society-driven aspirations.

University Education Abroad

Obtaining a bachelor's degree from a respectable university abroad is considered an attractive option, albeit an expensive one, to stand a chance of attending a post-graduate program in fields such as medicine, engineering, and computer science. The bachelor's degree can contribute to landing the "dream" white-collar job, possibly at a major corporation. Some employers, particularly global companies, give applicants bonus points in the hiring process if they have earned a degree from a reputable university abroad, particularly from universities in English-speaking countries. It is not uncommon for Korean global companies to recruit Korean graduates directly from U.S. university campuses. Oftentimes, job announcements include a statement indicating that the company is specifically searching for Korean applicants who graduated from university in the United States.

It is advantageous for candidates for teaching positions at Korean universities to have earned any degree, be it a bachelor's, a master's or a doctorate, from a university in an English-speaking country. Advantages include the fact that Korean universities require professors to publish research papers in English language journals for them to obtain tenure. Also, the ability to teach in English can earn candidates extra points in the job application process. Furthermore, it is common for university professors who teach in English to receive additional compensation.

Anecdotally, a Korean friend of mine who had earned a bachelor's degree from a Korean university decided to apply for a doctoral program in the United States. After she earned her degree, she applied unsuccessfully for a teaching position in several universities in the U.S. Then, she applied for a similar job at a top-tier university in Korea. Her application was successful after the first attempt. Subsequently, she was assigned to teach some of her major classes in English and was granted tenure after she published research papers in English journals.

The option to study abroad especially appeals to students who either have excelled academically or who have not earned the necessary test scores or grades to be admitted by a top-tier university in Korea, provided that their parents have the necessary financial means to pay for it. Parents are willing to make the sacrifice of paying for their children's tuition, travel, living, and incidental expenses. These expenses often add up to several thousands of dollars per month. Parents rely upon their savings or borrow money from family members or even banks. However, taking into consideration the high tuition costs for international students in the U.S, in addition to room and board costs, travel and incidental

159

expenses, and the fact that a bachelor's degree requires at least a four-year commitment, the reality is that education abroad remains a viable option only for wealthy parents.

Parents of students who wish to study abroad generally recognize that to increase the probability of their children's acceptance, they must seek university admission expertise outside of the school system. The exception to this rule is if the student is attending an international school, where these services are usually provided. The demand for this type of support has prompted entrepreneurs to provide college admission consulting services for a fee. Procuring this type of consulting services is analogous to the system of *hagwons* or private tutors, since the services purportedly give students an edge in the university admission process. These services may include guidance in choosing the appropriate high school courses, test preparation and test-taking advice, information about university selection and the admission application process, college admission research and specific college/university suggestions, and practical assistance with the application process itself. The efficacy of these consultants seems to be uneven, especially when it comes to advising seniors and their families on admission to U.S. universities. To be effective, college admission consultants must be thoroughly familiar not only with admission requirements and the application process for each university, but also the programmatic strengths and idiosyncrasies of universities and their campuses, in addition to the academic strengths, deficiencies, and preferences of the applicant. Most importantly, the consultant needs to guide the applicant through a strategic plan that will ensure admission to several institutions, based on the student's academic and extracurricular record. Then, the applicant and the family can make the final selection from these options.

Unfortunately, these consulting services do not always produce positive results. As an example, the parents of a senior valedictorian at the high school where I taught sought and paid for the services of a private consultant to give their daughter an edge over other university applicants. They hired the outside consultant, even though these services were expertly provided in-house by an experienced college counselor hired by the high school. In the end, the consultation process was a total failure. The student received rejection letters from the dozen or so universities in the U.S. to which she was advised to apply. Thus, the graduating senior spent the following year out of school, researching other options for the subsequent year. The additional expense incurred by this student's parents is yet another example of how far Korean parents are willing to go to support their children's education. They view these types of expenses as an investment in their children's, as well as their own, future economic wellbeing.

Regrettably, in the case cited above the effort was misguided. The question: "How misguided are some of these services in general?" is a valid one. Rumors appear to indicate that some consultants complete the applications and even write the required essays for the applicants. Do students who obtain assistance with the essay-writing process have an unfair advantage over students who lack this support? If universities in the U.S. are relying upon essays as one of several factors that determine academic potential and eventual eligibility for admission, are decisions being made on false premises when it comes to some international students who hire unscrupulous university admission consultants?

Korean students are keenly aware of the sacrifice and financial stress that their parents face because of the high cost of their private education. They are also cognizant of the need for them to deliver the result that their parents expect of them: being accepted by a prestigious university. Consequently, the students themselves are under enormous stress. As a result, some students resort to "intentional harm." They are particularly vulnerable to this psychological distress when admission to a reputable university fails to come to fruition. They are also understandably susceptible to a feeling of failure under such conditions. It is not surprising that this aforementioned intentional harm (suicide) was the leading cause of death among youth aged 9 to 24 from 2007 to 2017.[29] Again, although the correlation between education pressure and self-harm is not established on one-to-one ratio, the aligning factors suggest that some relationship must exist.

Academic Competition, Grade Inflation, Degree Inflation and Disenchantment

Holders of bachelor's degrees are finding it increasingly more difficult to procure employment after graduation, even when the student graduates from a top-tier university. Even though major corporations assign these graduates some sort of advantage, the job is by no means guaranteed. Some graduates recognize that a bachelor's degree not only does not ensure employment, but it does not necessarily even provide them with the needed career entry-level skills. Therefore, even some graduates from top-tier universities are enrolling in career and technical education programs to obtain the practical skills and corresponding certifications that will prepare them for entry-level jobs. The brutal competition for jobs is prompting this proactive action on the part of university graduates and is the result of the pervasive degree inflation that the democratization of higher education has produced. However, this initiative by university graduates, as well-intentioned as it is, in fact exacerbates the widespread degree inflation.

The myth that a university degree is the panacea for future economic and material success, the universal expectation for high school graduates to attend and graduate from university, and the democratization of higher education have contributed to both an absence of emphasis and a stigma associated with career and technical education programs. The end result is substantial degree inflation.

Because of the high percentage of individuals with a bachelor's degree, the country has an artificially high level of education. The reality is that the economy is unable to accommodate this excess of "highly educated" individuals in jobs that require a university degree. Consequently, those who are unable to secure a position in their area of expertise have the unenviable choice of being unemployed, underemployed or accepting a job at the minimum wage that requires less than their academic preparation would suggest. Those who choose to be unemployed or underemployed over working in the service industry out of pride, shame or any number of reasons, end up being a burden to the family.

One cannot underestimate the impact that the democratization of higher education in Korea has had on employment. Data published in an article that appeared in the *Munhwa Ilbo* on May 2, 2018 indicates that according to research conducted by the Korean Research Institute for Vocational Education and Training, in 1990, 20% of employees working at large corporations with at least 500 employees had a bachelor's degree. By 2015, that figure had skyrocketed to 60%.[30]

Degree inflation is especially felt at the higher echelons of education: the master's and doctoral degrees. According to the article cited above, there are 1.13 million people who hold a master's degree, a doctoral degree or both. The employment market, however, can only accommodate 250,000 people with such degrees. Consequently, there is an excess of 880,000 people with graduate degrees, clearly revealing an overabundance of overqualified individuals. Contributing to this excess number of people holding graduate degrees is the practice of furthering one's education by returning to school after completing the requirements for a bachelor's degree to obtain either a master's or doctoral degree. The assumption is that such a postgraduate degree will increase the chances of landing the "dream job." Also contributing to this degree inflation are individuals who, for one reason or another, are unable to find a job after obtaining their bachelor's degree. If their parents can afford to pay for graduate school costs, they opt to return to education to seek another degree out of desperation.

Unfortunately, the unintended consequences further exacerbate the degree inflation for the country. This situation causes a great deal of consternation and frustration for people who are unable to secure a job even after all the time, effort, money and sacrifice invested in obtaining a post-graduate degree. In the article cited above, Kim Ahn-kook, senior researcher at the Vocational Competency Development Center, suggests that a modification in the people's approach to higher education is needed.[31] Kim points out that this oversupply of overqualified individuals is a wasteful and inefficient use of resources. Furthermore, he underscores the short-term side consequences discussed in this section, which include unemployment, underemployment and settling for jobs that require much less qualification than the academic preparation obtained.

The gravity of the prevalent degree inflation is evident in a statistical report published recently by the Korean National Statistics Office (NSO). Based on May 2018 data reported on June 23, 2018, by the NSO, the number of unemployed citizens who graduated from 4-year universities has reached a record high. Per Labor Force Population Research conducted by the NSO, the number of unemployed workers holding a bachelor's degree or higher level of education in May 2018 was 402,000. This figure represents a year-to-year increase of 76,000 from 2017.[32] The 2018 numbers are the highest ever to exist since such statistics were first recorded in June 1999.[33] The number of unemployed workers with a bachelor's or higher degree represents 35.8% of the total unemployed population, which is 1,121,000 Korean citizens.[34] If the number of unemployed with a two-year vocational college degree is included, the percentage of unemployed with a higher education degree is a staggering 48.8%.[35] In comparison, in May 2000, the number of unemployed with a bachelor's or higher degree comprised only 14.2% of the total unemployed.[36] Therefore, the proportion of unemployed with a bachelor's degree to the total unemployed increased 2.5 times in 18 years. Such an increase is due to insufficient number of jobs for individuals with a bachelor's degree, which causes extreme competition in the job market, and degree inflation.

As of May 2018, the total labor force population, both employed and unemployed, who held at least a bachelor's degree was 9.32 million. This figure has also increased about 2.5 times from 3.79 million in May 2000.[37] Some young people have become disenchanted with the competitive nature of Korean society and the sacrifices that must be made by students and their families to have a fair chance in a system that appears to favor those who are financially well-off. Some of these disenchanted young people refer to Korea as *Hell Joseon*. They are rejecting some of the values that Korea represents. This topic is discussed more in depth in Chapter Eight.

Those students who gain admission into middle-tier or third-tier universities know very well that their chances of being hired by a major corporation are practically nonexistent. They are cognizant that they may be able to secure a job at a small or mid-sized company where the salary, benefits and job security are significantly lower than they had hoped for. As a result, the quality of life that these conditions may generate is not up to their standards. Also, many applicants feel that these conditions are not conducive to raise their future children to be successful in such a highly competitive environment. So, there is a feeling of resignation among these students, which may be reflected in their attitude and outlook. A Korean colleague of mine who teaches at a lower-tier university confided that many students at these universities are not only ill-prepared, but they have an attitude of entitlement. In many instances, they expect to pass courses even though they do the least amount of work possible. Students who do practically no work, attend class unprepared, put their head down on their desk, and go to sleep during class expect to receive passing grades. And they often do. Faculty are aware of the uphill battle faced by students in these universities, and attempt to give them a leg up by awarding better grades than they deserve, thus contributing to grade inflation.

Furthermore, university non-tenured faculties are at the mercy of student evaluations for job security, particularly faculty at the instructor or adjunct (part-time) level. It is not uncommon for faculty who are in their probationary period, instructors and adjunct professors, to award students a higher grade than they deserve in exchange for positive evaluations. Because job security for non-tenured teachers depends heavily on student evaluations, historically there has been such pervasive grade inflation at middle- and third-tier universities that the Ministry of Education has mandated that universities impose maximum percentages allowed for letter grades. As an example, the university that had jurisdiction over the high school where I worked implemented a policy that no more than 40% of final grades be "A" grades and

60% "B" grades for non-major classes of 19 or fewer students. For non-major classes of 20 or more students, the maximum percentages allowed of As is 30% and the combination of As and Bs cannot exceed 70%. These artificially imposed grade percentage restrictions raise questions on two counts: First, the questionable reality of academic freedom that the teaching profession is universally characterized by, and second, the universal belief that a grading system is supposed to recognize merit, not seat time.

During their university stay, students often repeat the courses in which they earned poor marks to improve their academic record, thus contributing further to grade inflation. Subsequently, once a course is repeated satisfactorily, the more recent grade is posted on the official transcript, and the original mark is usually expunged, thus giving the student a higher grade point average and concealing the fact that specific courses were repeated. This practice of deleting grades from an official transcript would be considered unconventional in the West because it is assumed that the official transcript reflects reality.

Some university students opt to perform volunteer work or participate in internships to distinguish their resumes. As indicated earlier, others choose to augment their academic or professional certifications, known in Korea as "specs," by completing certificate requirements above and beyond their degree, such as a computer operation license, CPA (Certified Public Accountant) license, Korean stenographer certificate and even foreign language training. The motivating factor is the belief that these additional qualifications will make them more competitive in the job search process.

Through this exercise of supplementing their academic and professional backgrounds, students can extend their university stay by one or two years beyond the traditional four-year sojourn. Even though these extended university stays take the pressure off the job market by delaying the graduates' job search, they come with an expensive price tag, which includes additional living expenses as well as university enrollment and tuition fees, not to mention possible additional *hagwon* and travel and tuition costs in the case of foreign language training when the program is undertaken in another country. The net result of these practices artificially raises the bar for job applicants and makes the competition even more brutal. Simultaneously, universities serve as "holding tanks" for the job market while students add qualifications to their resumes.

While they are in the process of applying for jobs, some university seniors choose to delay graduation to maintain their student status, even after completing their course requirements.

These students believe that their chances of success in the job search are better as students than as graduates. Naturally, extending the time at university requires students and their families to incur additional enrollment fees, expenses for books and supplies, and living expenses, which means that only those students whose families can afford the additional costs can take advantage of this extra time. Assuming the general belief that job applicants have a higher probability of landing a job with a major corporation as students than as graduates, the children of more affluent families appear to have an advantage since they can pay for the additional expenses generated by extended university stays.

If the conviction that job applicants have a higher prospect of obtaining the dream job as students than as graduates is accurate, then the time, effort, and expense that are directed toward extended university stays actually translate into a decided edge for the haves and a disadvantage for the have-nots. It is true that in other capitalist societies the wealthy are also able to gain an advantage over others by virtue of their privileged position, money, and social connections. However, in a country like Korea where annual job creation cannot accommodate the number of university graduates, where the competition for jobs is grueling, any edge is magnified. Furthermore, in Korea, the universities themselves seem to be permitting this gaming of the system to take place. In the United States, for example, universities, particularly state-funded universities, would not allow extended stays once students complete their graduation requirements. The premise in this case is that space at university is limited and they want to provide an opportunity to obtain an education to as many people as possible. Those who are cynical about the competitive nature of Korean society and refer to the country as *Hell Joseon* may view this practice of extending university stays as another point of contention. The concept of *Hell Joseon* is addressed in Chapter Eight.

Endnotes

1   "Population, total – Korea, rep.," *World Bank*, accessed 18 November 2019, *data.worldbank.org*.

2   "Parents Spend More and More on Private Tuition," *The Chosun Ilbo*, 27 March 2017, *english.chosun.com*.

3   Ibid.

4   Siobhan Fenton, "President Obama Praises South Korea For Paying Teachers as Much as Doctors," *The Independent*, 18 July 2015, *independent.co.uk.*

5   "Statistical Database," *Korean Statistical Information Service,* accessed 20 July 2019, *kosis.kr*.

6   "Monthly Spending on Private Education Up 33%," *The Korea Herald,* 17 March 2018, *koreaherald.com*.

7   "Gangnam District," *Wikipedia*, accessed 20 July 2019, *Wikipedia.com.*

8   "International Education Attainment," *NCES National Center for Education Statistics,* accessed 16 August 2019, *nces.ed.gov.*

9   "Monthly Spending," *The Korea Herald*.

10   Yim Hyun-Su, "Viewers Gush Over 'Sky Castle,' *The Korea Herald*, accessed 16 August 2019, *koreaherald.com*.

11   Ibid.

12   "Hit Drama Reveals Sky High Pressure of South Korean School System," *The Jakarta Post,* accessed 30 June 2019, *thejakartapost.com.*

13   Ibid.

14   Jin-Hai Park, "Sky Castle captures elite moms' education craze," *The Korea Times*, accessed 29 June 2019, *koreatimes.kr.*

15   "Monthly Spending," *The Korea Herald*

16 Ibid.

17 Reeta Chakrabarti, "South Korea's schools: Long days, high results," *BBC*, 2 December 2013, *bbc.com*.

18 Ibid.

19 "Total," *Statistics Korea*, accessed 16 August 2019, *kostat. go.kr.* and "Suicide No. 1 Cause of Death for S. Korean Teens, Youths," *The Korea Herald*, accessed 16 August 2019, *koreaherald.com*.

20 "Globally Mobile Youth," *The Power of International Education*, accessed 16 August 2019, *iie.org*.

21 "List of Countries by Population," Statistics Times, 29 July 2019, *statisticstimes.com*.

22 Ibid.

23 Bronwen Reed, "Wild Geese Families," Australian *Broadcasting Corporation*, 17 June 2015, abc.net.

24 "Enrollment in Vocational Schools Surges," *Korea Joongang* Daily, 23 January 2017, k*oreajoongangdaily.joins.com*.

25 Ibid.

26 Ibid.

27 Ibid.

28 Although these observations pertaining to Meister High Schools still apply, they should be viewed in light of recent developments described in the update below.

29 "Suicide No. 1 Cause," *The Korea Herald*.

30 Jun Jin-Young, "Master's and PhD. Market demand is only 250,000," trans. Young Lee, *Munhwa Ilbo*, 2 May 2018, *munhwa.com*.

31 Ibid.

32 "Did you go to college to do this? 1 in 3 unemployed," trans.

Young Lee, *Naver,* 23 June 2018, *naver.com.*

33   Ibid.
34   Ibid.
35   Ibid.
36   Ibid.
37   Ibid.

Chapter Four

An American High School in Korea

Profile of an American High School

This chapter examines the behavioral patterns and learning behaviors of the students at the American high school where I taught. First, however, it is essential to describe the school's profile to provide context for this educational setting. The school was accredited by the Western Association of Schools and Colleges (WASC), which made it a bona fide American high school and facilitated the students' application process to U.S. colleges and universities. During the academic year of 2012-2013, at the beginning of my tenure, the students were all of Korean descent and hailed from various locations throughout Korea including large cities like Seoul, Busan, and Daejeon. Some students came from the Korean education system, and others had attended school in a Western country where the language of instruction was English, such as the U.S., Canada, or Australia. Three years later, in fall 2015, only a handful of non-Korean students enrolled in the school. These non-Koreans had lived in the country long enough for them to be able to communicate fluently in Korean with other students and blend in with the rest of the student population. Therefore, it is safe to say that their presence did not disrupt the harmony and homogeneity of the student body.

Boarding facilities were made available for students whether their families lived in or outside of Jeonju. The percentage of boarding students varied annually from approximately 40% to 50% of the total student population, which was typically less than 100 students. The school was co-ed. It is important to note that many of the students were there primarily to have exposure to a Western style of education, to improve their command of the English language and to eventually graduate and gain admission into a reputable university in Korea, the United States, Canada, the United Kingdom, or other countries around the world. Clearly, the exposure to education in English, as well as exposure to the Western style of teaching, enhanced the graduates' chances of succeeding at a Western university. Instructors were native speakers of English. The majority of us received our teacher preparation training in either the United States or Canada. The administrative duties were split between a Korean administrator who also spoke English and an American principal who was bilingual-bicultural in English and Korean. Some instructors had experience teaching in the Korean education system, others had experience teaching in *hagwons*, and still others had neither.

Professional Experience

It is also important to note that this four-year professional experience in Korea was not my first teaching interaction with Korean students. Before teaching in Korea, I was a teacher and a guidance counselor in California for 15 years. I taught at a high school located in a city that was considered, at the time, a port of entry for new immigrants. Even though there were waves of immigrants from different parts of the world, most of the incoming students at that time were from South Korea. Subsequently, I had the opportunity to provide academic counseling for ten years at a top-notch community college. At this college, there was a high percentage of recent Korean immigrants, many of whom transferred to major universities both in and outside of California. Some, however, experienced difficulty adjusting to a Western style of education. These difficulties were made apparent by their less than stellar academic performance.

Therefore, my exposure to teaching and counseling Korean students over the course of my career is much more extensive than my recent four-year professional experience in Korea. The observations below about the learning behaviors of Korean students are based on my professional training, 28 years of professional expertise, and input from colleagues in various disciplines in the United States and at the American high school where I worked in Korea. Through my professional training and experience, I have learned that students' attitudes in a learning environment are influenced by several dynamics. These dynamics include cultural factors, the students' motivational level, their prior exposure to learning stimuli such as books and computers, the parents' level of education, home environment, and the pedagogical approaches to which they are exposed (e.g., teacher-centered, student-centered or learning-centered). Yet, many students exhibit an attitude that is conducive to learning even when some of the aforementioned factors are less than ideal.

Because of the relatively small number of students and the unique characteristics of this school, it is critical to avoid making generalized assumptions about Korean students based on only a small sample. The context of the educational experience is undoubtedly one of a few influential factors in student behavior. The environment of an American high school might evoke differentiating results from a typical Korean school. However, one may expect those behavioral patterns that have a cultural bias to reflect society at large. In other words, even though these Korean students who were immersed in a school that attempted to emulate an American environment with English instruction facilitated by Western instructors, a Westernized code of conduct and set of expectations, it would not be surprising for their behavior to still be influenced by their Korean upbringing. In fact, it would be natural for student behavior to reflect their culture in a similar situation regardless of their background. Therefore, it is totally feasible that their behavior could reflect values embedded in the Korean culture even as they are operating in a different environment.

Students' Behavioral and Learning Patterns

I, along with my colleagues, observed behavioral and learning patterns among the students with whom we worked. Initially, within these generalized behavioral paradigms, except for students who had prior exposure to a Western-style of education, generally speaking, students seemed to be uncomfortable in a student-centered environment. They hesitated when given the opportunity to operate in a participatory educational setting. In other words, they were more comfortable in a teacher-centered approach, where students could sit at their desk and listen to the teacher lecture, while taking notes and subsequently studying their notes to restate that information on a test. As students became more proficient in English and more comfortable, even adept, in a participatory environment and simultaneously more cognizant of teacher expectations, most students showed remarkable improvement in this regard. However, students accustomed to a teacher-centric approach found old habits difficult to overcome.

Furthermore, initially, students also froze when faced with the prospect of practicing their independent thinking ability. They assumed that all the correct answers had to come from the teacher and not from students. The concept of open-ended questions appeared to be new to them. Gradually, as teachers asked open-ended questions, encouraged students to pose questions themselves and express their opinion, students became more skilled at posing not merely average, but incisive questions as well. This development appeared to coincide with the improvements made in students' command of the English language and critical thinking skills.

The hesitation to ask questions in class appears to have cultural roots. In the West, students are encouraged to pose questions in class as it is considered a sign of intellectual curiosity as well as critical and independent thinking. Asking individual questions is diametrically opposed to the Korean concepts of unity and harmony, which are achieved when all students behave similarly. Based on the Korean paradigm, a student asking individual questions disrupts the unity and harmony of the classroom. Students learn at an early age in school not to ask questions during a teacher's lecture unless they are considered top-notch students. When one such student asks a question, the harmony is maintained by the concentrated attention of the rest of their classmates who honor not only the questioner who has earned the unspoken right to pose questions based on their academic prowess, but also the teacher who is viewed as providing knowledge and wisdom. By withholding questions, students avoid "wasting" both the time of the teacher and the other students, a concept that is related to efficiency. If only the best students ask questions, then the entire group benefits and class time is maximized. This model is further explained by the motto "대를 위한 소의 희생" ("For the large, sacrifice the small") or, "Each individual should act or sacrifice for the benefit of the group," which is discussed in more detail in Chapter One.

Similar observations have been made by Professor Justin Fendos, educational researcher at Dongseo University, about the lack of independent thinking and creativity among Korean students at the university level. In an article that appeared in The Korea Herald on October 15, 2017, Professor Fendos states: "There is no scientific proof that South Korean students are less creative than their Western counterparts; the main reason for this [assumption] is the lack of a reliable assessment that can quantify creativity."[1] Nevertheless, he shares that anecdotally, he and his colleagues:

have frequently observed a significant difference between Korean university students and foreign peers when they are put together into groups and asked to solve problems. The Korean students simply aren't good at solving problems they haven't experienced before and will often gape in amazement at the speed and ease with which their foreign colleagues can think up new solutions.

Assuming this difference is real, a conclusion both I and the Korean government agree on, it becomes paramount to identify the causes. When one studies the common experiences of Korean students, one thing becomes obvious immediately: the fact that creativity is largely discouraged in Korean classrooms at virtually every level.

Throughout primary school, Korean students are socialized to be submissive and do what teachers tell them.[2]

I would add to these comments the following: I firmly believe that the type of learning and social skills that Professor Fendos and his colleagues have identified as lacking in the repertoire of Korean students can be learned if they are nurtured. The possibility exists that the observed student habits and learning patterns are reinforced by the teaching and learning methodology employed by private tutors and *hagwon* instructors that specialize in test preparation. The learning in such an environment relies exclusively on repetition, rote memorization and teaching-to-the-test. The instructors' primary goal is to teach students to maximize their test time by answering questions quickly and efficiently and giving them lots of practice with test questions.

Realistically, tutors and *hagwon* instructors are doing what they are being paid to do. They are coaching students the most efficient strategies to approach a test so as to obtain the highest possible score. These practices and this behavior are not unique to Korea. What is unique, as with many other behavioral patterns observed among Koreans and discussed in this book, are the degree of intensity and pervasiveness of the behavior, which may very well be a byproduct of the competitive environment.

Obviously, in this environment, there is not much opportunity to emphasize creativity, independent thinking, inquiry-based learning or collaborative learning. By utilizing this teaching methodology in the *hagwons*, which are so prevalent in Korea, the unintended effect may be to enable this learning strategy in other settings, whether or not it is most effective for long-term assimilation and educational health.

Assuming that this spread of the *hagwon* culture is indeed happening, then the "golden goose" that laid the golden eggs, or *hagwons* and private tutors that help to make higher education accessible, in fact negatively impact the learning ability of Korean students. It is crucial for students and parents to recognize that the skills that provide access to university in a test preparation environment are not the same skills that will enable students to succeed in an educational setting that thrives on creativity, critical and independent thinking, inquiry-based learning, and collaborative learning.

Additionally, some students at the American high school exhibited a passive attitude when given the opportunity to collaborate with other students in group projects. Rather than working as a team, some students allowed a few who showed initiative to carry the entire workload. Again, this attitude is not unique to Korean students. As with other observed behavior, the difference is in its pervasiveness. In other educational settings, this behavior may be more closely associated with laziness or apathy. However, in the Korean educational setting these descriptors do not appear to apply as much as the element of efficiency. Students who relinquish their responsibilities to others recognize that by doing so, the group project will be performed by the most capable students and the group will reap the benefits by receiving a higher group grade. In reality, however, those students who abrogate responsibility benefit the least from the learning process, whereas those who actively participate benefit the most. The latter expand their critical thinking ability, develop or enhance their leadership skills, and build social skills as well as self-esteem.

One of the goals of education is to prepare students to become productive members of society. Educators who allow students to shirk responsibility do students on both sides of this dichotomy a disservice. The inherent message to students who relinquish their responsibilities is that they can get by in life doing the minimum. Conversely, permitting students who take the initiative to carry the entire workload instills an unhealthy attitude vis-à-vis their learning. It also allows those students to escape the challenges of working with a team by just doing what they always do: doing it themselves. By providing a safe environment where all are not only able but required to participate in the learning and discovery process, students recognize how stimulating learning can be while they contribute to the success of the group. Along the way, they also learn to accept responsibility by sharing the load equally. Also, their self-esteem and self-confidence are enhanced because they discover that their contributions matter.

In their behavioral habits, students display the quality that permeates throughout the Korean culture: the tendency to be efficient. They exhibit a preference for multiple-choice questions instead of essay, short answers and fill-in-the-blank questions. Multiple-choice questions seem to be preferred for two very simple reasons: Students can progress through multiple-choice questions much more quickly than essay questions, and they can probably earn a higher score on multiple-choice than on essay, short answer and fill-in-the-blank tests. Therefore, this process seems efficient to them. Teachers noted this tendency in most subjects. However, it was of utmost concern in mathematics and science courses, in which showing the step-by-step process of arriving at the correct answer is critical. This is particularly important in higher-level courses, such as AP (Advanced Placement) courses, which emphasize critical thinking and research-based curricula. Also, in these classes, inquiry-based learning and experiments are an essential part of the learning process.

Finally, students tended to "cram" for tests by subsequently "dumping," purposefully trying to "wash away," or forgetting most of what they learned before a test. The theory behind this process is the incorrect assumption that they have no more use for that information after the test. Students believe that they must make room in their short-term memory for new material instead of viewing the learning process as a set of building blocks. Students at the school where I taught may have invented their own euphemism and referred to this process as "brainwashing." I recall, on several occasions in my classes while teaching a new concept that related to something we had studied in class previously and had a test on it, students had no recollection of the material. When I reminded them that we had already covered the material and had been tested on it, they were quick to explain that because they had already tested on that concept, they had forgotten about it. Once again, this behavioral pattern appears to be driven by the cultural emphasis on efficiency.

Undoubtedly, some of these behavioral and learning patterns present themselves in other settings and cultural contexts, as well. However, they seem to be more pronounced and pervasive within the Korean cultural background. It is difficult, if not impossible, to assign a direct cause-and-effect relationship, such as attributing a behavioral pattern to culture rather than prior education experience, or even lack of interest or motivation. A combination of causes could be considered a distinct possibility, not to mention the stress and anxiety caused by being in a different educational environment and dealing with language acquisition. However, it is more important to recognize the existence of specific challenging, unfavorable behavioral patterns, identify the possible cause/s, and devise a plan to eradicate them, or, at the very least, counteract their negative impact on the learning process.

From a pedagogical perspective, without taking cultural influences into consideration, it is possible to eradicate these behavioral patterns by meeting students "where they are" in terms of their critical thinking and learning ability. First, students can be exposed to experiences that are supported by their learning preferences, to give them a taste of success and build their self-confidence. Gradually, if teachers introduce activities that are more challenging, students will learn to build critical thinking skills and enhance their communication and social skills. If the activities gradually escalate in difficulty to move students toward desired behaviors, the negative impact of efficient, short-term gain learning behaviors might be counteracted. Students may even discover the joy of learning.

To accomplish this, very specific and clear rubrics need to be embedded into the grading system and made explicit to students to ensure that they understand the teacher's expectations. In order to be effective, the grading system should not only be perceived as fair, but should include a reward system. The reward system should promote positive behavior and academic achievement. Adopting productive behavioral patterns will enable students to acquire the skills needed to succeed in a demanding academic setting, in higher education and eventually as productive members of society and the workplace.

As alluded to earlier, one of the missions of education is to prepare students to be successful, productive citizens, regardless of their chosen profession. In this particular institution, and while working in an American school, teachers espoused specific values that are ingrained in the fabric of Western culture. For example, businesses and industries in the United States seek employees who are independent thinkers and learners. As such, schools need to develop creative individuals with the necessary social skills to function effectively in an environment where teamwork is essential.

Culture Clash or Dance?

The American high school was a setting where Korean and Western cultures coexisted but often clashed. On the one hand, teachers came to the school espousing a Western set of values, norms, and expectations. On the other hand, the students, except for those who had lived in the West, parents, and certainly the Korean administrators came to the table with a Korean set of values. Moreover, Korean families and administrators obviously had a specifically Korean image of what an American school was supposed to be. The participants had plenty of opportunities to compromise, particularly in philosophical areas such as the enforcement of the student conduct code.

A disciplinary case concerning two students involved in a dorm fight exemplifies the divergent opinions based on cultural differences. The fight took place in the evening. One of the students was older than the other, which is an important consideration in the Korean culture, since traditionally younger students are expected to be respectful and subservient to older students. The following day, the administration notified the students' parents of the incident. The younger student was then taken to a hospital for examination, as he was complaining of pain in his ears. The diagnosis was a ruptured eardrum, which was most likely caused by a punch thrown by the older student. The two students were suspended temporarily until an investigation into the incident could be conducted and the facts established.

The administration investigated the facts surrounding the incident, and they presented the results to the disciplinary committee. The administration, as described earlier, consisted of a male Korean administrator and a bilingual-bicultural American principal. The committee was comprised of teaching faculty and the guidance counselor, all of whom were Westerners. The committee members reviewed the case following the guidelines established by the student conduct code. However, because of the committee members' background, their cultural lenses influenced their perception of the incident. After careful consideration of all the facts, the disciplinary committee recommended to the administration that the older student be expelled. The disciplinary committee recommendation was in line with the student conduct code, which was meant to discourage similar altercations and ensure the safety of students. In the meantime, the mother of the younger student called the administration and requested that the older student be given no punishment. She reasoned that the fight was a personal matter between the two students and she expressed a concern that the student body would ostracize her son if the older student were expelled. After reviewing the disciplinary committee's recommendation to dismiss the older student and after hearing the plea from the younger student's mother, the administration decided to side with the younger student's mother. They did not expel the older student despite the committee recommendation to the contrary. Instead, the older student was required to participate in daily physical exercises for a determined number of days under the supervision of the ROTC command.

This is an example of the balancing act that members of this learning community, which included students, parents, teachers, and administrators, had to perform in this bicultural environment. The disciplinary committee made a recommendation based on the facts, the student conduct code and their cultural reference. Since this was an American high school, the disciplinary committee's recommendation aligned with what a disciplinary committee would recommend in a United States school. However, the administration opted to overrule the committee's recommendation based on their perception that the student code of conduct had to be applied in the context of the Korean culture. Given the setting, this was a very wise decision. However, a deep analysis of the situation indicates that the outcome of this incident reflects a microcosm of Korean societal practice, from the younger student's mother's plea to the administration's decision to allow the older student to remain in school after inflicting bodily injury to another and possibly causing permanent damage to the student's eardrum, and receiving only a symbolic slap on the wrist. These two actions appear to parallel what happens in the Korean society at large in regard to the absence of strict enforcement of existing rules. This observation will become evident per the discussion in Chapter Six on man-made accidents and in Chapter Seven's discussion of recent industrial accidents.

Clearly, the administration had the authority to overrule the disciplinary committee since it was only considered an advisory group for the administration. The teachers on the disciplinary committee knew full well that once the decision was made not to expel the student, they had to accept it. They felt that the punishment applied by the administration did not go far enough. The concern among teachers remained that this decision would send the wrong message to the students. By allowing the student to remain in school, the administration conveyed that it was acceptable to fight, since the offenders would only receive a slap on the wrist. Furthermore, teachers were concerned that this incident, if left practically unpunished, would encourage students to engage in bullying. Since some of the teachers had worked in Korean schools and *hagwons*, they were aware that bullying exists and it could be a contagious phenomenon if left unchecked.

In addition to student interactions, the teachers also diverged from the parents and the administration when it came to grading. The parents and the administration expected that low grades (D and F) should be expunged from the student's transcript once the courses were repeated satisfactorily. The accepted practice in the West is to post the new grades, but leave the original grades on the school transcript with a notation indicating that those courses had been repeated. Then, on the transcript, the school either recalculates the grade point average (GPA) using only the repeat grades or averages the original grade and the repeat grade. Through this practice, the transcript truly reflects the reality of the student's progress, whereas the practice of expunging low grades from a student's transcript does not, even if the courses are repeated successfully with a higher grade.

The instruction at the school was delivered in English, except in the case of world language classes like Chinese and Spanish. Even though teachers used the lecture method, they did not rely on it entirely. Instead, it was one of many teaching pedagogies that the instructors had at their disposal. Other strategies used extensively were the Socratic Method, collaborative learning, class discussion, problem-based learning, scaffolding, group and individual projects, research projects and laboratory experiments in science classes. I am including this discussion of the teaching and learning methodologies espoused by teachers at this school not only to emphasize that the classroom environment was participatory, but also to present it as a backdrop for some of the adjustment difficulties experienced by new students to the school coming from the Korean education system.

As discussed earlier, students who had attended school in the Korean education system before transferring to this American high school initially experienced difficulty adapting to the more interactive methodologies employed by teachers. For example, when asked open-ended questions, students were usually at a loss to come up with an answer. Consequently, they would freeze even when there were no linguistic impediments to giving a response.

This "freezing" resulted from anxiety at being asked to think for themselves. Many students were more comfortable being fed the responses by their teachers. In this Westernized learning environment, they were being asked to become independent thinkers with little preparation for such. When assigned group projects, individual students had to be cajoled to participate, let alone take leadership roles to ensure that the group accomplished its objectives. The lack of initiative was exacerbated by the lackadaisical attitude of group members who would rather have one or two students do all the work than participate in and contribute to the learning process. To address this tendency, teachers would resort to assigning specific tasks to individual group members and allocating both individual and group grades to make everyone accountable. Eventually, after a semester or two at the school, students would become acculturated to a more participatory style of learning, as well as to an accountability system that held them responsible for their performance.

One reason that Korea has advanced so dramatically in science and technology since the end of the Korean War is that the country emphasizes education beginning at a very early age. Education and culture go hand-in-hand. Therefore, it is not surprising to see the cultural stress on efficiency and the overemphasis on multiple choice questions and standardized tests. Multiple-choice tests, by nature, lend themselves more to rote memorization and repetition than open-ended, short answer questions, fill-in-the-blanks, or essay exams in which critical and independent thinking skills are emphasized. As a result of the competitive nature of the education system, as well as the emphasis on efficiency, students have developed a tendency to work out solutions to mathematical problems on multiple choice tests by making a few calculations on paper, considering the given choices through a process of elimination, and choosing the answer without going through the entire step-by-step process. While this may result in finding the right answer, students can succeed on a test without being able to explain how to calculate the problems they are given.

On account of their training, the Western mathematics teachers employed by this school encouraged students to demonstrate the step-by-step process of arriving at the answer on paper. This practice enabled students to demonstrate their critical thinking process. Since the educational environment was interactive, the teachers who were aware of the students' emphasis on efficiency and who wanted to help them develop their critical thinking skills often chose to award students partial credit for showing the steps for solving a problem. The students would receive the credit even if the final answer was incorrect due to a mathematical miscalculation.

Other teachers encouraged students to explain the steps necessary to solve a problem to their peers. Students would demonstrate their problem on the board to reinforce method to the other students, while simultaneously improving their communication skills. These techniques were particularly helpful for students who planned to attend a university in the West. Practicing these types of skills, both progress-oriented and socially oriented, helped them assimilate more easily to a Western style of education at the university level.

There were other habits that students brought from their previous experience that were more deeply ingrained and consequently more difficult to eradicate than learning patterns. One of those habits was the tendency to put their head down on the desk to rest or take a nap either between classes or during class. Students who were new to the school incorrectly assumed that the practice would be condoned at this American high school. However, they soon found out that it was not. First, the school had a policy that discouraged sleeping in class, and second, the relatively small class size made it impossible for any student who fell asleep to go undetected. If students put their head down, teachers would instruct them to sit up. If students fell asleep in class, teachers would wake them up and issue a warning. If the attitude persisted, they either assigned detention or lowered the students' participation grade in class or both. In chronic cases, parents were contacted to determine whether a health issue was involved.

As indicated earlier, most of the students in this school came directly from the Korean education system. Even if only some of the students had the habit of putting their head down on the desk to rest or take a nap, the logical assumption is that this behavior was allowed in their former school experience. Assuming this observation is accurate, three factors seem to be possible contributors. First, the average class size in Korean schools is larger than at the particular school where I taught; therefore, it is easier for students to engage in this activity without being noticed. Second, when class size is an issue, to be able to cover the required material, there is a tendency to use less interactive teaching strategies such as the lecture method, which if used extensively tends to exhaust the students physically and mentally as a result of physical inactivity and short attention span. Third, teachers in the Korean education system may have a tendency to take a more indulgent attitude when it comes to this type of student behavior because they are well aware of the students' grueling schedules. The topic of demanding student schedules was discussed extensively in Chapter Three. Based on comments from some of my Korean faculty friends, this empathetic feeling is also one of the reasons why Korean faculty at second- and third-tier universities may be more generous with their grading system.

The grading system employed by teachers at the American school includes a small but significant percentage assigned to class participation. Naturally, students cannot participate if they fall asleep in class. As an example, in my world language classes, class participation comprised 10% of the final grade. To effectively learn a new language, students need to be active participants and to be able to engage in dialogue in the target language. This requirement made it impossible for students to earn a final grade of A if they failed class participation. In essence, final grades were based on merit and engagement, not on seat time. I also developed a class participation rubric that was distributed and reviewed with students when we reviewed the course syllabus on the first day of the semester. This practice made students aware of not only the grading criteria, but the criteria for assigning participation grades.

Since this was an American high school, participation in *hagwons* was not required. However, students enrolled in seven classes instead of six as is customary in California public high schools.

Also, students were required to participate in an activity, either a sport or a co-curricular activity after their seven classes were completed each day. These activities were either academic or physical in nature. The latter was an attempt to compensate for the fact that the school did not offer a physical education program due to facilities concerns. Sports facilities were under the jurisdiction of the university. Therefore, it was more feasible to offer all physical activities at once than offering them dispersed throughout the day. Also, the size of the student body made it impractical to facilitate a physical education program. The physical activities included sports such as basketball, fitness, golf, soccer, volleyball, and tennis. The co-curricular activities ranged from SAT preparation and AP mathematics and science preparation to Model United Nations and Yearbook. These activities ended just before dinner time, which means that the students had a much longer school day than students in American high schools in the United States. The consolation was that even though their day was long, it was not nearly as long as that experienced by their counterparts who were enrolled in Korean schools. There, most students attended *hagwons* after the regular school day is over. As previously mentioned, some of these cram schools could go as late as 10:00pm, 11:00pm, or in some cases, midnight. By contrast, after dinner at the American school, students were required to attend supervised night study if their grade point average (GPA) fell below a certain level. This activity gave students who were experiencing academic difficulties an opportunity to improve their proficiency in specific subject areas and thus improve their semester grades, which had an impact on their overall GPA. Students in good standing were rewarded by enjoying some free time or having the freedom to study in their dorm room on their own.

The constant battle with some students' somnolence reflects their excessively long day. The long hours were exacerbated for students who have poor study habits, which required them to stay up late studying after participating in an activity, eating dinner, and possibly attending night study. Some would take a short nap after dinner to have enough physical and brain power to keep going until the wee hours of the morning. Even though there was a dorm supervisor for the boys and another for the girls' side of the dorm, occasionally there were some disciplinary cases where individual or a small group of students would play video games in their room, when they were supposed to be studying, or sneak out of the dorm to smoke or buy alcoholic beverages. It is essential to note that the high school being described here was a boarding school, but most high schools in Korea are not. The addition of residency could make a difference concerning the level of supervision, concentration, and discipline.

Young Lee and I recognize that the discipline issues described in this section are not necessarily typical of high school students in Korea, and therefore, this behavior cannot and should not be generalized to other high school students. However, according to a study conducted by Statistics Korea, the smoking and drinking rates for middle and high school students in 2014 were 9.2% and 16.7% respectively.[3] By 2017, according to the Korean Statistical Information Service, the percentage of smokers dropped to 3.0% and 9.2% for middle and high school students respectively.[4] It is interesting to note that the downward trend in smoking for middle and high school students parallels the drop in overall tobacco use for the entire country. According to OECD data, the percentage of daily smokers for Korean 15 years of age and older was 20% in 2014, and 17.5% in 2017.[5] This decrease in smoking may be related to the sentiment toward smoking in the nation during the same period, which is reflected in the adoption of smoking ban laws throughout the country, specifically in Seoul:

> At the moment [November 26, 2017], there are 17,500 public areas where smoking is prohibited, which include some 3,400 areas close to education facilities such as kindergartens and day care centers. About 6,800 bus stops, 1,700 subway exits, 1,700 parks and squares are also designated as non-smoking areas.

> In addition, 57 streets in areas with heavy foot traffic, including Insa-dong and part of Gangnamdaero, are now non-smoking zones, and violators face fines of up to 100,000 won ($92).

> There are also another 23,900 indoor locations – buildings of public offices, restaurants, hospitals and some apartments – designated as smoke-free zones.[6]

Despite the impressive number of non-smoking and smoke-free zones in Seoul, Korea was cited by the World Health Organization (WHO) for "not properly implementing policies on protecting, enforcing bans and raising taxes, according to the WHO Report on the Global Tobacco Epidemic 2017."[7] The WHO recommended that Korea intensify their policies: "In September [2017], the World Health Organization recommended South Korea adopt more stringent regulations to ban cigarette smoking in public places and restrict tobacco advertising and promotions."[8] The recurring issue with the lack of stringent regulations and enforcement of existing laws will become more apparent in Chapters Six and Seven pertaining to accidents.

The poor sleeping habits of some of the boarding students caused them to wake up just in time to take a shower or wash their face, brush their teeth, get dressed, and walk to their first-period class, thus missing the most important meal of the day: breakfast. Meal costs may have been included in the tuition and expenses fees package selected by the parents at the start of the school year. Parents of boarding students had the option of including meal costs in the fees package. An element of efficiency appears to be present in this seemingly ordinary activity. Avoiding breakfast allowed the students to sleep more, and thus study or play computer games later into the evening. The lack of nutrition in the morning exacerbated the students' sleepiness at least until lunch. Per a social survey conducted by Statistics Korea, in 2016, only 57.7% of youth aged 13 to 24 ate breakfast.[9] Not surprisingly, when this statistic is broken down further, the younger population aged 13 to 19 showed a higher percentage who ate breakfast, 67.6%, versus those aged 20 to 24 at 45.8%.[10]

Commuting students at the school were in a better situation since they had more structure and supervision at home. They came to school with a full stomach, and their sleeping habits were more regular and effective.

It is important to reiterate that most students eventually overcame the learning challenges and counterproductive behavioral patterns described in this section, and adapted successfully to an American style of education. Some adjusted quickly, and others took a little longer. However, the result is that a significant number of graduates were admitted to a university in the United States, Canada, Korea and other parts of the world. Some of the graduates who gained admission to a university in the United States received scholarships based on their academic accomplishments and potential. It was heartwarming to see deserving graduating seniors receive a well-earned scholarship. In a couple of instances, the awards were in the $20,000-$25,000 range.

Clearly, learning to function successfully in and adapting to a new learning environment and culture are challenging processes. However, those students who had a clear vision of what they wanted to accomplish, showed adaptability and invested the time, effort, and hard work, in the end, received a well-deserved compensation.

Endnotes

1 [Justin Fendos], "Why Korean Students Lack Creativity," *The Korea Herald*, 15 October 2017, *koreaherald.com*.

2 Ibid.

3 "Youth," *Statistics Korea*, accessed 22 August 2019, *kostat.go.kr*.

4 "Current Cigarette Smoking," *Korean Statistical Information Service*, accessed 20 November 2019, *kosis.kr*

5 "Daily Smokers (indicator)," OECD, accessed 28 July 2019, *data.oecd.org*.

6 Kim Da-Sol, "Seoul Delays Plan to Ban Public Smoking, *The Korea Herald*, 26 November 2017, *koreaherald.com*.

7 Ibid.

8 Ibid.

9 "2017 Statistics on the Youth," *Statistics Korea*, accessed 22 August 2019, *kostat.go.kr*.

10 Ibid.

Chapter Five

The View from 30,000 Feet

During his administration, President Barack Obama praised the Korean education system on several occasions. The president, along with former Education Secretary Arne Duncan, asked why American education could not be more like the Korean model.

The answer has its roots in the divergent historical, social, economic and cultural factors unique to Korea and America respectively. Clearly, neither President Obama nor Secretary Duncan implied that the U.S. should duplicate everything about the Korean education system. Duplication would, of course, be difficult to achieve, not only because of the aforementioned factors, but because the homogeneity of Korea contrasts with the diversity of America. The prevailing cultural and ethnic diversity that permeates in the United States would make adoption of the Korean model of education impossible. One such difference is the Western emphasis on individuality as opposed to the Korean stress on unity and conformity. From a very young age, parents, teachers and other adults in the West praise and reward children for their independent thinking, for asking pertinent and incisive questions, for their individual accomplishments, for standing out, and for their pursuit of uniqueness from the clothes they wear to the career or profession they choose. Also, from a very young age, children in the West are given choices, from the food they eat to the talents they cultivate, be it in sports or in the arts or among brothers and sisters. For the most part, Western parents realize that happy and healthy children require a balance in their lives, a balance between study and play. However, in several of their public speeches, both Duncan and the President identified elements of the Korean education system that they felt America should emulate.

Needless to say, because people at these levels often speak in soundbites, not much detail or evidence is provided for their rationale when it comes to Korean education. Following is a brief discussion of the points they found admirable. Subsequently, an in-depth analysis of the more prominent education elements of Korean society is presented to explain possible outcomes and behavioral patterns that are learned at an early age and adopted as part of the modus operandi of individuals within the Korean cultural context. The principles of these behavioral patterns are then generalized and applied to everyday life.

A bird's-eye view is not the same as the view from the ground. Although it may seem simple for the President to suggest that Americans simply "adopt" elements of Korean education, this section explicates the ways that the Korean system has evolved as a unique embodiment of its cultural values.

Seriousness about Education

Secretary Duncan believes that the Korean sense of educational purpose is rooted in both policy and culture. In a 2014 speech, he made the following comments regarding the policy aspect of the Korean seriousness about education: "Korea is serious about developing and rewarding great teachers. That means recruiting top college graduates into teaching, training them effectively for the job, and making sure vulnerable students have strong teachers."[1]

Secretary Duncan went on to compare U.S. and Korean practice vis-à-vis teacher recruitment, teacher pay, and teacher training:

> In the United States, a significant proportion of new teachers come from the bottom third of their college class, and most new teachers say their training didn't prepare them for the realities of the classroom. So, underprepared teachers enter our children's classrooms every year, and low-income and minority kids get far more than their share of ineffective teachers.

> In contrast, in South Korea, elementary teachers are selected from the top 5 percent of their high school cohort. Teachers there get six months of training after they start their jobs. They are paid well, and the best receive bonus pay and designation as "master teachers."

...in Korea, according to an international study, students from low-income families are actually more likely than students from rich families to have high-quality teachers.

Why? Because teachers get extra pay and career rewards for working with the neediest kids. Their children who need more, get more. Our children who need more get less.[2]

After reading these comments, I, as an educator, am left with more questions than answers. For example, in order to compare apples to apples, it would be enlightening to find out whether new Korean teachers feel that their teacher training prepares them for the realities of the classroom. If it does, why do they receive six months of training after they start their assignment? Their response should then be compared to American teachers' responses for a more complete understanding of how well teacher training prepares educators. However, even this exercise of ensuring that survey protocols are identical, or at least similar, does not go far enough.

A comparison of school and classroom conditions in Korea and the U.S. needs to be taken into consideration as well. As an example, delinquency and violence appear to be more prominent in U.S. schools for several reasons, some of which are cultural in nature, including the legalized gun policy in the United States. This policy does not exist in Korea. The example of guns and violence only scratches the surface in terms of the differences in the cultural context for teachers in each country. Therefore, teacher training beyond delivery of instruction and classroom management must be different and address societal needs. Besides, societies are dynamic. Consequently, it is practically impossible for teacher training programs to prepare future teachers for every possible eventuality.

For example, at one of the high schools where I taught, a student brought a gun to school and shot himself in the classroom in front of the teacher and his classmates. I am certain that the teacher underwent teacher training, but did the training prepare her for that situation? Probably not. Therefore, because of the dynamic nature of societies, it is better to provide ongoing teacher training in addition to that provided by teacher education programs to better meet the needs of a changing society.

Parental Involvement

During his tenure, Secretary Duncan was fond of relating a story that took place in 2009 in which President Obama met with then-Korean President, Lee Myung-Bak (2008-2013). Reportedly, President Obama asked the Korean President what his biggest challenge was in education. Lee responded that parents in Korea are too demanding. Apparently, even the "poorest Korean parents demanded a first-class education for their children, and he [President Lee] was having to spend millions of dollars each year to teach English to students in first grade, because his parents won't let him wait until second grade."[3]

What the quote above does not tell the audience is that the primary motivator for "poor" Korean parents to demand a "first-class education" for their children is the gruelingly competitive environment of the university admission process. This admission process, as aforementioned, ultimately links to the brutally competitive nature of the job market. Therefore, by "demanding a first-class education," "poor parents" are advocating for their children. These parents want to ensure that their children have a fair chance to compete against those from families with the financial means to send their students to *hagwons* and private tutors from a very early age. The parents' desire for their children to succeed in this ruthless environment is understandable.

Therefore, the constant advocacy push-pull between wealthy parents and those with lesser means amounts to a process of upping the ante. For example, if public schools offer English education beginning in the fourth grade, wealthy parents will ensure that their children receive private English education earlier than the fourth grade, to ensure that their children have a head start over other students. At that point, parents who cannot afford to pay for private tutors or *hagwons* for English language instruction will demand that the government offer English education earlier than the fourth grade. Once the government agrees to this demand and subsidizes English language instruction starting in the third grade, it would not be surprising if the competitive nature of the culture motivates wealthy parents to pay for their children's private education focusing on English language instruction in the second grade or earlier. And so on. Viewed from a different perspective, if parents do not "demand a first-class education," their children run the risk of being at a greater disadvantage in this highly competitive environment. After all, their children's success determines at the very least the comfort level, and at most the economic survival, of the next generation.

I recall talking extensively to the father of a student at the American high school where I taught who insisted that his son be scheduled for physics the semester after transitioning from the ESL program into regular classes. The father was insistent, even though his son was clearly not ready at that particular juncture to succeed academically in such a high-level course. I recall that the only argument this father finally listened to was the explanation about the rationale of the sequential order of mathematics and science courses and the idea behind prerequisites.

His son would be more likely to succeed in physics after completing the appropriate prerequisites. Some of the student's teachers reported that the student exhibited some behavioral patterns that were of concern. His science teacher noticed that he studied using two chemistry textbooks side by side: the one in English that was issued to him by the school, and another he purchased in Korean. This study habit obviously demanded more time than if he had used only one textbook.

Also, it was evident that he was under pressure to do well in the chemistry class. Moreover, teachers noted that he often fell asleep during class, most likely a sign that he was not getting enough sleep at night even though he was a commuting student living at home under the supervision of his parents. It is also conceivable that living at home under parental supervision applied additional pressure on the student to perform at the highest possible level. Furthermore, teachers observed that he appeared to be detached from his peers; he kept to himself and did not take the initiative to associate with others. These symptoms gave us a reason to be concerned about the student's well-being.

A myriad of similar examples come to mind: For example, I met parents who visited the school to insist that their children be placed in higher level classes than their academic preparation called for, even when their children did not have the required command of the English language that would enable them to succeed in a rigorous academic program. The parents insisted on driving their students beyond their academic limitations at a particular time in their development. This insistence seemed to be fueled by the concern that their children would fall behind others in the same age group, and consequently be at a disadvantage academically for the foreseeable future.

I realize that the situation was unique. This was an American private school representing a small sample of Korean parents. Therefore, caution should be used when applying these generalizations to the entire Korean population. However, based on my observations, I can attest that the students' parents at this particular school were very much involved in their children's education as advocates. At times, I felt that some parents were so relentless in their desire for their children to advance academically that yielding to their wishes would be detrimental to the students' well-being and the integrity of the academic program. From my perspective, the competitive environment, and desire to provide their children with a competitive advantage, appeared to be at the root of what seems to be purely a "parental involvement" attribute.

Respect for Teachers

In his State of the Union Address on January 25, 2011, President Obama alluded to the respect accorded to teachers in Korea as a quality that the American education system should emulate. He stated:

> ...after parents, the biggest impact on a child's success comes from the man or woman at the front of the classroom. In South Korea, teachers are known as "nation builders." Here in America, it's time we treated the people who educate our children with the same level of respect. We want to reward good teachers and stop making excuses for bad ones.[4]

The President delivered a similar message in various other speeches, including in an address at Kenmore Middle School in Arlington, Virginia on March 14, 2011.

The respect for teachers that President Obama refers to translates to respect for the individuals as well as the profession. This respect includes acknowledgement of teachers' contribution to the education of the nation's youth, as well as a level of compensation for teachers that is commensurate with or at least relative to other professions.[5]

This concept is more evident in the President's remarks on the launch of ConnectHome Initiative at Durant High School in Durant, Oklahoma on July 15, 2015, where he stated, "...they [South Koreans] pay their teachers the way they pay their doctors – and they consider education to be at the highest rung of the professions."[6]

Young Lee and I agree that in Korea, the teaching profession is considered at "the highest rung of the professions," a view which contrasts with the perception of teachers in the United States. The teaching profession is highly regarded in Korea as a result of the inherent job security associated with the profession, the competitive nature of the field, and the difficulty entailed in landing a tenure-track position. However, elementary and secondary teaching positions are not considered well-paid jobs. The statement indicating that Koreans "pay their teachers the way they pay their doctors" even if accurate, which is highly questionable, is misleading to an American audience because their point of reference is that in the U.S. doctors are well-paid, but teachers are not.

According to the *U.S. News and World Report*, physicians rank 6th on the list of best-paid jobs for 2018. They are paid $196,380 on average.[7] Other medical specialists rank higher on the pay scale. However, teachers do not even make the top 25 best-paid jobs list. Historically, teachers in the U.S. have not received lofty salaries considering the amount of academic preparation and dedicated time the profession requires. The point here is not that teachers ought to be paid at the same level as doctors, but to point out the cultural context for each of the two countries and the dissonance between President Obama's statement and the image in the mind of his American audience. Traditionally, in the U.S. doctors have been at or near the top of the best-paid jobs. Therefore, when the American public hears the statement that Koreans "pay their teachers the way they pay their doctors," the logical assumption is that Korean teachers must have high salaries if they are paid at the same level as doctors. This is an incorrect assumption since Korean doctors are not as well compensated as their American counterparts are.[8]

Higher Expectations of Students

As far as the perception that Korean parents and schools place higher expectations on students than their American counterparts is concerned, both President Obama and Secretary Duncan seemed to agree.

In a speech delivered on January 13, 2014 to the National Assessment Governing Board's Education Summit for Parent Leaders, Secretary Duncan referenced the poor performance of students on standardized tests in the United States in relation to other countries. For example, he indicated that "America now ranks 22nd in math skills and 14th in reading among industrialized countries—and our achievement gaps are not narrowing."[9] The Secretary also alluded to the precipitous decrease in college completion rates which saw the U.S. drop from the number one position to number 12 in the time frame of one generation.[10]

Interestingly, the U.S. was replaced as the number one country in the college completion rate category by none other than Korea.[11]

As a result of these sobering statistics, Secretary Duncan took the opportunity to underscore the major differences between American and Korean education that, in his opinion, tip the balance in favor of Korean students in the achievement gaps. The Secretary identified the demands placed upon Korean students as one of the factors contributing to their achievement edge. He reiterated the following:

> South Korea—and a few other countries—are offering students more, and demanding more, than many American districts and schools do. And the results are showing, in our kids' learning and in their opportunities to succeed, and in staggeringly large achievement gaps in this country.[12]

Since his audience was composed primarily of parent leaders, the theme of demanding more from schools, teachers, and students was restated several times throughout his speech. However, Secretary Duncan clarified that he was not proposing that the U.S. should imitate everything Korea does in education. In fact, he noted without going into detail that in Korea, "the pressure to study can get out of hand."[13]

However, the tone of his speech is in the context of: "Why can't Americans be more like Koreans?" This is clearly the message when he reiterates to his audience that "we need to act on what we know about countries that are out-educating us."[14]

However, he conceded that Korean students are exhausted.[15] Nevertheless, he did not mention that "intentional harm" among 9 to 24 years of age has been the leading cause of death for some years, which may be the result of the pressure placed upon them.

Also, notably absent from Secretary Duncan's remarks were comments regarding the high percentage of families' income that Korean parents spend on private supplemental education and test preparation. Nor did he mention that it is this emphasis on test preparation that has made Korean students outstanding test takers. Another notable omission from the Secretary's remarks is the Achilles heel of the Korean education system, which Korean parents have complained about: the lack of emphasis on creativity.

This concern is magnified if private education through *hagwons* and private tutors is included in the mix given their emphasis on repetition, rote memorization, and test practice. Finally, when the Secretary singled out Korea's accomplishment as the country with the highest college completion rate, he neglected to acknowledge the negative impact on the economy of the oversupply of individuals with a bachelor's degree or higher, not to mention the emotional impact on the overqualified individuals who are unable to obtain a job commensurate with their educational qualifications, or worse yet, who are unable to secure a job at all.

Clearly, public speeches by government leaders and other dignitaries have a purpose. Some are meant to convince the public or sway public opinion, or promote or advocate for a program, idea or belief. The portrayal of Korean education described by President Obama and Secretary Duncan focuses almost exclusively on the positive aspects and understates the vulnerable points of the Korean education. Essentially, it is an oversimplified and incomplete image, which can only be captured from a very high altitude where contrasts are non-existent and details are perceived as inconsequential. The danger for an uninformed public is to be swayed by arguments based on incomplete and superficial representations.

I find this argument about the effectiveness of Korean education akin to tourists posting pictures of the magnificent places they visited during their trip to a foreign country and leaving out the photos of the not so appealing places. Also, posting only photos limits the travelers' ability to share details such as the sounds and smells that did not quite agree with them or the insects that bit them. In reality, the viewers of those photos will have an incomplete image of those places, unless they have been there themselves. Depending on where they live and how they feel about their homeland, those representations may compel the viewers to visit or wish they could live there.

Longer Hours of Instruction and their Impact on Students

President Obama believed that one of the reasons why Korean education has an advantage over its American counterpart is

216

the difference in the amount of time Korean children spend "in school." In his remarks to the Hispanic Chamber of Commerce delivered on March 10, 2009, President Obama lauded the Korean education system for requiring students to spend more time in the classroom than American schools. His pointed remarks about the antiquated calendar of the American education system as compared to its Korean counterpart read as follows:

> We can no longer afford an academic calendar designed for when America was a nation of farmers who needed their children at home plowing the land at the end of each day. That calendar may have once made sense, but today it puts us at a competitive disadvantage. Our children – listen to this – our children spend over a month less in school than children in South Korea – every year. That's no way to prepare them for a 21st century economy. That's why I'm calling for us not only to expand effective after-school programs, but to rethink the school day to incorporate more time – whether during the summer or through expanded-day programs for children who need it.
>
> …the challenges of a new century demand more time in the classroom. If they can do that in South Korea, we can do it right here in the United States of America.[16]

Many Koreans reacted swiftly in disbelief to the President's comments suggesting that the U.S. look to their country's education as a model to emulate. One day after the President's comments, on March 11, 2009, their reaction was summed up in a piercing statement in an article that appeared in *The Korea Times*:

> Obama's remarks came as a surprise to many South Koreans as the country's education system has been under constant public criticism due to its lack of creativity and heavy dependence on private tutoring.[17]

It is true that Korean students attend classes for more hours than their American counterparts. However, it is also true that many of these additional classes are supplemental to those provided by the Korean education system. As a result of the extended hours in "crammers" and tutorial sessions, Korean students give up activities that otherwise would make up a balanced teenage life.

The unfortunate intentional harm figures cited earlier are not surprising, given that since at least 2010 Korean school-aged youngsters have scored poorly when compared to their counterparts in other OECD (Organization for Economic Cooperation and Development) countries on satisfaction surveys.[18]

In 2010, *The Chosun Ilbo* reported that:

> Children and adolescents in Korea are the least satisfied with their lives among 26 member countries of the OECD. According to a survey released on

Tuesday by a research center affiliated with Yonsei University and a foundation named for educator Pang Jong-hwan, only 53.9 percent of 5,435 schoolchildren from fourth grade to 12th said they were satisfied with their lives. That means one in two Korean children and adolescents are dissatisfied.[19]

The article goes on to specify: "The greatest source of stress was school work, followed by physical appearance and problems with parents."[20]

Five years later, in 2015, *The Chosun Ilbo* reported that:

A whopping 50.3 percent of Korean kids are stressed about their studies, the highest proportion among 30 countries surveyed, according to an analysis by Kim Mi-sook of the Korea Institute for Health and Social Affairs…

Only 18.5 percent of kids in Korea said they are "very happy" at school. Korea comes fifth from the bottom…

The happiest kids were in Ireland (42.5 percent), Romania (41.6 percent), Lithuania (39.0 percent), Norway (38.8 percent), and the Netherlands (38.4 percent).[21]

The article quotes Kim Mi-sook, the analyst, as saying:

> We need to lighten their [the students'] burden of study and give youngsters more free time and more things to do with it... We should also learn what we can from countries like the Netherlands, where kids are happy and perform remarkably well.[22]

Spending such an inordinate amount of time studying in *hagwons*, or with private tutors beyond regular school hours, has turned Korean students into sedentary human beings at a very early age.

In 2016, *The Chosun Ilbo* reported that Korean youngsters spend only half an hour a day outdoors.

> Korean children spend only 34 minutes outdoors a day on average, a survey shows. That is a mere third of the time spent outside by their counterparts in the U.S. (1 hour and 59 minutes) and Canada (1 hour and 40 minutes).

> The Environment Ministry surveyed 8,000 children and adolescents...

> Korean children between three and nine years of age spend most of their time indoors, going to crammers, playing games or watching TV.[23]

The pattern of reported unhappiness or dissatisfaction and lack of exercise by Korean teenagers appears in statistics even as late as 2017, when *The Chosun Ilbo* reported the results of worldwide surveys conducted among 15-year-olds. The article reports that:

> Korean teenagers rank at the top in the OECD when it comes to academic performance but are among the unhappiest in the club of rich countries. They also start private tuition earlier than in any other country, suggesting that public education is failing them, talk less to their parents and spend the least time exercising…
>
> Compared to 48 countries including non-OECD member nations, they still ranked at the bottom…
>
> …they start trudging to crammers at the age of nine, sooner than anywhere else. The average age was 11…
>
> But they spend very little time engaged in physical activities, with only 46.3 percent playing a sport either before or after school, ranking at the bottom. One out of five does not spend even a day exercising the minimum of 60 minutes, like walking and cycling…[24]

In summary, as aforementioned, Korean students do spend more time in the classroom than their American counterparts; however, a significant portion of the extra classroom time is dedicated to supplemental, enrichment education, and test preparation.

Consequently, it is very likely that Korean students are better test takers than American students. As a result of the enormous amounts of time spent in "crammers" and tutorial sessions, Korean students have little time left for outdoor activities or physical activity, sports, and even talking with their parents. They spend most of their time indoors either studying in "crammers," playing games or watching television.

What is the cost of this imbalanced way of life? Based on the factors that Young Lee and I have examined, Korean students pay dearly by being either the most or among the most dissatisfied children with their lives among OECD countries. They are also some of the most stressed about their studies. This pattern is not new, however, it seems to be gaining momentum in recent years based on self-harm counseling data. According to *The Chosun Ilbo*:

> Self-harm is on the rise among Korean teenagers, suggesting that stress levels are rising in the country's brutally competitive education environment.
>
> The Ministry of Gender Equality and Family analyzed records from 230 youth counselling and welfare centers across the country and found that counsel[l]ing for self-harm rose from 4,000 in 2015 to 28,000 last year [2018].[25]

Preparing for Exams vs. Preparing for University

The extreme reliance on testing compels students to resort to cramming for tests. Consequently, retention of learned material past a certain test is more challenging. I recognize that the practice of cramming for a test is a universal technique used by students everywhere, but Korean students have taken cramming to a new level.

For example, as aforementioned in Chapter Four, students at the American school where I taught would often use the euphemism "brainwashing" to describe the process of forgetting after a test everything they had crammed before the test. They believed that "washing" their brain of old information enables them to better retain new material for the next test. One unfortunate outcome of this process of making room for new information by forgetting previously learned material is that it ignores that the most effective learning is achieved when viewed as a set of building blocks.

As discussed in my observations of behavioral patterns of Korean students earlier in Chapter Four, they are very adept at picking the correct answers on a multiple-choice test but very poor at demonstrating the step-by-step process by which they arrive at the correct answer, a highly-coveted skill in American high schools and universities. In an article written by Alan Singer and published in *HuffPost* on March 18, 2010, he shared the experience of Clay Burell, an American humanities teacher living in Korea, who reports that:

Korean students are forced to study in 'hagwons' – private night, weekend, and summer classes where the overwhelming emphasis is on learning English. The Korean Education Ministry estimates that as a percentage of GDP, South Korean parents spend four times more on average on private education than their counterparts in any major economy. [As discussed earlier, this figure may be underestimated on account that private tutor fees are mostly paid in cash; therefore, they are not reported in government generated statistics.] Most of what they study is 'worksheet-based, scripted, and devoted to passing college examination tests, the SAT, TOEFL, and all the other tests these classes teach to.' What Burell finds ironic is that despite all of this investment and high test scores, Korean students are notoriously poor at reading, writing, and speaking English. In other words, they can't use what they are supposed to have learned and what they test well at.[26]

As a result, Alan Singer argues that "years of extra tutoring prepares Korean students for college entrance exams but not for acquiring a college education."[27] To support his argument, the author quotes Dr. Samuel Kim's research on American university dropouts. According to Singer, Dr. Kim is a senior research scholar at the East Asian Institute at Columbia University. He reports:

44% of Korean students who enter 'top' American universities drop out before graduating. This is much higher than the dropout rate for students from China (25%), India (21%) and even the 34% dropout rate for American students at the same universities.[28]

The lesson from observations, testimonials, and statistics in this and previous chapters about education in Korea is that both the preparation for and skills needed to succeed in a testing environment are very different from those needed to thrive in a university environment. The reality is that learning does not stop when students walk out of the testing room of a university entrance examination or when they receive their college entrance exam score or when they receive their notice of admission from their dream school. The building blocks of the learning process continue to accumulate and the joy of learning reaches yet a higher dimension once students begin their college experience. Students who prepare for both will maximize the learning and adapt more easily to any learning situation.

The assumption that one education system is better than another requires an in-depth analysis that includes identification of appropriate, culture-bias-free objective criteria. The fact that Korean students are good test-takers does not imply that the Korean education system is better than its American counterpart. This is particularly true, given the fact that a significant aspect of Korean education is the extensive utilization of private tutoring and "cram academies" that focus on test preparation and rely heavily on repetition, test practice, and memorization. It is not surprising, then, that Korean students perform well on multiple choice tests. The "cram academies" and private tutors that focus on test preparation, in general, appear to be doing a good job of elevating the students' test-taking ability. However, test-taking ability represents only one portion of the entire education spectrum. The most enduring portion of education is the experiential piece which takes place in a safe academic environment where students can exercise their individuality while collaborating with others, demonstrate a hunger for discovery and learning, and an inexhaustible ability for creativity and even experimentation.

If "cram schools" prepare students for the test-taking portion of education, but not for the experiential piece, is the rest of the Korean formal education preparing students for the experiential piece? If results on multiple choice tests are used to compare student performance, we need to ask ourselves: what role do test practice and teaching-to-the-test play in temporarily influencing test scores? Are test practice and teaching-to-the-test the most effective methodologies? Do they promote long-term retention? Do we espouse a system that emphasizes rote memorization as its primary method of teaching and learning? Or, do we embrace a system that fosters creativity, critical and independent thinking, self-expression and problem-solving?

As aforementioned, in the four years I spent working at the American high school in Korea, the most common complaint from the American and Canadian teachers was that some of the students were very good at identifying the correct answer on a multiple-choice test. However, the same students were very poor at demonstrating the steps they took to arrive at a given answer. Also, teachers complained that the students were not

226

independent thinkers and expected the teacher to provide them with the "correct answer." Moreover, they were not very adept at collaborative learning, i.e., teamwork. This does not mean that Korean students cannot acquire these skills. They can and they do, when given the appropriate environment and practice.

Cause-and-effect is a rather difficult relationship to ascertain in a complex environment, like education, where numerous factors can influence an outcome. The fact that Korean families spend more money than their American counterparts on private education does not necessarily translate to better-prepared students for a higher education environment that upholds such values as creativity, critical and independent thinking, and collaborative learning.

When comparing education systems from two different countries, one must be cognizant of the myriad of variables that can influence student performance. In examining the Korean and American education systems, the two most glaring differences are first, the amount of time, money and effort spent in Korea on private education. Secondly, one must take into account the fact that the Korean education system is composed of students who come from a homogeneous society, language and culture, whereas American students are as heterogeneous as can be. Korean students do come from different socio-economic backgrounds; however, in addition to having diverse socioeconomic backgrounds, their American counterparts report to school with a wide range of learning behaviors, and most importantly, varied levels of exposure to the mainstream culture as well as the language of instruction.

These differences can help or hinder the success of students even before they cross the threshold of the school gate in kindergarten, thus potentially perpetuating social inequality. However, the fact that in the American education system a student who starts middle school with enormous cultural and socioeconomic disadvantages, including lacking the knowledge of the English language, can somehow become not just bilingual-bicultural, but trilingual, and earn a doctoral degree, and eventually become a successful higher education administrator is a testament to the accessibility of the American education system, and the power of determination, dedication, love for learning, and mentoring from those who saw a diamond in the rough. That student is I. My chances of replicating this feat in the Korean education system, which favors children from families who can afford the high cost of private supplemental education and tutoring, would have been minimal to nonexistent.

Endnotes

1   Arne Duncan, "Parent Voices for World-Class Education: Remarks of U.S. Secretary of Education Arne Duncan to the National Assessment Governing Board Education Summit for Parent Leaders," U.S. Department of Education, 13 January 2014, ed.gov.

2   Ibid.

3   Ibid.

4   Barack Obama, "Remarks of President Barack Obama in State of the Union Address," *The White House Office of the Press Secretary*, 25 January 2011, *obamawhitehouse.archives.gov.*

5   Barack Obama, "Remarks by the President on Education in Arlington, Virginia," *The White House Office of the Press Secretary*, 14 March 2011, *obamawhitehouse.archives.gov.*

6   Barack Obama, "Remarks by the President on the Launch of ConnectHome Initiative," *The White House Office of the Press Secretary*, 15 July 2015, *obamawhitehouse.archives.gov.*

7   "Best Paying Jobs," *U.S. News and World Report*, accessed 30 Aug 2019, *money.usnews.com.*

8   Given the 2017 OECD data on teacher salaries, Korean starting teacher salaries both at the elementary and secondary level are much lower than their American counterparts. At the 15-year experience mark, the salary gap remains considerably wide between the two, with American teacher salaries remaining higher than those in Korea. However, Korean teacher salaries at the top of the scale in the two segments of education are higher than those of American instructors. Therefore, it appears that

229

in preparation for President Obama's speech, the analysis for the comparison between teacher salaries in the two countries was made at the top of the pay scales without consideration to salaries at the starting point or the 15-year mark. These statistics support President Obama's argument that Korean teacher salaries are higher than their American counterparts. However, for the sake of accuracy and full disclosure, the comparison should be made at various points in the salary scale. One such option is as follows: starting salaries, after 15 years of experience, and at the top of the scale. This analysis would begin to draw a full picture of the teacher salary comparison argument. However, for this assessment to be complete a thorough discussion of other factors such as cost of living, fringe benefits, teacher retention, and longevity in the profession would be in order. Absent these considerations, the teacher salary comparison is inconclusive.

9   Valerie Strauss, "Arne Duncan: Why Can't We Be More Like South Korea?" *The Washington Post*, accessed 31 July 2019, *washingtonpost.com*.

10   Ibid.

11   Ibid.

12   Ibid.

13   Ibid.

14   Ibid.

15   Ibid.

16   Barack Obama, "Remarks by the President to the Hispanic Chamber of Commerce," *The White House Office of the Press Secretary*, 10 March 2019, *obamawhitehouse.archives.gov*.

17 "Obama Lauds Korea's Education of Children," *The Korea Times*, accessed 9 November 2019, *koreatimes.co.kr*.

18 "Korean Kids Unhappiest in OECD," *The Chosun Ilbo*, 6 May 2010, *english.chosun.com*.

19 Ibid.

20 Ibid.

21 "Korean Kids Most Stressed in the World," *The Chosun Ilbo*, 12 March 2015, *english.chosun.com*.

22 Ibid.

23 "Korean Kids Spend Barely Half an Hour a Day Outdoors," *The Chosun Ilbo*, 11 May 2016, *english.chosun.com*.

24 "Korean Teenagers Study Hard but Feel Unhappy," *The Chosun Ilbo*, 25 April 2017, *english.chosun.com*.

25 "Self-Harm on the Rise Among Korean Teens," *The Chosun Ilbo*, 27 July 2019, *english.chosun.com*.

26 Alan Singer, "Obama, Korea, and American Schools," *HuffPost*, 18 March 2019, *huffpost.com*.

27 Ibid.

28 Ibid.

Chapter Six

Man-Made Accidents

April 16, 2014 – *Sewol* Ferry Disaster

On April 16, 2014, I came home to find out that a boat accident had claimed the lives of over 300 people. Most of these people were high school students who were on a field trip to Jeju Island. My first thought was, "My students and I could have been among the victims!" I also thought about how devastating the accident would be for a school, the victims' families, and the whole country. Some people were shocked; others appeared traumatized. I knew at that very moment that I would write a book about Korea. Such was my initial reaction to the *Sewol* ferry accident, one of Korea's worst tragedies in the recent past. As of this writing, a total of 304 people lost their lives. Nine bodies have not been found.

Efficiency

Today, our world is undergoing profound changes. Many of these changes have come about from advancements in technology. Volumes have been written about the impact that technology has had in our lives; therefore, I will not go into detail here. Suffice it to say that the profound impact the Digital Revolution has had on humankind is akin to that of the Industrial Revolution. The fundamental difference is that the influence of the former is more profound and ubiquitous. It is influencing humanity at a more personal level; it is changing not only how we work, but how we live and how we think. Technology has both forced us and enabled us to assess how we perform tasks daily in industries from business to health care, banking, tourism and hospitality, entertainment, and even education.

As we incorporate technology into our daily lives, we become so comfortable with it, and accustomed to it, that we take it for granted. When ATMs were first introduced, some of us distrusted their technology. Concerns about the machine's ability to conduct a secure, private transaction delayed our acceptance of the new machines. Now, for better or worse, we have embraced even the smartphone, which we use for almost every aspect of our lives. Despite our very same privacy concerns, we turn to our smartphones for everything from selecting our commute to monitoring our bank accounts, our pulse, our physical activity and the quality of our sleep, planning our day's activities based on weather forecasts, conducting financial transactions, and deciding where we vacation, where we shop, and where we eat. Technology has made almost everything that touches our lives more convenient and accessible, thus making us more efficient.

Korean culture, of all cultures, recognizes the value of efficiency. I would dare to say that efficiency is a way of life for Koreans as evidenced by the pervasive "*pali pali*" culture. For Koreans, efficiency is everywhere, from how students arrive at the answer to a math problem to the use of student rankings to determine candidates for top-tier universities and for hiring purposes at major corporations, from driving habits to the saturation of love motels, and from at-home cooking to restaurant dining.

Work Ethic

One of the practices that caught my attention is the work ethic. Generally, Koreans work six days per week. Furthermore, it is not uncommon for entrepreneurs and small business owners to work seven days per week. I recall one Sunday during which I experienced a drain problem in my apartment. I called a handyman to resolve the issue. Not only did he come and promptly take care of the problem, but he did not even ask to be paid overtime for a Sunday visit. I had a similar event with my telecommunications service under similar circumstances. In my experience, a weekend service interaction like these would be unheard of in the United States.

According to the Organization for Economic Cooperation and Development, in 2017, Koreans were second only to Mexicans in the number of hours they worked per year with an average of 2,024 to Mexico's 2,257. By comparison, Americans and Japanese averaged 1,780 and 1,710 hours respectively. Of the 35 OECD countries reporting data, the average total of working hours was 1,759. Therefore, Koreans worked 265 more hours than the average of all 35 OECD countries.[1]

The last year I resided full-time in Korea was 2017. In Chapter Two, I observed that in 2017, residential and non-residential construction was ongoing in Jeonju, the city where I lived. I also noted that it was not unusual to observe construction sites constantly in operation, even on Sundays and late evenings. By contrast, in the U.S., construction tradesmen working on Sunday seems to be uncommon. As I walked by these Korean construction sites, I often wondered about the propensity for safety concerns when construction workers work long hours for seven days each week. As aforementioned, I cannot confirm whether the workers labored longer than eight hours per day or they were on a rotating schedule, thus allowing them to cover the extended hours utilizing overlapping shifts. As my stay in Korea progressed, but particularly after the *Sewol* ferry tragedy, I became more conscious of man-made accidents in general, not just those that occurred in and around construction sites.

Natural disasters are caused by uncontrollable forces such as a hurricanes, typhoons, floods, volcanic eruptions, earthquakes, landslides, or lightning. Because these disasters are not preventable, people can and should prepare for such incidents. The preparation may include storing fresh potable water, which is safe for drinking and food preparation, having sufficient canned food to last several days, and maintaining a well-supplied first aid kit.

With the advent of industry, man-made disasters began to occur more frequently. Because man-made tragedies are usually associated with human error, they are preventable but nearly impossible to predict. Given the appropriate attentiveness to safety standards and precautions, their frequency should diminish. These types of disasters include any freak accidents, train derailments, building and bridge collapses, oil spills, traffic accidents on land, on water or in the air, gas leaks, environmental pollution, and nuclear meltdowns. Depending on the circumstances, the people involved, the people affected, and the scale, some of these incidents could be categorized as industrial accidents. I will discuss those in Chapter Seven.

As I began to research man-made accidents that happened in Korea prior to the *Sewol* ferry incident, the causes cited and the recurring themes that connected most of them intrigued me. However, it was the potential and unnecessary loss of innocent lives that motivated me to continue to conduct research and eventually write this book. I have lived long enough to recognize the basic premise of man-made accidents: Although preventable, they can occur anywhere, anytime. Korea has certainly had more than its fair share of them.

My sincere hope is that the identification of the recurring themes can help to prevent future man-made tragedies, not only in Korea but across the globe, by sensitizing people to the responsibility we all have: We must take the necessary precautions to prevent them.

In the chapters about education, I identified how the emphasis on efficiency and overreliance on test preparation can lead to the misidentification of the means as the ends, as well as the acquisition of learning habits that are detrimental to experiential learning, which I find to be the most profound aspect of learning.

In the chapters about man-made and industrial accidents, we will see how efficiency continues to play a central role as the conduit for short term financial gains, greed, and skirting public safety laws. From a humanistic perspective, one of the unfortunate outcomes of efficiency in man-made and industrial accidents is the loss of innocent lives. Humankind's existence on this planet has become so precarious that we need to minimize the risk factors by genuinely caring for one another and upholding public safety to avoid adding to the perils of natural disasters including those caused by extreme weather patterns attributable to global warming. Minimizing risk factors may mean that we need to reduce our emphasis on efficiency, recognize that greed is self-serving and not in the best interest of humanity, and ensure that our safety regulations are current and strictly enforced.

Rapid Urbanization

As expected, along with the remarkable macroeconomic success and the technological advancements in Korea beginning at the end of the Korean War, the country underwent amazing urbanization and migration from rural to urban areas between 1960 and 1990. According to the World Bank, in those 30 years alone, the urban population experienced a remarkable 46% net increase from 28% to 74%. By comparison, in the following 28 years from 1990 to 2017, the urban population increased at a more moderate pace, only growing nine percent from 74% to 83%.[2]

Figure 1: Percentage of urban population[3]

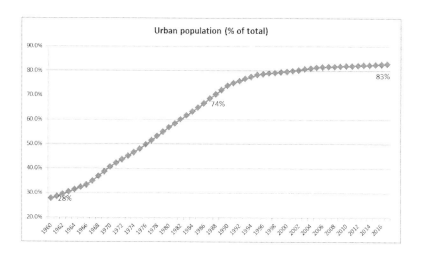

The annual percentage of the urban population increase in the 30 years from 1960 to 1990 was between 3.3% and 7.5%. By contrast, the percentage increase in the subsequent 27 years from 1991 to 2017 ranged from .057% to 2.5% with a percentage increase of less than 1% being registered in each the last fifteen years from 2003 to 2017.

Figure 2: Urban population growth[4]

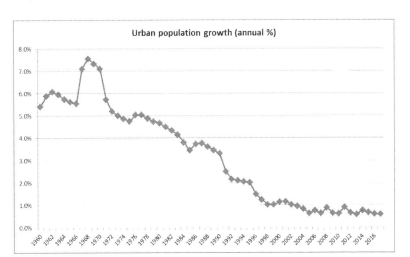

Because of the rapid and unprecedented migration from rural to urban areas, the construction industry experienced a windfall never seen before in Korea. This was particularly true in housing, as well as in general infrastructure development. Furthermore, when Seoul was named host of the 1988 Summer Olympics, the required infrastructure development placed additional pressure on the already overstretched construction industry. In that period, moreover, the country had in place protectionist policies which required that Korean companies complete all construction. The construction expansion provided unique opportunities for Korean entrepreneurs to generate profits of extraordinary proportion. Unfortunately, these conditions also opened the doors to opportunities for greed, corruption, and disregard for public safety.

Man-Made Accidents

In this section, I analyze three man-made accidents and reference several others which took place during this period of rapid urbanization and economic expansion which took place between the 1960s and 1990s.[5] In the same period, the Korean economy grew at an average annual rate of nearly nine percent, and per capita income increased more than a hundredfold. The purpose of this section is not to provide a complete inventory of incidents, or even a thorough examination of the specifics surrounding each of the selected events. Doing so would be beyond the scope of this book. The goal of this section, as with the entire book, is to identify the behavioral patterns surrounding those three events and determine whether similar patterns resurfaced in accidents that happened in more recent times from 2014 to 2018.

Given the parameters of this book, I also purposely avoid discussing the specific disaster response for each event even though its effectiveness, or lack thereof, may have contributed to the number of unfortunate casualties. Korea, a developing country during the period of economic expansion, lacked the technology, rescue equipment and disaster response appropriate for responding to emergencies. Korea also lacked a systematic rescue system and the seamless communication system between governmental agencies that is so critical during emergencies.[6] Therefore, it would be inappropriate to draw conclusions about a technologically advanced Korea in the 21st century based on events that took place at a time when the nation was still considered a developing country. For this reason, I minimize the emphasis placed on incidents that happened during this earlier period. However, I do not minimize the tragic loss of innocent lives during that timeframe. Recognizing the reappearance of similar behavioral patterns at a later stage of development serves to provide a genuine reflection about the society's level of advancement. By advancement, I here specify that it is not economic or technological, but define advancement in terms of ethics, consciousness, and values, such as compassion, and the importance given to public safety.

The list of accidents from that period is plentiful and the loss of innocent lives tragic. In addition to the three incidents selected for analysis, the list includes the partial collapse of a bridge over the Han River, a gas explosion in Daegu, a fire in a subway station in Daegu, a train derailment near Gupo station in Busan, a gas explosion in a hotel in Seoul, a dynamite explosion in a train station, and the crash of a Korean Airlines plane in Guam, human error being the primary cause of the latter. The human toll for these man-made accidents alone amounts to at least 865 innocent lives.[7] The selection criteria for the three incidents identified for discussion in this section is as follows: The events were similar to other more recent accidents either in context or in regard to patterns of behavior associated with the cause of the accidents. Also, I considered the intent and scope of this book in the selection process.

Three Man-Made Accidents that Typify the Prevailing Conditions during the Period of Rapid Urbanization and Economic Expansion

Because of the prevailing environment that included unprecedented build-up of infrastructure and housing to accommodate the extensive urbanization which caused many projects to be ongoing concurrently during this period, "together with other stimulants such as greed for fast money, [these projects] are believed to have led to compromises of several building codes both by the companies and authorities."[8] As a result, structures erected during this period, and those that remain, were and continue to be susceptible to structural failure.

April 8, 1970 - The Wawoo Apartment Building Collapse

From the late 1950s through the 1960s, the beginning of the rapid urbanization period, Seoul was forced to accommodate the unprecedented influx of citizens from rural areas who were living in illegal settlements. As a result of the demand for housing,

> ...many buildings and houses were constructed without permits... President Park Chung-Hee ordered the mayor of Seoul, Kim Hyun-Ok, to build citizens apartments and house the people from these illegal settlements in them. The mayor... had the nickname "Bulldozer" because during his time many areas in Seoul got erased and replaced by modern large-scale structures, such as apartments, wide

243

roads and elevated freeways. Seoul [began] to [lose its] historic streetscape, a small labyrinth-like and organic road network.[9]

An example of a structure erected "more rapidly than usual" and whose history concluded in a tragic disaster is the five-story Wawoo apartment building which collapsed on April 8, 1970, four months after completion.[10] Reports indicate that the building was constructed in six months, from June to December 1969.[11] The investigation conducted following the collapse shows that:

> ...the foundation columns were not resistant to the self-weight of the apartments. An insufficient amount of rebar in the foundation constructed along the mountain slopes was the direct reason for the collapse.[12]

Other contributing factors cited include "poor and too quick construction, mistakes in the static calculations, bad quality of the concrete and mountain runoff water."[13]

The Wall Street Journal reports that per the government's *Encyclopedia of Korean Culture*, the Wawoo apartment building collapse "was a man-made disaster caused by corruption of construction firms and supervision agencies."[14]

This incident took the lives of 33 people and injured 40.[15]

Evidence of the widespread construction deficiencies and disregard for safety standards during this period of rapid urbanization is reflected in the results of "an inspection of the citizen apartment[s] [which] showed that 75% of the existing buildings [did not] fulfill safety standards."[16]

October 1993 – The Sinking of the *Sohae* Ferry

The *Sohae* ferry sank in the waters of the West Sea near Wi-Do Island in October 1993 with 400 passengers and crew members.[17] The ferry was carrying 362 passengers, 141 over its capacity, plus heavy freight.[18] The accident caused 292 people to drown. Various sources point to overloading of passengers and baggage, improper maintenance of the boat, and reckless navigation in extreme weather conditions as factors that contributed to the sinking of the boat.[19]

June 29, 1995 - The Sampoong Department Store Collapse

A structure which exemplified the feverish urbanization pace and almost euphoric feeling of economic well-being that permeated the affluent was the fashionable Sampoong department store located in the wealthy Seocho district of Seoul. Construction of the nine-story building (five floors above ground and four underground) that housed the Sampoong department store began in 1987 and concluded two years later.[20] The building collapsed on June 29, 1995. In this case, the changes made to the original blueprint design caused structural flaws. Furthermore, because the building was erected "on a landfill site that was poorly suited to

245

such a large structure," the foundation itself made the building susceptible to instability.[21]

The blueprint design changes included the addition of a fifth floor above ground, conversion of the fundamental purpose of the building from residential apartments to a department store with open space and a reduced number of columns, the addition of escalators, and a food court which required heavy restaurant equipment. Also, a 45-metric ton air conditioning unit was installed on the roof further adding to the weight and pressure placed on the columns:[22]

> The completed building was a flat-slab structure, without crossbeams or a steel skeleton, which effectively meant that there was no way to transfer the load across the floors. To maximize the floor space, Lee Joon [Sampoong chairman and owner] ordered the floor columns to be reduced to be 24 inches (61 cm) thick, instead of the minimum of 31 inches (79 cm) in the original blueprint that was required for the building to stand safely. In addition, each column was 36 feet (11 m) apart to maximize retail space, a decision that also meant that there was more load on each column than there would have been if the columns were closer together...As a result of the fifth floor's presence, the columns held up four times the maximum weight that they were supposed to support.[23]

To get these radical building design changes approved, the owner bribed government officials.[24] The Sampoong department store collapse killed 502 people and injured 937.[25]

As if corruption in the form of bribery and making fundamental blueprint design changes against the advice of the contracting firm were not enough, the elements of greed, irresponsibility, and disregard for human lives also describe the actions of the corporation chairman on the morning of the collapse. The superstore had become a hub for upper-middle-class families, primarily homemakers. It averaged 40,000 shoppers per day during the building's five-year history.[26]

Actions taken in this case exemplify not only greed, corruption, and poor judgment but also the *gap* and *eul* relationship discussed in detail in Chapter One. Having more authority, influence, and resources than Woosung, the original company hired to construct the building, Lee Joon, the chairman of Sampoong, ordered the construction company to make unreasonable structural changes to the blueprints. When Woosung refused to make the changes, Lee Joon fired the contractor and brought in his own company to complete the project. Cracks in the building began to appear on the fifth floor months before the collapse: "The management all but ignored the warning and only moved merchandise that was stored in the fifth floor to the basement to relieve it of some weight."[27] Various sources also report that management ordered the air conditioning units to be turned off to minimize the vibration and prevent further widening of the structural cracks.

The day of the collapse, engineers were called in to conduct a cursory inspection of the building after cracks that had begun to appear in April of the same year began to widen. They declared the building unsafe. Subsequently, the board of directors met. They advised Lee Joon, the chairman, to evacuate the building but he refused, citing potential revenue losses: "By the mid-1990s the store's sales amounted to more than half a million U.S. dollars a day."[28] However, Lee himself left the building before the collapse.

In the aftermath of the deadly collapse, Lee Joon and his son, Lee Han-Sang, "were convicted and sent to prison for 10 1/2- and 7-year terms respectively. Twelve local building officials were found guilty of taking bribes of as much as $17,000 (U.S. equivalent) for approving changes and providing a provisional use certificate."[29]

Following the Sampoong department store building collapse, "a government survey of high-rise structures found 14% were unsafe and needed to be rebuilt, 84% required repairs, and only 2% met standards."[30] These astounding findings are a clear indication of the alarming state of affairs of building structures in Korea at the time.

The incidents discussed above are but three of the many tragedies that took place during the rapid urbanization and economic expansion period (1960s-1990s). The section that follows examines some of the man-made accidents that occurred from 2014 to 2018. The causes and circumstances surrounding the incidents selected represent cultural and behavioral patterns that recur not just in these accidents, but also in those that occurred during the economic expansion. The criteria used to select these accidents include most recent timing and the profound societal impact. The intent and scope of this book are factors that played a crucial role in the selection process.

Recent Man-Made Accidents

April 16, 2014 – *Sewol* Ferry Disaster: Perfect Conditions for an Accident

The Korean coast guard concluded that the primary cause of the *Sewol* ferry tragedy was an unreasonably sudden turn to starboard.

The *Sewol* ferry was retrofitted two years before the accident to increase its capacity by 239 extra tons, thus making it more prone to tip over on account of the imbalance between the port and starboard side of the ship. On the day of the tragedy, the ship was overloaded with freight. Based on the prosecutor's findings, it was carrying 2,142 tons of freight, or almost twice the maximum limit of 1,077 tons.[31] Also, per the prosecutor's findings, the freight was not safely secured. Reports indicate that the freight was not securely tied to save time during the unloading process. This attitude supports Korea's emphasis on efficiency, which produces a general disregard for or minimization of safety concerns. Because the freight was not securely tied, the shift undergone by the cargo made the tilt and imbalance more pronounced when the ferry made the sharp turn. As the ferry tipped over, some of the cargo fell and blocked the exits, consequently making it more difficult for passengers to evacuate.

Moreover, the ship "was also possibly crewed by insufficiently trained personnel."[32] This assertion is supported by survivors' statements indicating that the crew had repeatedly directed the passengers to stay put while the ferry sank.

The ineptitude, poor judgment, and irresponsibility of the captain and crew of the ferry is poignantly described in an editorial piece published in *The Korea Herald*:

> The most unfortunate thing was that the Sewol and its passengers had an utterly incapable and irresponsible crew. Had they acted how any ordinary, average maritime officer, not a hero, would have in such a situation, many more passengers could have jumped off the ship in time and gotten picked up by boats that responded to the distress call.
>
> The captain and two other crew members were arrested... three days after they abandoned their own ship, leaving hundreds of young students and passengers behind. It still is a mystery why they kept advising the passengers to stay inside their cabins for about two hours even after the ship began listing.
> It is certain that the Sewol's crew lack not only the capability to operate a ferry that can carry up to 956 passengers and make proper judgment calls in an

emergency but also the minimum level of professional ethics and sense of responsibility.[33]

An article published by *Foreign Policy* on April 16, 2014, the very same day as the *Sewol* ferry accident, even before the details that lead to the sinking of the ship were out in the open, titled "Why Do So Many People Die in Ferry Accidents," describes almost to the letter the circumstances surrounding the tragedy:

> Ferries in the developing world are often overcrowded, which can throw off a boat's balance or make it top heavy and more prone to capsizing. And when crewmembers are inadequately trained they are uncertain of how to respond in the event of a disaster, exacerbating these problems. Moreover, government safety regulations are far less stringent – or go unenforced – in developing nations.[34]

It is remarkable to note that even though the article cited above appeared on the day of the *Sewol* ferry tragedy, it could very well describe the conditions under which the *Sohae* ferry sank two decades earlier. Furthermore, the most striking point the author makes in this paragraph is that the circumstances he describes apply to "ferries in the developing world" or "developing nations." Therefore, theoretically, the conditions should have applied to Korea in 1993, the year the *Sohae* ferry went down, and 292 people drowned. These conditions should no longer have been applicable in Korea circa 2014, the year the *Sewol* ferry accident actually happened. In other words, in spite of the country's unprecedented economic and technological advancements, people lost their lives due to circumstances that did not have parity with the nation's progress.

As expected, given the ease of access to information in our day and age, details surrounding the *Sewol* ferry incident are much more readily available than about the sinking of the *Sohae*. Despite these information accessibility differences, and given what we know, what can we surmise from the conditions surrounding the *Sohae* and *Sewol* ferry tragedy vis-à-vis Korea's economic and technological achievements in the two decades between the two tragedies? In my opinion, the resurfacing of similar behavioral patterns and motivating factors twenty years into an astronomical economic and technological advancement means that progress in the less tangible areas—values and levels of consciousness—do not move at the same pace as economic and technological progress. Unlike economic and technological progress, cultural values and attitudes are deeply ingrained in the fabric of the society. The public needs to work deliberately to ensure that values and levels of consciousness keep pace with economic and technological progress. Unless parity is reached in all areas, innocent lives will continue to represent the price that societies pay for the disparity between them.

In the aftermath of the *Sewol* ferry accident:

» The Prime Minister, Chung Hong-won, resigned.
» The principal at Danwon High School, where many of the students studied, committed suicide.

» The CEO of Cheonghaejin Marine, the company responsible for operating the *Sewol* was blamed for violating safety rules. The company had modified the ship to enable it to carry more passengers. These modifications made the ship more vulnerable to tipping over. The firm's CEO was sentenced to ten years in prison.

» Lee, Joon-seok, the captain, was convicted of murder and sentenced to 36 years in prison for professional negligence causing death.

» The *Sewol's* engineer was sentenced to 30 years in prison.

» Crew members received sentences between five and 20 years.

May 26, 2014 – Goyang Bus Terminal Fire in Gyeonggi

On May 28, 2014, as the Korean people mourned the death of more than 300 passengers in the *Sewol* ferry catastrophe, seven people were reported dead and more than 50 others were injured in a fire. The fire began on the first basement level of the Goyang Bus Terminal in Gyeonggi. Welding sparks generated by contractors hired to remodel the site to build a food court may have caused the fire. By law, companies wishing to complete a building renovation or expansion that would change the safety features of the site must submit a construction plan. They must also obtain permission from both a city government agency and a district fire station before commencing the work. Allegedly, the contracting company, in this case, began the work before obtaining approval from the local fire station.

Furthermore, reports indicate that the contracting company requested permission from the local fire station to alter the fire prevention shutters. The fire station did not approve this request. One such shutter apparently malfunctioned, which caused toxic smoke to leak into the second floor. This leak caused the bulk of the casualties resulting from smoke inhalation. It is unclear whether the fire shutter malfunctioned or whether construction workers deliberately tinkered with it to prevent it from working properly. Experts believe that if the fire shutter had worked, fewer fatalities would have been registered.

January 10, 2015 – Apartment Fire in Uijeongbu, Gyeonggi Province

On January 10, 2015, a fire in the ten-story Daebong Green Apartment complex in Uijeongbu killed four people and left 124 others injured, 14 in critical condition. A total of 226 people lost their homes.[35] The criminal investigation conducted jointly by the police department and the National Forensic Service (NFS) found that the fire started on the first floor near the ignition of a four-wheel motorcycle belonging to a Mr. Kim. After reviewing CCTV security video footage, the investigating team determined that Mr. Kim had applied fire using a lighter to remove the key from the ignition. Apparently, it was frozen due to extreme cold weather conditions. Reportedly, the four-wheel motorcycle caught on fire and strong winds caused the blaze to spread to the cars parked on the ground floor and then moved quickly to the structure including the upper floors: "[The investigating team] showed the footage to Mr. K and he acknowledged that he applied heat to the key box with a lighter and the fire occurred due to his carelessness. The investigation team booked him on charges of suspicion of negligence in a fire and negligence resulting in injury and death."[36]

The fire quickly spread to two adjacent residential buildings, one a 10-story, and the other, a 15-story building. In addition to the fatalities, estimates indicate that 20 vehicles in the above-ground parking lot of the apartment building were totaled.[37]

Figure 3: The charred remains of the Daebong Green Apartment complex in Uijeongbu.[38]

Figure 4: Firefighters attempt to put out the fire on the first floor of the Daebong Green Apartment complex in Uijeongbu.[39]

Fire officials reported that the Uijeongbu fire spread quickly from the first-floor parking lot to higher levels because of the highly flammable materials used to cover the outer walls of the building.[40]

An article that appeared in *The Dong-A Ilbo* covering the apartment fire in Uijeongbu refers to the exterior cladding used in the buildings in question as "dryvit method." However, the generic designation for this process is exterior insulation finish system (EIFS) since "dryvit" actually refers to a brand name of exterior cladding. According to *The Dong-A Ilbo*:

> The method is preferred by building owners, because it is cheaper by more than 50 percent than the use of stone to finish the exterior wall, and the construction period can be cut nearly in half.[41]

The Washington Post substantiates the inexpensive qualities as well as the energy-efficient characteristics of this exterior insulation finishing method:

> Dryvit is a brand name for a type of exterior cladding known as EIFS — for exterior insulation and finish system. It consists of rigid foam insulation board attached to the wall, topped by a base coat of synthetic stucco reinforced with mesh and a textured finish coat of synthetic stucco. It's waterproof, highly energy-efficient and relatively inexpensive.[42]

Benjamin Haag explains why EIFS has been so popular in building construction. He describes the popularity of the process as follows: "Exterior Insulation Finish System (EIFS) is a non-load bearing exterior wall treatment which due to its excellent insulation properties and design flexibility has been a popular choice for exterior building cladding for several decades."[43]

The flammability of EIFS, however, seems to outweigh the energy-efficient and low-cost nature of this type of building cladding. Haag further explains that structures that are clad with EIFS present a real challenge for firefighters when they catch on fire. He describes the flammable features of EIFS and some of the challenges they present to firefighting personnel:

> Due to the polystyrene foam insulation component, EIFS is considered combustible. Polystyrene foam is a thermoplastic material which means it will melt

and flow when heated. 'Polystyrene foam will produce combustible and toxic gases at approximately 570°F and will ignite in a range between 900°F and 1,000°F' (Spadafora, 2015). When ignited, a polystyrene fire will create high heat conditions, rapid flame spread, and dense black smoke. The heat release rate for thermoplastics can be three to five times higher than those of ordinary combustibles such as wood or paper. The heat of combustion for ordinary combustibles generally ranges between 6,000 and 8,000 Btu/lb (13,960-18,600kj/kg). The heat of combustion for plastics generally ranges between 12,000 and 20,000 Btu/lb (27,900-46,520kj/kg). (FM Global, 2015).[44]

The technical figures cited above may leave the reader wondering how flammable polystyrene foam is. An experiment conducted in 2010 by the Korea Institute of Construction Technology, and described by *The Dong-A Ilbo*, gives the reader a more concrete and dramatic image of the combustibility of this material:

The Korea Institute of Construction Technology tried to set fire to [the] inside of [a] wall measuring three meters wide and six meters long after installing exterior material... using [the] dryvit method... [The] wall caught fire in a matter of just 90 seconds. The fire completely engulfed the exterior wall in four minutes, with intense flames reaching as high as six meters, generating black toxic gas. The situation was [similar to the apartment] fire in Uijeongbu.[45]

Based on reports regarding the speedy spread of the fires both at the apartment building in Uijeongbu and at the sports complex in Jecheon discussed below, which both billowed black smoke, as well as judging by the number of victims that were hospitalized in critical condition after inhaling toxic fumes, the fires behaved in a manner consistent with this type of cladding.

Also, two other factors contributed to the rapid spread of the fire. One was the absence of a sprinkler system. Apparently, only 11-and-higher-story buildings were required to have a sprinkler system at the time of the fire.[46] The second factor was the building's pilotis-style structure. It is termed "pilotis" for the support columns or piles used to raise a building, usually to the second floor, to maximize the space for parking, storage or both. However, this type of structure has the potential to create hazardous situations, particularly in fires that begin on the first floor, as was the case with this particular fire, because of the possibility of the blaze spreading to cars in the parking area. This scenario has a high probability of destroying and blocking the first-floor exit, thus preventing residents from evacuating the building as well as blocking firefighting personnel accessibility. Additionally, the structure is susceptible to enabling the spread of heat, fire and toxic gas to the stairwell and elevator pit.

All of these challenges appear to have been present in the inferno of the Daebong Green Apartment complex in Uijeongbu. A report in the *Korea JoongAng Daily* describes in great detail what happened and how residents reacted to the emergency after being trapped in the building when the fire broke out:

The flames obstructed the main doorways on the first floor and smoke billowed up inside the buildings. Most of the trapped victims evacuated to the rooftops and waited for helicopters to rescue them. Others who lived on the lower floors jumped out of their windows or climbed down the outer walls before firefighters arrived at the scene.[47]

Finally, after the Uijeongbu fire and calls for stricter codes involving EIFS-clad buildings, "the Public Safety and Security Ministry vowed to start a campaign to **crack down** on the use of exterior materials that are susceptible to fire." According to *The Dong-A Ilbo*, "the ministry [planned] to oblige building owners and builders to use fire retardant materials, **irrespective of the building's height or use** when installing insulation materials on the exterior wall."[48] Furthermore, *The Dong-A Ilbo* reported that under existing law at the time of the Uijeongbu fire, building contractors and owners were not required to use fire retardant materials, "except in high-rise buildings, [factories,] and facilities used by the public within commercial districts."[49]

In the end, the government passed regulations prohibiting the use of flammable cladding in the construction of buildings six stories and higher.[50] These new regulations, however, only apply to ongoing new construction. Thus, the regulations leave existing buildings that contain flammable materials intact. These buildings with flammable materials are the structures that present formidable challenges for firefighters and a threat to the population at large.

At the conclusion of the police department investigation of the cause of the apartment fire in Uijeongbu, the investigating team announced that it had "charged 15 [people] including the person who, unintentionally, started the fire… [The] team released a report on the findings through the press saying that it would send the case to the prosecutor with the intent to prosecute."[51]

December 21, 2017 – Sports Complex Fire in Jecheon, Chungcheong Province

29 people were reported dead and 37 injured in a fire that started on the first-floor parking lot of a sports complex. The fire quickly engulfed the eight-story building and spread to approximately 12 cars parked in the parking lot. The building also housed a sauna, a gymnasium, and several restaurants.

On December 25, 2017, *The Korea Herald* reported that:

> National forensic experts concluded Saturday [December 23, 2017] the fire started from the first-floor ceiling of the parking lot, quickly engulfing eight stories in just seven minutes. Among the dead, 20 suffocated from toxic smoke in the female sauna.[52]

Also, the media reported that experts pointed to the external cladding material used in the construction of the building as the prime suspect for the rapid spread of the fire. They specifically named dryvit cladding as the culprit because they consider it to be "cheap but highly flammable finishing material."[53] They also

261

pointed out that it emits highly toxic gases into the atmosphere in fire situations, thus causing lung problems for people who inhale them.[54]

These materials reduce building costs significantly. They supposedly reduce construction time as well. Furthermore, since winters are rather cold in Korea, contractors utilize energy-efficient materials like EIFS in building construction. However, given the highly flammable qualities of EIFS cladding, it stands to reason that more substantially fire-resistant materials should be used.

Also, reports indicate that firefighters found that Electrical Piping Shaft (EPS) walls were not fireproof, although fireproof EPS walls are required to obtain city approval. Fireproof EPS walls are supposed to delay a fire from reaching the higher floors. Evidently, the lack of fireproofing enabled the fire to reach the higher levels more quickly, thus potentially causing more casualties. It appears that the city approved the use of the building regardless.

According to *The Korea Herald*, "also problematic was the structure of the building, which was raised above ground on pillars."[55] As discussed above, this type of building structure is termed "pilotis":

> [A pilotis structure] is susceptible to fires that start on the ground floor as staircases act like smokestacks, causing flames to spread upwards... The incident is invoking comparisons with a fire which erupted three years ago [in January 2015] at an apartment in Uijeongbu, Gyeonggi Province. The building

also contained the flammable material and was constructed in a similar style.[56]

Many buildings in Korea have a comparable structure. Therefore, the potential for similar incidents in the future may be quite significant.

Figure 5: Firefighters and forensic investigators examining the first floor of the eight-story building that housed the sports complex in the city of Jecheon.[57]

Reportedly, in July 2017, the son of the building owner conducted a fire safety inspection. Apparently, the fact that the second-floor emergency exit was blocked because the space was being used as storage facilities went unreported. Supposedly, the fire department conducted a building inspection in October 2017. From existing reports, it is not clear whether the emergency exit issue went unreported then. Fire-fighting experts believe that some of the fire victims might have been saved if the second-floor exit had been accessible.

On December 23, 2017, the *Yonhap News Agency* reported that the owner had purchased the building in August 2017 and had "remodeled it to house a gym, public sauna and other facilities."[58]

Two days later, on December 25, 2017, the agency reported that after raiding the homes of an owner and a manager of the fitness center "to investigate if they were negligent in preventing… [the] disaster… The police appeared set to press charges of manslaughter caused by professional negligence and violation of the fire law against the 53-year-old owner, while they will push for charges of manslaughter against the 50-year-old manager."[59]

Contributing Factors

Other issues appear to have contributed to the casualties in the fire. Some of these factors reportedly included a non-functioning sprinkler system, which is a violation of fire prevention laws. Other factors included insufficient emergency exits, and illegally parked cars. The latter prevented the fire trucks from accessing the site as quickly as possible. Reports indicate that it took authorities about 15 minutes to move some of the cars that were illegally parked to enable fire trucks to reach the building. Once the vehicles were removed, there was insufficient space for the firefighters to maneuver the delivery of water to the raging inferno. Days after the Jecheon fire, people reportedly continued to park illegally on the same street where the burnt sports complex was located.

It is clear that one of the reasons why people continued to park illegally, still blocking access to emergency equipment, was the relatively low probability of getting a parking citation. Even in the rare instance of receiving a parking citation, the fine was minimal. In this case, a potential fine was clearly not an effective deterrent. Before August 2018 in Korea, violations for parking within 15 feet of a fire hydrant used to run approximately the equivalent of $40-$50. In the United States, by contrast, parking violations may cost as much as $150. The fee amount varies depending on the city. As of this writing, parking within 15 feet of a fire hydrant would cost a driver $53 in Santa Monica, $68 in Los Angeles, $77 in Baltimore, $110 in San Francisco, and $150 in Chicago.

Additionally, drivers in the United States would be responsible for late penalties. In Korea, it is common practice for owners of these illegally parked cars to escape with a simple warning from the police or emergency personnel. In the United States, however, the car is issued a citation and no second chances are given. Because a parking citation in Korea is seldom issued, the concept failed as a deterrent. Some Koreans recognize the low probability of being fined for breaking the law; therefore, when faced with a choice to park illegally near a fire hydrant and risk the low likelihood of being fined or be inconvenienced by the less efficient option of having to walk farther to their destination, they clearly opt to break the law and take a chance of incurring either a warning or a fine.

Korean law allows for emergency departments to move illegally parked cars if necessary, but before August 2018, this was rarely done. It was unclear as to who was responsible for paying towing and storage or impound fees. In the United States, by comparison, the car owner is responsible for paying these fees, which can be quite significant and may even surpass the amount of the parking citation fee by a considerable margin. In Korea, before August 2018, if the emergency personnel had to break the windows of a car to perform their duties, their department was responsible for the damage. This may explain the emergency personnel's hesitation to break the windows of vehicles that obstructed their work. Recently amended pertinent laws, however, give "firefighters on the field… more discretion and authority in emergency situations."[60]

In similar instances in the States, the insurance company would not cover the damages caused by firefighting personnel to an illegally parked vehicle that is obstructing the performance of their duties because of owner negligence. Ameriprise Auto & Home Insurance Company, for example, defines negligence as failure "to demonstrate the appropriate amount of care or responsibility for the situation. The failure to take appropriate precautions can cause [the insured] to be liable for the damage."[61] Therefore, the car owner is the responsible party.

To facilitate communication with car owners, Koreans frequently tape their cell phone number on the dashboard. That enables anyone who needs an illegally parked car moved to communicate with the owner. This is done for the convenience of drivers who may habitually park their vehicle illegally. Therefore, the burden is on the driver who is inconvenienced rather than the inconsiderate driver.

Figure 6: Typical image of double-parked cars in Korea.[62]

Figure 7: Typical image of illegally parked cars in a residential area in Korea.[63]

The Seoul fire department has confirmed that factors contributing to the fire in Jecheon are present in the city of Seoul as well. Following the Jecheon fire, the Seoul fire department inspected 319 buildings that house public bathhouses and sauna businesses. 120, or 37%, of the buildings inspected failed safety standards. Many of the buildings inspected did not have accessible emergency exits, either because they were blocked or for another reason. Some of the buildings had the fire sprinkler systems disabled to prevent their operation.[64] If the percentage of buildings that failed safety standards found in Seoul holds for the entire country, the total number of affected buildings is staggering, even for a small country like Korea. However, Young Lee and I fear that the percentage of buildings that do not meet safety standards may be higher outside of the capital.

January 19, 2018 – Sejong Hospital Fire in Miryang, South Gyeongsang Province

Almost a month after the sports complex fire in Jecheon, which killed 29 people, a fire erupted at Sejong Hospital in the city of Miryang. This fire killed 46 people including one doctor, one nurse, and one nurse assistant. Yonhap News Agency reports a total of 146 injuries.[65] Initially, the press reported 37 fatalities; however, the death toll rose after the preliminary reports because some of the injured were in critical condition. Reports indicate that toxic fumes inhalation caused most of the casualties. The media reported that faulty wiring started the fire in the ceiling of the pantry room, which doubled as a changing room. This room was located on the first floor of the main building of the hospital.

At the time, the hospital complex included the six-story main building and an annex, which housed a nursing hospital for the elderly and served as a nursing home.

On January 29, *The Korea Times* published a litany of possible safety code as well as emergency guideline violations. The first indication of a possible violation of safety guidelines was the six victims who had perished in the elevator and were later discovered by firefighters. Universal building safety guidelines indicate that elevators are not to be used in case of fire or emergency evacuation. If elevators are used, the elevator shaft could act as a conduit for toxic gases and fire moving upward. The discovery of these victims is an indication that the staff may have failed to alert them against using the elevator.

Below is a series of additional possible safety violations that appear to reflect cost-cutting measures:

> On Friday [January 19, 2018], the 99 patients at the hospital with 95 beds were under the care of only one doctor and eight nursing staff, indicating one medical staff member was responsible for about 11 patients. The hospital had three doctors, only two of whom worked full-time, and 23 nursing staff, in violation of the law which states that at least six doctors and 35 nursing staff members were required for a hospital of that size. Putting too many patients in one room was also a contributing factor that prevented swift evacuation. The hospital put 20 patients in one

room, which according to some surviving patients caused difficulties when entering, leaving or moving around it. The amount of fee-for-medical services for admitting a patient a hospital can seek from the National Health Insurance Service is the same, regardless of the number of patients a room holds. This has been the primary reason for the hospital to put as many patients as possible in a limited space.[66]

The article also discloses that Sejong Hospital had illegally remodeled the building in 2006. Subsequently, the city government issued a fine to the hospital in the amount of 30 million Korean won (~$28,000) for the aforementioned illegal building remodeling.

Hospital administrators came under fire from the public and the press for the lack of a sprinkler system, which might have helped reduce the number of casualties. However, at a press briefing, Song Byeong-cheol, Hospital Chairman, "argued that his hospital was not subject to the mandatory installation of sprinklers due to its small size."[67]

Government officials from the ruling and opposing parties offered the customary condolences to the victims' families and pledged support for the victims and their families. Representatives from various ministries were deployed to the scene of the accident to assist with the aftermath of the tragedy. They also pledged to conduct a thorough investigation to identify the cause of the fire as well as the responsible parties. Moreover, government officials "pledged to carry out sweeping measures to enhance public safety."[68] As of this writing, the term that no one has operationally defined is "sweeping measures."

In March 2018, in the aftermath of the fire, 12 people who were deemed either directly or indirectly responsible were indicted. These people included the hospital administrator as well as former and incumbent government officials: "The defendants include[d] the head of the hospital's board, who [was] accused of violating the Building Act, the Medical Service Act and a number of other laws in the course of running the hospital..."[69]

Eventually, the chair of the hospital board and the general manager were imprisoned for illegally renovating the hospital and not following safety rules.

Tougher Measures

After the two latest deadly incidents that happened within the same month, including the sports complex blaze in Jecheon and the Sejong Hospital fire in Miryang, especially given the public's complicity in many of the man-made accidents I researched, it became evident to me that a radical change is needed to seriously modify the public's attitude toward fire prevention and the preservation of public safety.

Following these two deadly fires, the government announced that it would conduct safety inspections on approximately 60,000 "high-risk" facilities throughout the country. According to *The*

Korea Herald, included in the "high-risk" category were "small- and medium-sized hospitals, nursing homes, flophouses, postnatal care centers, public bathhouses and traditional marketplaces."[70] These businesses were classified as "high-risk" because many of them were located in buildings that were exempt from meeting stricter safety regulations because of their size.

The plan called for two rounds of inspections. In the first round, local governments would provide inspectors with a checklist of 20 to 30 items. Subsequently, a second round of random inspections would take place to ensure that the first reviews were conducted properly. Reportedly, identified repairs and reinforcement work would be funded through local governments' "disaster management funds and fire safety subsidies."[71] However, it is not clear whether the repair and reinforcement costs would be borne by local governments or by the business owners themselves. *The Korea Herald* reported: "After the inspections, the government [would] follow up on whether the managers of the facilities [had] redressed the safety problems as ordered by the inspectors."[72]

These two tragedies finally motivated legislators to amend the Framework Act on Fire-Fighting Services. The amendment served to minimize the impact of future fires. The intended effect of the revised law was to address some disconnects between the law and actual practice in terms of ensuring public safety. One such disconnect was exemplified by drivers who fail to yield to fire trucks in traffic, even though the trucks sound their sirens. Another disconnect was the aforementioned incessant and illegal random parking, which often obstructs access to fire hydrants, fire equipment, and firefighters. If strictly enforced, the most invaluable contribution of the law will be to change the public's attitude toward fire prevention, firefighting, and the protection of public safety.

The amendment, which went into effect on June 27, 2018, and was implemented on August 10, 2018 by the Seoul metropolitan government, at least, authorizes local police departments to designate no-parking zones within five meters of fire hydrants. It also increases fines for both drivers who obstruct fire-fighting trucks in traffic and who park their vehicle either within five meters of fire hydrants or in fire-truck-only zones. The penalty was set at one million Korean won (~$896). The substantial increase in the fine sends a clear message to drivers that the government is serious about enabling the work of firefighters by establishing clear guidelines and punishing obstructionists to curtail future fire catastrophes.

Below are two of the amendment's key points in paragraphs four and five of Article 25 of the Framework Act of Fire Services. These paragraphs clarify prior uncertainties associated with the removal of vehicles that obstruct the effort of firefighters, and related costs. The adoption of this amendment is well-intentioned. However, its success will be determined not by its intention but by the effectiveness of its enforcement and its impact on the general public's attitude toward communal safety, as the paragraphs explain:

(3) When making urgent mobilization for fire-fighting activities, the director general of a fire-fighting headquarters, the head of a fire station, or the fire brigade commander may remove or move any parked or stopped vehicles, objects, etc. that hinder the passage of fire engines or the fire-fighting activities.

(4) The director general of a fire-fighting headquarters, the head of a fire station, or the fire brigade commander may request the relevant agency, such as the competent local government, to provide assistance regarding tow trucks, human resources, etc. in order to remove or move any parked or stopped vehicles hindering fire-fighting activities under paragraph (3), and the relevant agency so requested shall provide the assistance except in extenuating circumstances. <Newly Inserted by Act No. 15532, Mar. 27, 2018>

(5) A Mayor/Do Governor may pay expenses to the persons providing tow trucks, human resources, etc. pursuant to paragraph (4), as prescribed by municipal ordinance of the City/Do. <Newly Inserted by Act No. 15532, Mar. 27, 2018>[73]

Concluding Thoughts about Man-Made Accidents

Reports indicate that the Sejong Hospital Fire in Miryang, the latest in a long string of man-made accidents and mishaps going back to the *Sewol* ferry catastrophe, eroded the people's confidence in the country's safety standards. In the wake of the most recent accidents, Koreans are beginning to recognize the repetitive patterns surrounding the incessant breach of safety rules and regulations. However, imposing even the most stringent of safety regulations alone will not prevent accidents. The public actually must adopt a mindset that accepts not only safety regulations, but understands and internalizes the spirit and intent behind them. Most importantly, the cultural values must inherently incorporate an intention to obey rules because doing so is in everyone's best interest.

Many of these catastrophes appear to have been caused by multiple factors that involve safety code violations. These codes were not only violated by directly responsible parties, but by the general public. The public displays a disregard for safety rules by utilizing facilities for something other than their intended purpose and pushing the limit of facilities and equipment to a breaking point with the sole intent of maximizing efficiency, and thus financial profits. The general public's behavior in many instances appears to be a contributing factor, and one that exacerbates the challenges of an accident site. Parking illegally in front of hydrants or in front of building entrances, thus blocking access to emergency vehicles, contributes to accident casualties in tangible ways.

National Reaction to Catastrophes

Typically, the Korean public has a three-prong reaction to catastrophes. First, after the initial shock and period of mourning, the response of the citizenry to these accidents evinces outrage. There seems to exist a strong demand to identify and punish the main culprit/s or parties in charge. Second, there is a demand for a heartfelt public apology from responsible individuals, whether the individual is the CEO of the company or the president of the country. Third, there is frequently a call for the government to intervene and "fix the problem."

Outrage and a desire to identify and punish the culprit/s

Even though perpetrators are identified and punished, man-made accidents caused by a disregard for public safety continue to reoccur. An examination of the causes of the various accidents seems to indicate that the patterns of disregard for public safety also repeat cyclically: Violating safety codes, exceeding the capacity of facilities, equipment or vessels, utilizing facilities for unintended purposes, remodeling buildings or vessels without the proper permits or inspections, or lacking inadequate safety inspections that are meant to uphold compliance with safety regulations all continually contribute to fatal accidents in Korea.

In some cases, the general public's behavior and attitude toward safety standards seem to have contributed to accidents. As such, a fundamental question is in order: Does the society support the idea of reducing the number of man-made catastrophes that are caused by disregard for safety regulations, with the understanding that adherence to strict safety standards will require a shift in the mindset of the nation?

Shifting attitudes to emphasize safety and careful planning, rather than efficiency, will not only inconvenience many people but more importantly most likely cause a reduction in profits and increase costs associated with such areas as construction, housing, transportation, health care, entertainment, and food. If the answer is no, then the discussion and debate end there. If the answer is yes, then how effective and practical is the national reaction to catastrophes?

Is the aforementioned public response to tragedies a knee-jerk response based on emotions? Or, is this response an efficient way of dealing with unfortunate and painful situations? Does the pattern of response address the core reasons why these types of accidents keep recurring? Or does the entire nation need to be more self-reflective and critical and ask: What are we, as a society, doing wrong? What is the general public's attitude toward safety standards, regulations, and penalties? How can we as a nation prevent unnecessary loss of innocent lives? Should the country continue to focus on identifying the key culprits and parties in charge, demand their punishment and go on with a business as usual attitude? Should the identification and punishment of key law-breaking individuals and responsible parties be sufficient to exculpate the general public so people can keep approaching safety standards, safety regulations and penalties in the same disdainful manner?

Young Lee and I recognize that the question of what to do about public safety issues generates controversy with people on both sides of the aisle. Some demand reform and strict adherence to safety regulations. Others say after a catastrophe: "Let's move on with our lives, once the perpetrators are brought to justice." The driving force behind the general public's attitude toward safety standards, regulations and penalties appears to be a desire for efficiency. This desire has personal convenience, self-interest, greed and economic prosperity at its root. The result, time and time again, is the loss of innocent lives. From an outsider's perspective, the unfortunate, sad, and frustrating nature of these "accidents" is that the cultural desire for efficiency takes precedence over human safety. The ache for personal convenience and strenuous striving for material wealth will outweigh the inconvenience of occasional tragedy. In other words, some people believe that for the country to maintain its economic viability, some sacrifices are inevitable. As previously discussed, historically, sacrifices have played an essential role in achieving the miracle on the Han River. What is the takeaway here? Is it that efficiency for the sake of profits must be the guiding principle for Korea? Or that disregard for safety standards and regulations is acceptable if you do not get caught? Or both? Or is it something else?

One segment of the population seems to espouse the idea that for the economy as a whole to move forward, and for the entire country to benefit, some sacrifices by a few will have to take place along the way. Therefore, some innocent lives will be lost in the process of achieving financial prosperity. These lives, in this viewpoint, are a sad but unavoidable price to pay for the benefit of all. This mentality may be derived from the historical attitude of applauding national sacrifice, which helped Korea rise from the ashes after the Korean War.

However, the Korean economy is now well past the developmental stage. Today, Korea remains among the elite economies of the world. Has the time come for Korea to deemphasize competitiveness and the efficiency-at-all-costs approach, and place more emphasis on actions that benefit all human lives? Viewed from an objective and humanistic perspective, these man-made accidents could be more consistently avoided if the nation adopted a more balanced mentality, one that values both financial benefits as well as universal safety. In this manner, the tendency to "cut corners" and disregard safety standards and regulations could be lessened, if the penalties for perpetrators are significantly high enough to be viewed as actual deterrents. However, Koreans, in general would need to forgo the financial benefits and conveniences that are generated by the disregard for public safety standards.

Demand for a heartfelt apology from responsible individuals

The absence or even the delay of a sincere apology after a national catastrophe or incident that receives national attention in some instances has caused public outrage. However, demanding and receiving the customary public apology does not go far enough. These apologies merely smooth over the latest incident, while avoiding an examination of the fundamental issues. This national nearsightedness is a denial of the complicity of the general public in these incidents. The nation needs to recognize the fundamental flaw of the widespread disregard for safety standards and regulations. A clearer message needs to be conveyed, one which clarifies that the temptation to "cut corners" and the *gap* and *eul* relationship all contribute to catastrophes and abuses.

Until this mentality is eradicated and the public grasps the concept that safety regulations have a purpose, and it is in the public's best interest to abide by them, these man-made accidents will continue to punish the country's psyche. In addition, if the general public is interested in decreasing, as much as possible, abuses and catastrophes caused by disregard for safety standards and regulations, the country needs to undertake a national campaign to undo decisions made in the past. Practices in areas such as building construction, which took place in the past in pursuit of efficiency and saving money on construction costs, must be eradicated. Such a "clean-up" campaign would be costly and would most likely increase the price of goods and services. The general public would have to bear this additional cost, but the revenue could very well create jobs. Young Lee and I understand that CEOs and the nation's president should be held responsible for ensuring public safety, but one person cannot change the general public's attitude toward public safety. The citizenry must recognize that public safety is everyone's responsibility. They must give this concern the attention it deserves. One person, or one leader, cannot achieve this alone.

Demand for the government to "fix the problem"

The truth of the matter is that legislators can adopt strict safety regulations, but if the public disregards them and continues to emphasize efficiency for the sake of financial profit, no safety regulations will be effective unless they are both enforced and carry severe financial consequences for lawbreakers. Similarly, some Koreans are concerned that legislators will not pass legislation that negatively impacts major corporations, out of fear that the economic momentum will be stymied. In reality, baby boomers and some conservative young people who recognize the contribution of the *chaebols* to the economic vitality of the country tend not to want the government to adopt laws that would impede the viability of the conglomerates. There is a widespread perception that the economic well-being of the country depends on the financial viability of the *chaebols* or family-run conglomerates because they are viewed as the engine of the Korean economy, and the job creators.

This belief may be deeply rooted in the Korean culture where historically, the group is more important than the individual. The mindset appears to have been promoted in the decades of the 1960s and 1970s under President Park Chung Hee (1963-1979), when the country was undergoing major reconstruction. Korea was attempting to undergo substantial recovery from the ravages of the Korean War as well as infrastructure build-up. His motto 새마을운동[*Sae ma eul eun dong*] or, "Let's rebuild the country," provided a cry for unity. However, once again, Young Lee and I reiterate that Korea is at a different stage now than in the '60s, '70s, '80s, and '90s. Today's economy is much larger; societies both in Korea and abroad are more complex, and globalization is here to stay. Young Lee and I also recognize that the existence of conflicting interests results in a more difficult decision-making environment for government leaders. However, the fundamental question remains: What does the general public want? Do they prefer to maintain the status quo or do they wish to move Korea to a more balanced level of advancement, whereby ethics, values, and the level of consciousness are in line with the strength of the economy and the technological progress?

Poor decisions, greed, corruption, and blatant disregard for public safety are symptomatic of a developing nation. These are some of the trends that existed during the period of rapid economic expansion and urbanization. As a result of the prevailing conditions during Korea's transitional period from a developing nation to a technologically advanced society, the Korean people had to cope with some tragic and life-changing man-made accidents. Regrettably, some of the practices and attitudes vis-à-vis public safety that were evident during this transformational period have remained deeply ingrained in the culture and have resurfaced in more recent accidents. The fact that some of these practices and attitudes keep reappearing indicates that societies which are in transition from a developing stage to a more advanced economic and technological level need to work deliberately to ensure that ethics, values, and the degree of consciousness keep pace with the rest of the advancements. In other words, old attitudinal habits and behavioral patterns are more difficult to eradicate than wrinkles, imperfect noses, and old technology.

According to University of Southern California History Department Professor, Hwang Kyung Moon, who wrote a piece titled "Lessons from Disasters" following the *Sewol* ferry accident, Korean people underwent a period of reflection and soul searching after the tragic accidents that took place during the period of economic expansion. He makes the following assertion:

> Koreans... came to understand that such behavior [The behavior associated with the collapse of the Sampoong Department Store.] was symptomatic of a more expansive problem in their society and culture, and that, somehow, they all shared responsibility for it.

> Societal elites and common people alike took a closer look at the mentalities and ethics of the period of rapid economic growth over the previous several decades. They wondered whether, in the rush to achieve industrialization, the country had lost its collective soul, willing to take too many shortcuts or failing to consider the broader, less tangible costs of chasing wealth.[74]

Given the almost incessant accidents in the more recent period from 2014 to 2018, and the recurring behavioral patterns associated with these incidents, is it time for the Korean people to undergo yet another period of reflection and soul searching to determine whether they are still chasing wealth at all costs and whether the lessons from the past have fallen on deaf ears. Is it time for Koreans to ask themselves: "What role do we, as a society, play in this accident-prone environment?"

Following the *Sewol* ferry catastrophe, *The Korea Herald* published an article titled "Culture closely tied to Korea's vulnerability to disasters," wherein the author, Kim Hoo-ran, identifies two cultural factors that have contributed to man-made disasters. The first factor is a failure to follow rules, and second is the "*pali pali*" culture. These are two of the characteristics permeating the Korean culture that I have also noted throughout my observations from everyday life, from work, eating and driving habits to education:

> Failure to stick to the rules has been a major contributing factor in most of Korea's man-made disasters… Some of the accidents that could have been foreseen and prevented had the relevant rules and regulations been observed…

> The culture of "ppalli ppalli," or "hurry hurry," is a byproduct of the era which saw economic development as the overarching goal. The whole country was in overdrive, disregarding rules and procedures if necessary, as it pursued accelerated economic development. Following decades of such circumvention of laws, Korean society became desensitized to the risks it was taking.[75]

These are all very accurate assertions. However, the most critical point that Koreans today need to recognize is that the country has moved on from that period of rapid economic expansion to a more stable stage of development. This evolution has contributed to the country's prominent position among the developed nations of the world. The strategies that helped to propel the country to its current position are, to say the least, misaligned with the current stage of development. At most, these strategies are counterproductive. The cultural evolution process must now give higher priority to intangibles such as sensitization to the value of human life, and the raising of consciousness to the level whereby actions are dictated by the collective well-being instead of individual convenience or materialistic wealth.

Update

Since the initial writing of this book, man-made accidents have continued to occur. Most notably, around 2:30 in the morning of July 27, 2019, two Korean nationals were killed and 17 injured when the loft of a night club in Gwangju collapsed.[76] Among the injured were foreign athletes competing in the July 12-28 FINA (Fédération Internationale de Natation or International Swimming Federation) World Championships in Gwangju located approximately 330 kilometers (~205 miles) south of Seoul.[77] According to reports, there were about 370 patrons inside the night club when the accident happened and approximately 100 of them were "on the loft area, which was 2.5 meters [~8.2 feet] above the lower floor."[78]

Initial reports by news sources including *Yonhap News Agency*, *The Korea Herald*, and *The Korea Times* indicate that at least a portion of the loft was "illegally" expanded "without the city's authorization."[79]

A follow-up report appearing in *Chosun Media* indicates that:

> …according to the Gwangju Police Department, the night club operator expanded and fixed the illegal structure on the second floor three times. The report also points out that the welding process was performed by an acquaintance of the club owner who did not have a welding license or qualified experience. Consequently, the police booked him on manslaughter charges.[80]

This latest accident presents yet again another example of behavior patterns reflected in actions taken without regard to public safety and the proper permits. As in other incidents, these actions appear to have a similar motive: financial gains, which are actualized by cutting corners and through efficiency.

Deadly accidents, such as, the sports complex in Jecheon, the apartment fire in Uijeongbu, the hospital fire in Miryang, and the night club in Gwangju provide the public with a reality check about the potential proliferation of the construction issues. Usually, after these types of incidents the government conducts inspections of similar facilities to determine the possible extent of the problems. After the loft collapse in the night club in Gwangju, *Dong-A Media* reporters conducted an investigation of night clubs in three cities:

> *Dong-A Media* reporters reviewed the public records of night clubs in Seoul, Busan, and Daegu. The team

randomly selected and visited 35 night clubs. They found that 25 of the 35 clubs added illegal structures such as a balcony. They also found that 10 of those 25 clubs were cited by government officials and ordered to clear or detach the illegal structures. However, they did not comply with the order and continued to operate the business.[81]

Furthermore, the article cited above states bluntly the reason why night club operators fail to comply with government orders to remove illegal expansions. The article asserts: "They are not following the demolition orders because the revenues from illegal expansions are much higher than the penalties they have to pay when they are caught in crackdowns."[82] This explicit statement supports an observation that Young Lee and I have made regarding the role of fines as deterrents in areas such as illegal parking which prevents firefighters from performing their duties, and substandard construction that endangers people's lives. Fines as deterrents of illegal acts, or actions that place public safety at risk, must be high enough for them to be effective.

However, the most important takeaway from the investigations by government officials after other deadly accidents in general, and the investigation by *Dong-A Media* reporters pertaining to unsanctioned structure additions in night clubs is the assessment of the potential extent of problems with existing structures and risk to the general public. Given these findings, it is clear that the potential for further loss of lives is there, even if all future construction and remodeling is done following strict safety guidelines by licensed contractors who obtain the required permits. The fact that these types of findings are being shared with the public, however, is a step in the right direction. It remains to be seen whether the government, building owners, and the general public take the necessary steps to implement an effective risk management program that includes undoing years of misguided decisions.

Endnotes

1   "Hours Worked," OECD Data, accessed 5 September 2019, *data.oecd.org.*

2   "Urban Population (% of World Population)," *The World Bank*, accessed 5 September 2019, *data.worldbank.org.*

3   Ibid.

4   "Urban Population Growth (annual %)," *The World Bank*, accessed 5 September 2019, *data.worldbank.org.*

5   See graphs above on urban population and urban population growth.

6   Sang-Soo Jeon, "Man-Made Disasters in Korea: Case Histories and Improvement Plans," *International Journal of Scientific and Research Publications* vol. 4, no. 7 (July 2014).

7   This figure does not include injuries, of which there were many more.

8   Benjamin Elisha Sawe, "The Sampoong Department Store Disaster of 1995, *WorldAtlas*, 25 April 2017, *worldatlas.com.*

9   Nikola, "The Last Citizen Apartment of Seoul, *KO-JECTS*, 23 November 2015, *kojects.com.*

10 Ibid.

11 Ibid.

12 Sang-Soo Jeon, "Man-Made Disasters in Korea."

13 Nikola, "The Last Citizen Apartment of Seoul."

14 Kanga Kong, "South Korea's History of Building Collapses," *The Wall Street Journal*, 18 February 2014, *blogs.wsj.com.*

15 Nikola, "The Last Citizen Apartment of Seoul."

16 Ibid.

17 A minor discrepancy as to the exact date of the accident exists

in the various reports. Some news sources indicate that it took place on October 10, and others claim that it happened on October 12. Sang-Soo Jeon, "Man-Made Disasters." "List of maritime disasters in the 20th century," *Revolvy,* accessed 5 September 2019, *revolvy.com.*

18   Ibid.

19   Ibid.

20   Sawe, "The Sampoong Department Store Disaster of 1995."

21   "Sampoong Superstore," *Failure Case Studies – The University of North Carolina at Charlotte*, last accessed 6 November 2019, *eng-resources.uncc.edu.*

22   Sawe, "The Sampoong Department Store Disaster of 1995."

23   "Sampoong Department Store Collapse," *The Distributed Wikipedia Mirror Project*, last accessed 31 March, 2017.

24   Andrei Lankov, "The Dawn of Modern Korea: Collapse of Sampoong Department Store," *The Korea Times*, 14 October 2004, *times.hankooki.com.*

25   Ibid.

26   Sawe, "The Sampoong Department Store Disaster."

27   Ibid.

28   "Sampoong Superstore," *Failure Case Studies.*

29   Ibid.

30   Ibid.

31   Jeon Su-Yong, "Prosecution Investigation on Sewol Ferry Accident," *The Chosun Ilbo*, 7 October 2014, *chosun.com.*

32   Per Liljas, "Investigations into the South Korea Ferry Disaster Reveal a Litany of Errors," *Time*, 24 April 2014, *time.com.*

33   "[Editorial]: Preventing Disasters," *The Korea Herald*, 20

April 2014, *koreaherald.com*.

34 Elias Groll, "Why Do So Many People Die in Ferry Accidents?" *Foreign Policy*, 16 April 2014, *foreignpolicy.com*.

35 "Fire at apartment block kills 4, leaves 124 injured," *Korea JoongAng Daily*, accessed 11 February 2019, *koreajoongangdaily.joins.com*.

36 Seul Lee, "Police closes investigation of Uijeongbu fire, "*Newshankuk*, 26 March 2015, *eng.newshankuk.com*.

37 "4 dead, 100 injured in apartment fire in Uijeongbu," *The Korea Times*, 11 January 2015, *koreatimes.us*.

38 Ibid.

39 "Police closes investigation of Uijeongbu fire," *Newshankuk*.

40 Hyun-Jeong Lee, "Police launch probe into Uijeongbu fire," *The Korea Herald*, 11 January 2015, *koreaherald.com*.

41 "Dryvit method suspected as cause of instant spread in Uijeongbu fire," *The Dong-A Ilbo*, 13 January 2015, *donga.com*.

42 Jeanne Huber, "Why does the inside of this door keep getting damaged by rain?" *The Washington Post*, accessed 5 September 2019, *washingtonpost.com*.

43 Benjamin A. Haag, "Exterior Insulation Finish Systems: Hazard Considerations for the Fire Service," *University of Cincinnati*, 10 February 2016, *ceas.uc.edu*.

44 Ibid.

45 "Dryvit method," *The Dong-A Ilbo*.

46 "Fire at apartment block," *Korea JoongAng Daily*.

47 Ibid.

48 Emphasis my own. "Dryvit method," *The Dong-A Ilbo*.

49 Ibid.

50 Se-Hwan Bak, "[Newsmaker] South Korean gyms face

scrutiny after Jecheon deadly fire," *The Korea Herald*, 25 December 2017, *koreaherald.com*.

51 "Police, closes investigation of Uijeongbu fire," *Newshankuk*, 26 March 2015, *eng.newshankuk.com*.

52 Se-Hwan Bak, "South Korean gyms."

53 Soo-Sun You, "Electrical spark started fire in Jecheon," *The Korea Times*, 6 September 2019, *koreatimes.ko.kr*.

54 Ibid.

55 Ibid.

56 Ibid.

57 Ryu Hyo-Jin, "Electrical spark," *The Korea Times*, 6 September 2019, image.

58 "(LEAD) State crime lab confirms Jecheon fire started from ceiling," *Yonhap News Agency*, 23 December 2017, *en.yna.ko.kr*.

59 Ibid.

60 Lee Jae-Min, "Liberal parking not condoned practice," *The Korea* Herald, 9 January 2018, *koreaherald.com*.

61 "Understanding negligence and liability," *Ameriprise Auto & Home Insurance*, accessed 5 September 2019, *ameriprise.com*.

62 Kim Jin-Kyu, "Double parking is common in parking lots in Jinju, South Korea," *NEWSIS*, 20 May 2009, *news.naver.com*.

63 Lee Jae-Ho, "Unenforced illegal parking laws in Gwangju residential area are inconveniencing residents," *Asia News Agency*, 20 February 2013, *anewsa.com*.

64 Park Jin-Young, "Fire Inspection of Bath Houses in Seoul: One Out of Three Fail Inspection," trans. Young Lee, *KBS*, 1 February 2018, *naver.me*.

65 "Death toll from hospital fire in Southern Korea rises to

46," *Yonhap News Agency*, 6 February 2018, *m-en.yna.co.kr*.

66 Lee Kyung-Min, "Miryang hospital faces probe over safety breaches," *The Korea Times*, 29 January 2018, *koreatimes.ko.kr*.

67 "Hospital apologizes for deadly blaze, but claims compliance with fire prevention rules," *Yonhap News*, 26 January 2018, *en.yna.co.kr*.

68 Choe Sang-hun, "South Korea Hospital Fire Kills at Least 37 People," *The New York Times*, 25 January 2018, *newyorktimes.com*.

69 "12 indicted for hospital fire in southern S. Korea that killed dozens," *The Korea Herald*, 16 March 2018, *koreaherald.com*.

70 Kim Hoo-ran, "Safety checks on 'high-risk' facilities begin next week," *The Korea Herald*, 2 February 2018, *koreaherald.com*.

71 Ibid.

72 Ibid.

73 "Framework Act on Fire-Fighting Services, Article 25," *Korea Law Translation Center*, accessed 26 November 2019, *elaw.klri.re.kr*.

74 Kyung Moon Hwang, "Lesson from Disasters," *The Korea Times*, 30 April 2014, *koreatimes.co.kr*.

75 Kim Hoo-ran, "Culture closely tied to Korea's vulnerability to disasters," *The Korea Herald*, 13 May 2014, *koreaherald.com*.

76 (3rd LD) Loft collapse inside Gwangju night club kills 2," *Yonhap News Agency*, 27 July 2019, *en.yna.co.kr*.

77 Ibid.

78 Ibid.

79 Ibid.

80 Kwon Oh-Eun, "The collapsed structure at Gwangju night club was built by an acquaintance of the owner who does not

have a license," trans. Young Lee, *The Chosun Ilbo, naver.me.*

81 Ko Do-Yea, "25 out of 35 two-story night clubs added structure without permit," trans. Young Lee, *The Dong-A Ilbo,* 30 July 2019, *naver.me.*

82 Ibid.

Chapter Seven

Recent Industrial Accidents

The reasons for including a separate chapter on recent industrial accidents in addition to the man-made accidents discussed in Chapter Six are threefold. First, the environment and circumstances associated with these incidents are different from those examined in Chapter Six, in that they occur while performing work-related duties, particularly for industrial companies. Also, most industrial accidents happen as a result of unsafe conditions or unsafe acts or both. Furthermore, industrial accidents have the potential to affect a large number of people or a large area. However, not all accidents that affect a large number of people are industrial accidents. The sinking of the *Sewol* ferry and the collapse of the Sampoong Department Store were not industrial accidents although they affected many people and both unsafe conditions and unsafe acts were present. Second, recent industrial accidents are currently producing profound repercussions in Korean society; and third, the potential to raise the level of consciousness of an entire country to the necessity of improving working conditions and uphold public safety has begun to materialize. Before delving into the specifics surrounding the events selected for discussion, the following two definitions of industrial accidents will help to clarify the parameters used to identify the incidents discussed in this chapter.

The *Collins English Dictionary* provides two definitions of an industrial accident:

1. An accident that happens to an employee of an industrial company during the course of their work.
2. A large-scale accident that is caused by an industrial company and affects a lot of people or a large area.[1]

In this chapter, I will focus exclusively on accidents that fall under the first definition. The samples will be limited to those accidents that happen to "employees of an industrial company during the course of their work."

The second definition comes from *Career Trend*:

Industrial accidents are severe mishaps that result in injuries to people and damage to property or the environment. For example, an explosion or fire at a pyrotechnics manufacturing facility is an industrial accident, as is the accidental release of toxic chemicals to the environment when a storage tank fails. Types of industrial accidents vary from one place to the next, but **most are a result of unsafe conditions and unsafe acts**.[2]

The "unsafe conditions and unsafe acts" portion of this definition is critical, because without these unsafe conditions and unsafe acts, the predisposition for accidents is significantly reduced.

As with man-made accidents in the previous chapter, the number of accidents that fall within the definition of industrial accidents remains sizable. However, as aforementioned in earlier chapters, this book focuses primarily on behavioral patterns within the Korean cultural context, not exclusively on accidents. Therefore, as I considered the potential incidents for inclusion and their related circumstance, I looked for patterns which epitomize the cultural norms to arrive at the specific events discussed below.

The Contractor-Subcontractor Relationship and Industrial Accidents

In the case of construction and other industrial accidents, select individuals, such as safety managers from the contracting and subcontracting company, are usually identified as responsible parties and prosecuted. If contracting and subcontracting companies are involved in the accident, the latter has traditionally absorbed the financial liability for accident risk. This absorption had been the practice for years, primarily to provide some legal and financial protection for large corporations or *chaebols*. Both government and citizens viewed these corporations as the engine of the Korean economy because of their enormous job creation power.

Conversely, in this relationship, individual subcontracting companies were essentially sacrificed. The government and the public viewed them as less powerful, less influential, and less able to create jobs on their own, and therefore, less likely to significantly impact the economy than major corporations were. This dynamic exemplifies the *gap* and *eul* relationship. Recognizing the invaluable contributions of the *chaebols* to the unparalleled rise of the Korean economy after the Korean War, the public historically condoned the special treatment given to *chaebols*. For years, this unconditional support derived primarily from baby boomers who lived through the difficult times during and after the Korean War. The baby boomers were those citizens who witnessed the critical role of the *chaebols* in the miracle of the Han River. However, given the recent number of fatal industrial accidents involving partnerships between contracting and subcontracting companies, an increasing number of critics of the status quo, particularly millennials, have raised their voices.[3] They demand a halt to the practice of "outsourcing of dangers" by enacting and enforcing laws that prevent the shifting of responsibility from contracting to subcontracting companies.[4]

Under the traditional arrangement, large corporations outsource projects to the subcontracting companies that submit low bids in a competitive process. Once a contract is secured, these subcontractors often cut corners on safety measures to remain afloat and make a profit. Cost reduction may include the hiring of low-cost irregular, contingent laborers to avoid having to pay benefits and avoid providing appropriate safety training. It may also involve performing tasks with fewer employees, even when safety measures call for workers performing their job in pairs. Each of these cost-cutting measures results in unsafe conditions.

Such was the case in the death of Kim Yong-kyun, a temporary worker at the Taean Thermal Power Plant operated by Korea Western Power (KOWEPO), who died on Tuesday, December 11, 2018 "after getting stuck between a conveyer belt and machinery while working his night shift alone."[5] His assignment "should have been done by at least two people for safety reasons," but since he was working alone, no one was available to shut down the equipment when Kim was trapped.[6] Unfortunately, the circumstances surrounding this incident are not unique; other workers have died while working alone, even though safety regulations require them to be working in pairs.

Some sources point to the disproportionate number of accidents in Korea associated with irregular or temporary workers. *The Korea Herald*, for example, reported that:

> In 2014, irregular workers, who accounted for 20 percent of the workers at conglomerates with more than 300 staff members, made up nearly 40 percent of those who died of fatal work accidents, according to the Labor Ministry.[7]

In an article published on June 2, 2016, *The Korea Times* reported a similar statistic for 2015. The article makes the following assertion:

Deaths of workers from subcontractors are not new. According to the Ministry of Labor and Employment, such deaths accounted for 40.2 percent of the total worksite deaths from industrial accidents last year [2015], up from 37.7 percent in 2012.

Out of seven workers who died at construction sites of Hyundai Heavy Industries this year [2016], five were subcontractor workers.

In Korea, [it is] legal and common for prime contractors, mostly big builders or transportation operators, to hire subcontractors because it is cost efficient and the subcontractors take charge of worker management instead of them.[8]

The statistics evidence a commonality between the percentage of irregular workers in large companies and the percentage of those who die of fatal industrial accidents. This link appears to give credence to critics of the subcontracting practice who maintain that conglomerates are outsourcing dangerous work. They insist that this practice engenders insufficient and ineffective safety training at best, and total absence of safety training at worst. Also, critics point to poor management of irregular workers as evidenced by lax supervision and persistent disregard for safety standards.

Judging by the results of a survey of 791 temporary workers conducted in 2014 by the National Human Rights Commission of

Korea, "irregular workers are more vulnerable to work [- related] accidents because they tend to be assigned heavier workload[s] and more dangerous jobs."[9]

Seoul Metro Accidents

I will begin the discussion of recent industrial accidents with those incidents that took place from 2013 to 2016 at Seoul Metro, which oversees the day-to-day operations of lines 1-4 of the Seoul subway.[10] Seoul Metro experienced four deadly industrial accidents from 2013 to 2016: 1) January 20, 2013 at Seongsu Station, 2) August 29, 2015 at Gangnam Station, 3) May 28, 2016 at Guui Station, and 4) September 3, 2016, near Seongsu Station. All of these accidents resulted in fatal tragedies, and each tragedy meets the criterion specified by the Career Trend definition of industrial accidents: They were the **result of unsafe conditions or unsafe acts**. They also meet the Collins English Dictionary definition of an industrial accident in that they happened **to an employee of an industrial company during the course of their work**.[11]

In all four cases, the individuals who were killed performing job-related duties were members of subcontracting firms contracted by Seoul Metro, which is part of the Seoul Metropolitan Government (SMG).[12]

January 20, 2013 – Seoul Metro Accident at Seongsu Station

Although information about this particular accident is rather sketchy because of the time elapsed since the occurrence of the event, reports indicate that on January 20, 2013, an inspector was killed at Seongsu Station while performing an inspection alone on subway screen door sensors.

According to the *Korea JoongAng Daily*, after this tragedy, Seoul Metro implemented new guidelines to prevent future "accidents involving screen doors."[13] Therefore, this accident marked the before-and-after era of requiring that maintenance workers perform their duties in pairs "at all times when repairing screen doors."[14] In other words, "working alone on screen doors became a violation of safety guidelines."[15] Also, "workers are supposed to only work on the outside of doors during subway operation hours and report to the station before working inside the doors."[16] However, because accidents under similar conditions kept occurring, it was evident that workers were not following the new guidelines consistently. As a result of the persistent accidents at Seoul Metro, the general public has questioned the effectiveness of the safety training and oversight of the company's subcontractors.

August 29, 2015 – Seoul Metro Accident at Gangnam Station

Soompi reported that according to the *KBS* (Korean Broadcasting System) *News*, Mr. Cho, a 28-year old maintenance worker was killed by a subway train while performing repair work on a screen door at Gangnam Station on August 29, 2015. Based on this report, Mr. Cho was working alone even though subway safety regulations require that "at least two workers [be] present at all repair sites."[17]

The report goes on to state other regulations related to operations, including the stipulation that:

> No repairs are ongoing while the subway is in operation, and that in the case of a repair that must be done during hours of operation, a report is made and appropriate measures are taken.[18]

However, the article also states that there are no consequences for breaching the regulations.

> A Seoul Metro representative stated, 'There is no penalty for not following the rules. There is simply a clause that states that in the case of an accident, the service company is to take full responsibility.'[19]

The paragraph cited provides beneficial insight about an environment that is prone to accidents. First, safety rules exist, but they are not enforced. Second, as noted by the company representative, there are no penalties for not following the rules. The first two points are patterns of behavior in Korean society that were observed and extensively discussed in previous chapters. These patterns concern such activities as driving and illegal parking, which are also related to public safety. Third, the Seoul Metro representative quoted above alludes to the contractor-subcontractor relationship as it relates to liability. In case of an accident, the subcontractor bears the full responsibility. As stated earlier, this practice appears to be in place to protect major corporations, including the *chaebols*, and by its very nature, it is analogous to the *gap* and *eul* relationship. In such a dualistic situation, the entity with the most influence, power, and resources receives better treatment or the most concessions. Fourth, the last statement attributed to the Seoul Metro representative implies that Mr. Cho, the maintenance worker killed in this accident, may have been employed by a subcontracting company. An article published by *The Korea Times* covering this accident confirms that Mr. Cho was indeed "an employee of the operator's subcontractor."[20] The operator was, of course, Seoul Metro.

The Korea Times reported that Mr. Cho "opened the door manually at around 7:30pm to run a check on it, although it was during subway operation hours."[21] A train arrived while he was working on the track side of the platform. Consequently, he was jammed between the door and the train. As a result, Mr. Cho sustained fatal injuries.

In *The Korea Times*'s article cited above, the writer quotes a Seoul Metro official as saying:

> Repair workers can open the door, but during subway operation hours, they are supposed to only work on the platform side, not on the track side.[22]

This statement naturally underscores the lax supervision of subcontracting workers by both Seoul Metro and the subcontracting company, and it suggests the possibility of lacking or inadequate training. It is unclear whether Mr. Cho was aware of the regulation or not. *The Korea Times* also reported that according to the Seoul Metro official, no one contacted the operations control center requesting a temporary halt to the operations.

Furthermore, he is quoted as saying:

> According to safety requirements, two or three workers should conduct repairs work during subway operation hours, but Cho undertook the job alone.[23]

However, the article based on *KBS News* presents a very different picture. The article, includes Mr. Cho's fiancée's statements, which appear to confirm the pressure applied by the subcontracting company and the unsafe conditions faced by maintenance workers. She is quoted as saying:

> He [Mr. Cho] used to complain that he was instructed to work alone during subway hours of operation. Since he was the youngest employee, he often took care of simple repairs and inspections by himself.[24]

Given the incongruence between the statements attributed to the Seoul Metro officer and Mr. Cho's alleged actions, one must question the level of supervision provided by Seoul Metro over the operations of the subcontracting company and its employees.

May 28, 2016 – Seoul Metro Accident at Guui Station

A 19-year old mechanic by the last name of Kim was killed by an arriving train while repairing a platform safety door at Guui Station on line two of the Seoul Metro. As in the previous two fatal accidents, Mr. Kim was reportedly working alone. However, safety guidelines call for this work to be performed by two individuals so they can look out for one another and thus avoid oncoming trains. Mr. Kim, along with 124 other employees of Eunseong PSD, a subcontractor of Seoul Metro, was "assigned to fix 7,700 platform safety doors at 97 stations."[25] According to an article that appeared in *The Korea Times*:

> In 2014 alone, platform doors on the four lines [lines 1-4] had some 12,000 malfunction reports, an average of more than 30 a day. Upon receiving a report, mechanics should arrive at the station in less than an hour or face penalties, according to the contract.[26]

This information indicates that the pressure placed on the maintenance workers caused by human resources shortage and time constraints was substantial and impactful. The article reveals that "The subcontractor [Eunseong PSD] refused to increase manpower to save costs."[27] However, the *Korea JoongAng Daily* reported that after Mr. Kim's death at Guui Station, the requirement to complete the repairs within one hour of a reported malfunction was eliminated.[28] If implemented, the elimination of this requirement would relieve some of the pressure on the mechanics.

According to *The Korea Herald*, in June, following the fatal accident at Guui Station, which was the third in three-and-a-half years under similar circumstances, "Seoul Metro admitted that [the accident] was due to lax safety standards and [a] flawed management system."[29] Also, after this incident, Seoul Metro finally began to enforce strictly the requirement that all mechanics work in pairs.[30] In other words, in order for Seoul Metro to finally enforce a basic safety rule, three-and-a half-years passed, three subcontracting workers died, and public pressure mounted to a point of no return.

After the deadly accident at Guui Station, the topic of outsourcing of safety and maintenance-related work received a great deal of national attention. For example, public leaders kept the pressure on Seoul Metro and other companies engaged in this practice by calling for a "halt [to] outsourcing practices."[31] Justice Party Chairwoman Sim Sang-jeong, for example, was quoted as saying, "Seoul Metro's irresponsible, indiscriminate corner-cutting practices caused the death [at Guui Station]. Furthermore, Seoul Metro is not the only company with such dangerous practices."[32] This statement amounts to a public chastising of Seoul Metro and an acknowledgement of the pervasive nature of outsourcing in Korea. The Chairwoman took the argument a step further by calling on Koreans to instigate profound societal change in order to prevent future tragedies when she said, "We must fundamentally change our society that keeps producing preventable tragedies."[33]

Working Conditions Update – One Year after the Guui Station Accident

One year after the fatal accident, *The Korea Times* published an update on the working conditions at Seoul Metro. The update included actions taken by the company to avert recurrences of similar accidents, as well as a report on the legal consequences associated with the Guui Station event.

According to the update, "the team-of-two rule [was] being strictly followed."[34] However, irregular workers were still "overworked and underpaid":

> Regular workers are guaranteed a rest after a nine-hour shift, but irregular workers often have to work 15-hour shifts, which entails frequent night duties.[35]

If accurate, these work conditions border on inhumane. Not only are they ethically unsound, they place workers and the public at risk, since the duties assigned to the mechanics impact public safety. Common sense suggests that the more hours that employees work without taking a break, the more prone they are to make mistakes. In industries dealing with public safety, an error might be fatal for the workers and, directly or indirectly, the general public.

Compensation

As far as pay is concerned, regular workers' monthly salary reportedly increases based on seniority, while "that of irregular

308

workers remains stagnant."[36] The victim's monthly salary was 1.44 million Korean won ($1,286) or 17.28 million won (~$14,532) per year.[37] This amount is dwarfed by the average annual salary of Seoul Metro permanent employees who earn "nearly 70 million won ($61,865)."[38] After 20 years on the job, the yearly salary gap between a regular and an irregular employee is 24 million won (~$20,402).[39]

It is not surprising, then, to find a high attrition rate among subcontracting workers at Seoul Metro. In 2017, *The Korea Times* reported that the company was "allowed to hire 206 irregular workers;" however, "the number… rarely exceeds 190, as many quit because of the excessive workload."[40] Based on the salary figures quoted above, low pay of subcontracting workers would seem to contribute to the high attrition rate.

Legal Ramifications

After the accident at Guui Station, both Seoul Metro and Eunseong PSD were held liable by the government. The prosecution charged officials from both contracting and subcontracting companies with serious professional crimes:

> The prosecution has indicted nine officials at Seoul Metro and Kim's employer, subcontractor Eunseong PSD. The two companies have also been indicted.

> The Seoul Eastern Prosecutors' Office said the nine are charged with professional negligence resulting in

death for failing to follow safety guidelines and [to send] officials for regular on-site safety inspections.[41]

Public Outcry

Because of both this instance and prior incidents at Seoul Metro, the public began to call for the company to stop outsourcing high-risk duties and to "hire all of its safety and maintenance workers as full-time employees."[42]

Pressure on Seoul Metro mounted even further, when the media reported irregularities involving both Seoul Metro and Eunseong PSD. News sources revealed that Eunseong PSD "was forced to hire retired officials from Seoul Metro, many without real mechanic skills, forcing the regular mechanics to cover more shifts and put their lives at risk."[43]

Further details of the irregularities were revealed by the press. Reportedly, at the time of this accident, Seoul Metro was subcontracting with four other companies besides Eunseong PSD. Reports indicate that all five subcontractors were forced to hire former Seoul Metro officials. According to an article that appeared in the *Korea JoongAng Daily* on June 17, 2016:

> There are 136 former officials of Seoul Metro currently employed at its five subcontractors including Eunsung PSD. Of them, 106 are aged 60 or older, and most of the remaining 30 are in their 50s...

All of the 136 were rehired at subcontractors under conditions that their mechanic skills and expertise were not to be tested; that they receive at least twice the salary of regular employees of the subcontractors; and that should the subcontractor go bankrupt, or if their contract with them ends, they can be rehired at Seoul Metro.[44]

Reportedly, Seoul Metro's practice of requiring subcontractors to hire former company officials was not new in 2016. The *Korea JoongAng Daily* reported that this practice dated back to 2008 when the company began outsourcing maintenance work. In that year, the number of retired Seoul Metro officials working at subcontracting companies was as high as 407.[45] The question here is "What is the impact of this unorthodox practice by Seoul Metro on public safety?" Clearly, the positions taken up at subcontracting companies by retired Seoul Metro officials with unspecified qualifications as a result of forced hiring means that subcontracting personnel had to perform the same amount of work, dealing with public safety, with fewer qualified employees.

The practice of requiring subcontractors to hire former Seoul Metro officials is certainly not normal business practice and may be classified as unethical at best and possibly corrupt at worst. Even if this is an isolated incident, higher orders of government have struggled with ethical issues.[46] [47] Although no causal link exists between the potential unethical/corruption issues at Seoul Metro and at higher societal levels, it seems likely that the cultural structure is particularly prone to these types of abuses.

The unfortunate consequence of this level of unethical practice is the stasis that results: The country cannot move forward and shake off the "developing country" image that Korea held in the decades following the Korean War.

September 3, 2016 – Seoul Metro Accident near Seongsu Station

On September 3, 2016, only three months after the fatal accident at Guui Station, another industrial incident within the jurisdiction of Seoul Metro claimed the life of a 28-year old irregular worker. The news article only shares the last name of the deceased, Park. Mr. Park fell to his death from a bridge near Seongsu Station. At the time of the accident, Mr. Park and four other workers from 3s Engineering, a subcontracting company for Seoul Metro, were performing bridge reinforcement-related work. They were reportedly "removing the supporting fixtures" from the bridge when the accident happened.[48]

Other Recent Industrial Accidents

The following stories about recent industrial accidents are related to employers other than Seoul Metro. The reason for including them is to demonstrate that specific behavioral patterns surrounding industrial accidents are observed in a variety of contexts and they involve different players. In other words, they are not exclusive to Seoul Metro. The inclusion of these stories is particularly important since the observations made in this book about the

Korean culture and society are based on patterns of behavior that have a tendency to recur.

June 1, 2016 – A Subway Construction Site Collapses at a Station in the City of Namyangju, Gyeonggi Province

A preliminary report indicates that a gas tank explosion in the city of Namyangju may have caused the collapse of an underground construction site. This incident killed at least four and injured ten people. Every single victim was employed by Maeil ENC, a subcontractor hired by POSCO Engineering & Construction to erect subway rails.[49]

As to the cause of the blast, *The Korea Times* reports:

> According to police, the explosion occurred because of the overnight leakage of propane gas from a tank, and it was the fault of the workers who failed to move the tank to a separate place the previous day as required by law.[50]

This statement lends credibility to the claim by critics that the emphasis on profit margins over public safety is the primary motivating factor behind the practice of subcontracting. The critical assumption is that this practice engenders inadequate or non-existent safety training, lax safety standards, and flawed management.[51]

The subway construction site collapse in the city of Namyangju is yet another example of an industrial accident stemming from a business practice between a major corporation and a subcontracting company. This and other recent industrial accidents aroused the public's concern about "lax safety standards."[52] Increasingly, the public seems to acknowledge that these standards result in "dangerous working conditions" leading to frequent fatal accidents involving subcontracting workers, and the practice of outsourcing dangerous work by major corporations.[53]

Per the frequent fatal industrial accidents, the country-wide accepted practice of subcontracting received widespread criticism. The Korean public, the academy, representatives from an occupational and environmental health agency, and even a representative from the United Nations Human Rights Office all voiced their opinion against these practices.

Professor Park Chang-geun from Catholic Kwandong University comments specifically about the subway construction site collapse in the city of Namyangju. *The Korea Times* quoted him as saying: "The workers at the subway construction site would not have been aware of the safety manual."[54] Professor Park teaches in the Civil Engineering Department at Catholic Kwandong University and he is a member of the Safety Evaluation Committee of Korean Infrastructure Safety Corporation, a government entity.

In the article cited above, in which he reacts to the same incident and searches for solutions that would stop the rash of fatal industrial accidents, the author credits the following statement to

314

Hyun Jae-soon, director of planning at the Wonjin Institute for Occupational and Environmental Health:

> The government should prevent big companies from entrusting safety work to a subcontractor. Also, the punishment for those responsible should be tougher so that an accident like this could bankrupt the company.[55]

The seemingly incessant fatal accidents involving prime contractors and subcontractors did not go unnoticed by the international community, even the United Nations. *The Korea Times* reports:

> The issue of subcontracting was also raised by the United Nations delegates who were visiting Korea to study business and human rights. Michael Addo, a member of the United Nations Human Rights Office, indicated Wednesday [June 1, 2016, the same day as the subway construction site collapses in the city of Namyangju] that prime contractors should bear more responsibility for things that happen down the chain of contracts.[56]

Each of these statements by individuals from very different backgrounds addresses disconnects in the existing paradigm of outsourcing of dangerous work. This relationship reveals the following repercussions: 1) inadequate or non-existing safety training of subcontracting workers, 2) the role of the government in permitting the outsourcing of safety work by prime contractors,

3) the relatively light consequences for violators, and 4) the abrogation of responsibility on the part of prime contractors in accident cases. These four areas should serve as the impetus for more effective outsourcing and the adoption of a paradigm that values public safety as much as profit margins.

In an article that appeared in the *International Business Times* (*IB Times*) regarding the subway construction site collapse in the city of Namyangju, analysts note: "Many safety problems in South Korea are due to poor regulation of the existing laws, and also wide ignorance that persists regarding safety in general."[57]

This assertion confirms Young Lee's and my observations about the litany of accidents, both man-made and industrial, that have plagued Korea for many years, especially in the recent past from 2013 to 2018. The country's technological advancements are in sharp contrast with the apparent disregard for public safety produced by an inclination toward efficiency and short-term financial gains. Financial gains along with profit margins attained through efficiency are vital in ensuring the viability of a company. At the macroeconomic level, they are the lifeblood of a nation's economy. When managed and reinvested properly, they enable a company and a country to generate economic growth. Young Lee and I are cognizant of the vital role that financial gains have played in Korea's economic and technological advancements. What we are suggesting is a paradigm that balances financial gains with public safety.

Subcontracting is a business strategy that generates financial gains, not just in Korea but in many countries around the world:

> In 2018, the global outsourcing market amounted to $85.6 billion. However, it's been estimated that as many as 50 per cent of outsourcing deals end badly. This isn't a reason to reject outsourcing. It simply proves how important it is to carefully choose an outsourcing partner and manage your supplier relationship.[58]

In reference to the industrial accidents reviewed in this chapter, especially those that happened in Seoul Metro's jurisdiction, particularly the incident at Guui Station since the company was reported in the press as admitting that the accident was as a result of "lax safety standards and [a] flawed management system," it is critical to reiterate the emphasis placed on managing the relationship with the supplier.[59]

A number of business sources, including MicroSourcing and Customer Think, cite the results of the Deloitte 2016 Global Outsourcing Survey to show the reasons why businesses engage in outsourcing world-wide. The top four reasons and their respective percentages are as follows:

> » Cost Cutting Tool – 59%
> » Enables Focus on Core Business – 57%
> » Solves Capacity Issues – 47%
> » Enhances Service Quality – 31%[60]

Based on the industrial accidents presented in this chapter, it appears that Korean companies that engage in outsourcing are in line at least with the top reason provided by the 2016 Deloitte survey respondents.

June 25, 2016 – Air Conditioner Technician Falls to his Death

Per a report from the June 25, 2016 episode of the major Korean news program *MBC News Desk*, a 42-year old air conditioner technician fell to his death from the third floor of an apartment building in Seoul. He was employed by a company which subcontracted for Samsung Electronics.

Reports indicate that the technician was required to make 60 repairs per month for a base monthly salary of 1.3 million Korean won (~$1,217).[61] The technician also received additional incentive bonuses of $5-$35 for jobs over the 60 base repairs.[62] The pressure to complete a fixed number of repairs and a chance to earn extra money to support his two children resulted in a distinct rush to complete the assigned jobs, plus more. According to the news broadcast, a good portion of the technician's salary was used to pay for his children's supplemental and enrichment education costs at *hagwons* or possibly university tuition. To earn the most money possible, the technician allegedly disregarded the use of required safety equipment such as a helmet and safety ropes. Reportedly, he also performed the work alone rather than with a partner.

Because the technician was working for a subcontracting company, Samsung Electronics does not bear any responsibility associated with the accident.

Sadly, this is not an isolated incident whereby an air conditioning technician loses his life in the course of performing his duties to earn a living.

July 9, 2017 – Air Conditioner Technician Dies

On July 9, 2017 yet another air conditioning technician surnamed Kim who worked for a subcontractor under contract with Samsung Electronics collapsed while performing a work-related assignment under similar circumstances.[63] He eventually died in the emergency room. According to his wife, Kim had not had a day off in four months.[64]

It is notable that both this and the previous air conditioner technician incident happened during peak season when temperatures and the humidity in Korea are high and the demand for air conditioning repairs spikes.

Aside from demonstrating the pervasive aspect and negative impact of the subcontracting practice in Korea, these examples provide a window to the human side of these tragedies, the pressure that these workers are under, and the sacrifices that they must make to support themselves and their families. In the end, some make the ultimate sacrifice in this subcontracting arrangement that seems to value short-term financial gains over working conditions and human lives.

December 11, 2018 – A Subcontractor is Killed in a Thermal Power Plant in Taean

Kim Yong-kyun was a 24-year old maintenance worker with Korea Engineering and Power Service (KEPS). KEPS was a subcontractor to the state-run Korea Western Power (KOWEPO). Mr. Kim died at a thermal power plant in Taean, South Chungcheong Province, approximately 130 kilometers or 81 miles southwest of Seoul, after being trapped by a coal conveyor belt. The young worker, who was into the fourth month of his temporary job, suffered a gruesome death when the conveyor belt, which was running at a speed of 16 feet per second, decapitated him.[65]

The Korea Times reported the following: "According to police, [Mr.] Kim was inspecting the conveyor belt alone although guidelines state at least two workers must do on-site work together for safety reasons."[66] The news outlet also reported that "[Mr. Kim] lost contact with the office around [10:00] p.m." on Monday, December 10, and his body was found at 3:20 a.m. of the following day."[67] Basic math reveals that the body may have been lying on the ground for five hours before being discovered.

Reports indicate that Mr. Kim received only "three hours of safety education before being deployed on the conveyor belt."[68] A similar statement from Mr. Kim's co-workers reported in *The Korea Times* appears to corroborate the claim of insufficient safety training at the site. Furthermore, his co-workers reportedly filed "28 complaints asking for improvements in the hazardous working environment but they were all rejected as they could cause 'facility damage.'"[69]

By skipping out on the full process of safety training for a particular project, which would be required for their own employees, large corporations save money. As such, they capitalize on the savings generated by hiring subcontractors instead of training their own workers. This arrangement enables subcontractors to hire irregular workers for lower wages and avoid paying benefits, thus indirectly saving even more money and increasing profits for large corporations. *Labor Notes* reports:

> …[Mr. Kim] had to pay out of pocket for a safety helmet and a flashlight while taking home less than $1,500 a month without benefits. This was less than half the wage[s] of regular workers, not even factoring in [the] benefits they can earn.

> At the time of his death, [Mr.] Kim's backpack contained a broken flashlight and three cups of noodles, the only meals he could afford.[70]

These statements encapsulate the low wages and harsh working conditions associated with contingent, short-term labor. Furthermore, they underscore the desperate situation that young people in Korea find themselves in when they fail to land a permanent position in a major corporation. In the broader context, these conditions begin to explain the emphasis that Korean families place on education. If children do not succeed in education, not only will they be unable to land a high-paying corporate job, but literally will put their lives at risk when forced into the undesirable option: working for a subcontractor.

Industrial accidents involving subcontractors are not rare occurrences and do not take place only at this particular plant. As per *The Korea Times*, 97% of accidents in the five years before this incident involved subcontract workers. Furthermore, in the previous eight years, 12 subcontracted workers lost their lives at the plant.[71] In spite of these statistics, the power plant received a clean bill of health from the government. In fact, the Korean government designated the plant as a "zero accident workplace" for the last three years. This designation is assigned when a company avoids major accidents or deaths. Moreover, "the government had also exempted KOWEPO from paying the premium for industrial accident insurance worth 220 million won ($1.9 million) for five years until 2017," as a result of the "workplace-without-accidents" certification.[72] *The Korea Herald* corroborated this information in an article published on December 16, 2018, titled: "Original contractors should be responsible for subcontractor accidents." The article confirms not only the savings amassed by KOWEPO resulting from the company's "safety" record, but also the government's practice of ignoring industrial accidents against the primary contractor when a subcontractor is involved:

> Korea Western Power, the company that operates the power plant, was given tax reduction benefits

based on its safety record because accidents involving subcontract workers are not recorded against the original contractor.[73]

The certification system only considers the accidents of workers hired by the company, but does not "count" subcontract workers. Consequently, the system incentivizes major corporations to expand their money-saving subcontracting practices by waiving industrial accident insurance premiums when no company employees are involved in accidents, regardless of the number of subcontractor accidents. Critics point to this disconnect as a way for major corporations to underreport industrial accidents, not only save money, but remain eligible for safety accolades. The unfortunate outcome of this "inaccurate" reporting process is that it perpetuates an unsafe environment for workers and for the public. Instead of working toward promoting public safety, the traditional and current system works against it.

Following Mr. Kim's incident, newspaper outlets reveal that the Korean public began to question the rigor of safety inspections at the plant. *The Korea Times* reports that two months before the accident, the Korea Safety Technology Association had conducted a safety inspection. This inspection included the conveyor belt involved in the deadly incident. The plant passed such review. Consequently, the publication surmised that "the inspection was carried out superficially."[74]

This incident received a great deal of attention from the public because Mr. Kim's death was the latest in a series of fatal industrial accidents. The frequency and persistence of these accidents underscores the country's emphasis on efficiency and quick financial returns at the expense of safety standards. Reports indicate that Mr. Kim's death is far from being an aberration. Instead, it appears to reflect the norm.

> [Mr.] Kim was collateral damage as the country has turned into a predatory economy that feeds on its temporary workforce. In South Korea, in an average year more than 1,000 workers are killed in accidents at their workplaces, the highest fatality rate among the 36 OECD member countries. **About 76 percent of these deaths are of temporary workers.**

> The alarming official figures likely understate the actual fatalities of temporary workers, as their accidents often go unreported.[75]

On June 27, 2016, the publication *Hankyoreh* published an article which exposed the reasons for the paradox between the relatively low industrial accident rate and high work-related fatality rate. The disparity in these rates is reflected in the data submitted for Korea, when compared to the OECD average. In 2013, Korea had an industrial accident rate of 0.59%, while the average for OECD countries was 2.7%, which implies that the work environment in Korea was significantly more safe than the rest of the OECD countries. The accident rate is calculated from the reported number of accidents per 100 workers. Conversely, Korea had a work-related fatality rate of 6.8 out of 100,000, the highest among OECD countries.[76]

The incongruity between Korea's remarkably low industrial accident rate and its significantly higher work-related fatality rate indicates the true state of Korean workplace safety. According to *Hankyoreh*:

> The explanation of this paradox is that South Korean industrial accidents are being covered up. That is to say, industrial accidents are not being called industrial accidents until death makes them impossible to conceal.[77]

An article titled "S. Korea industry's deadly conditions built on culture of cover-up" written by Bryan Harris, Song Jung-a and Kang Buseong published on December 5, 2017 by the *Financial Times*, corroborates the concern over the discrepancy between Korea's low industrial accidents rate and its high death rate compared to other OECD nations. The article reports that "labour experts, activists and even official government reports… allege that companies cover up the incidents" for the reasons already discussed.[78] Furthermore, corporations save significantly when they receive government waivers for insurance payments. Another reason behind the alleged accident cover-up is to avoid "damage to their brand."[79] The latter reason for the suspected accident cover-up makes sense since Korea depends so much on its conglomerates for national economic viability.

The critical question is this: How extensive is the cover-up of industrial accidents and illnesses? Although the *Financial Times* article quoted above focuses on acknowledged hidden industrial accidents and illnesses at Hankook Tire, the authors indicate that allegations of a "failure to protect workers" extends to other major companies.[80] This group includes the semiconductor division of Samsung Electronics, which has been snarled in a dispute with approximately 240 workers "who say exposure to chemicals triggered a host of diseases, including leukemia, lymphoma and brain tumors."[81]

In order to identify the root of the cause behind the issues with industrial accidents in Korea, the authors of the *Financial Times* article quote a member of the academy, Paek Do-myung. Mr. Paek works as a public health expert at Seoul National University, and explains the situation in the following manner:

> South Korea's industrial accidents problem is… more serious than other manufacturing powerhouses… individual safety and workers' rights have traditionally taken a back seat to the country's economic development and corporate competitiveness.[82]

This statement alludes to a contributing factor behind the miracle on the Han River: the national fervor for the country's economic development since the end of the Korean War, an unwavering commitment to a national cause despite the high toll paid in innocent lives. The national fervor is evident through the cultural element embedded in the statement. Koreans are unusually willing to make personal sacrifices for the advancement of the country. These two perspectives are discussed in detail in previous chapters.

As aforementioned, one of the financial incentives for underreporting industrial accidents is lower or waived premiums for industrial insurance. Another incentive "is the government's practice of giving higher [priority] to companies with lower industrial accident rates during the 'prequalification' assessment of companies that mean to make a bid for large construction projects."[83]

In 2018, thanks to mounting public pressure, Korea finally adopted an integrated system which requires contractors and subcontractors to share responsibility for industrial accidents. However, the policy only applies to "limited industries, including production, railroads and subways and those with more than 1,000 full-time workers. Other industries such as energy production, mining and shipping have been exempted."[84] Although the new system is a step in the right direction, it does not and cannot completely address the fundamental cultural issues underlying the safety problem.

The "Kim Yong-kyun Bill"

Subsequently, on December 27, 2018, "after a week of public outcries and protests following Kim's death," the Parliamentary Environment and Labor Committee passed an amendment to the Occupational Safety and Health Act (OSHA) (a.k.a. Industrial

Safety Act), also referred to by the media and the public as the "Kim Yong-kyun Bill."[85] The nickname honors the 24-year old maintenance worker who lost his life in the KOWEPO thermal power plant in Taean. Indeed, the purpose of this bill is to prevent future industrial accidents by "expanding the duties of the company hiring subcontractors… by holding it responsible for the safety management of the subcontractor employees and strengthening the punishment of the employer and company when a worker dies in a work-related accident."[86] For additional stringent measures, "the amendment bans corporations from subcontracting 22 types of high-risk job[s] such as metal plating."[87]

The adoption of the "Kim Yong-kyun Bill" is a crucial step, in terms of preventing future industrial accidents involving contractors and subcontractors. The question remains: Does the new law go far enough? Even though the punishment, both imprisonment and fines, for violators of safety regulations has increased in some instances in the recently approved amendment, the bill falls short of its initial intent. *The Kyunghyang Shinmun* reports that it remains a watered-down version of the original draft.[88] Most likely, the terms of the approved bill represent a compromise between the various political factions.

In the case of a fatal industrial accident when a contractor and subcontracting company are involved, the original draft called for an increase in the maximum number of years of imprisonment from the current seven to ten years.[89] Instead, the final bill maintains the current limit of seven years.[90] However, it does incorporate a new stipulation that when "the same crime is committed within five years, the sentence can increase by up to a half of the original sentence."[91] Nevertheless, the new law significantly increases the fines in a fatal industrial accident involving a contractor and subcontractor from the current 100 million won (~ $89,022) to one billion won (~ $889,742). Also, "when the company hiring the subcontractor fails to fulfill its safety and health measure obligations," the original draft called for a maximum punishment of five years imprisonment and fines up to 50 million won (~ $44,511).[92] However, the final language of the bill stipulates up to three years imprisonment or a fine up to 30 million won (~$26,706). Even though the punishment for violators specified by the newly passed amendment is less than the original draft stipulated, it is nevertheless significantly higher than the current "up to one year imprisonment or a fine up to 10 million won (~$8,900)."[93]

The adoption of this amendment signals that Korea is making progress toward decreasing the number of industrial accidents. As with any new law, however, it is yet to be determined how strictly the regulation is actually enforced and whether it achieves the desired purpose. In the broader context, Korea has indeed passed the "Kim Yong-kyun Bill" and other recently adopted laws to protect workers and make primary contractors more accountable. This new legislation indicates that Korean society is undergoing a subtle, long-overdue but profound shift in consciousness. In the long run, this shift will benefit the entire country. A profound change in priorities is beginning to take place.

Endnotes

1   "Industrial accident," *The Collins English Dictionary*, accessed 9 September 2019, *collinsdictionary.com*.

2   Emphasis added. Deb Dupree, "Definition of industrial accident," 27 December 2018, *careertrend.com*.

3   Our definition of millennials is as follows: Anyone born between 1981 and 1996 (ages 23 to 38 in 2019) is considered a millennial. Michael Dimock, "Defining generations: Where millennials end and Generation Z begins," *Pew Research,* 17 January 2019, *pewresearch.org*.

4   Choi Young-ae, the Chief of the National Human Rights Commission, was quoted in an article written by Jo He-rim and published in *The Korea Herald* on December 16, 2018 calling "for an amendment to the Occupational Safety and Health Act (OSHA) to ban 'outsourcing dangerous' work at infrastructure sites and to mandate that prime contractors take responsibility for accidents that occur at work sites." He was reported as saying, "To cut down labor costs, society is outsourcing even the responsibility to prevent accidents and disasters to subcontractors – 'outsourcing the danger.'"" Jo He-rim, "Original contractors should be responsible for subcontractor accidents," *The Korea Herald*, 16 December 2018, *koreaherald.com*.

5   This industrial accident is discussed below in more detail. Ibid.

6   Ibid.

7   Ock Hyun-ju, "Explosion at a subway construction site

kills 4 workers, injures 10," *The Korea Herald,* 1 June 2016, *koreaherald.com.*

8   Kim Se-Jeong, "Subcontracting causes accidents through negligence," 2 June 2016, *koreatimes.co.kr.*

9   Ock Hyun-ju, "Explosion at a subway construction site."

10   Cho Han-Dae and Esther Chung, "Subway workers are still hustling," *Korea JoongAng Daily,* 17 June 2016, *koreajoongangdaily.joins.com.*

11   Emphasis added.

12   Lee Kyung-min, "Subway accident shows safety ignored," *The Korea Times,* 1 June 2016, *koreatimes.co.kr.*

13   "Metro worker crushed by train," *Korea JoongAng Daily,* 30 May 2016, *koreajoongangdaily.joins.com.*

14   Ibid.

15   Ibid.

16   Ibid.

17   Leejojoba, "Young Korean Man Loses his Life in Subway Accident; Was Doing Repair Work Alone Despite Regulations," *Soompi,* 1 September 2015, *soompi.com.*

18   Ibid.

19   Ibid.

20   Kim Rahn, "Worker dies while repairing screen door at subway station," *The Korea Times,* 30 August 2018, *koreatimes.co.kr.*

21   Ibid.

22   Ibid.

23   Ibid.

24   Leejojoba, "Young Korean Man."

25   "Subway accident shows safety ignored," *The Korea Times,* 1 June 2016, *koreatimes.co.kr.*

26 Ibid.

27 Ibid.

28 Cho Han-Dae and Esther Chung, "Subway workers are still hustling."

29 Kim Da-Sol, "Subway maintenance worker dies during repairs," *The Korea Herald,* 4 September 2016, *koreaherald.com.*

30 Cho Han-Dae and Esther Chung, "Subway workers are still hustling."

31 Lee Kyung-min, "Subway accident shows safety ignored."

32 Ibid.

33 Ibid.

34 Lee Kyung-min, "One year after Guui Station accident, not much has changed," The Korea Times, 28 May 2017, *koreatimes.co.kr.*

35 Ibid.

36 Ibid.

37 Ibid.

38 Yang Young-yu, "Looking into the mirror," *Korea JoongAng Daily,* 24 October 2018. *koreajoongangdaily.joins.com*

39 Lee Kyung-min, "One year after Guui Station accident."

40 Ibid.

41 Ibid.

42 Lee Kyung-min, "Subway accident shows safety ignored."

43 Cho Han-Dae and Esther Chung, "Subway workers are still hustling."

44 Ibid.

45 Ibid.

46 Choe Sang-hun, "Park Geun-hye, Ex-South Korean Leader, Gets 25 Years in Prison," *The New York Times,* 24

August 2018, *newyorktimes.com*.

47   Joyce Lee, "South Korean court raises ex-President Park's jail term to 25 years," *Reuters*, 23 August 2018, *reuters.com*.

48   Kim Da-Sol, "Subway maintenance worker dies during repairs."

49   Ock Hyun-ju, "Explosion at subway construction site."

50   Kim Se-Jeong, "Subcontracting."

51   This claim derives from the information published in *The Korea Times*, which is factually correct to the best of our knowledge.

52   "Explosion at subway construction site," *The Korea Herald*.

53   Ibid.

54   Kim Se-Jeong, "Subcontracting."

55   Ibid.

56   Ibid.

57   Nandini Krishnamoorthy, "South Korea: 4 dead, 10 injured in explosion near Seoul," *International Business Times*, 1 June 2016, *ibtimes.co.uk*.

58   "Outsourcing," *NIBusinessInfo.Co.uk*, accessed 9 September 2019, *nibusinessinfo.co.uk*.

59   Kim Da-Sol, "Subway Maintenance Worker."

60   "The Ultimate List of Outsourcing Statistics," *Microsourcing*, 28 February 2019, *microsourcing.com*.

61   Shin Jae-woong, "Fell to his death during air conditioning installation, working without safety devices because of pressure due to tight schedule," trans. Young Lee, 25 June 2016, *n.news.naver.com*.

62   Ibid.

63   Gang Hee-Yeon, "Collapse during installation…Repeated

tragedy every high demand season for air conditioning," trans. Young Lee, 13 July 2017, *n.news.naver.com*.

64   Ibid.

65   Yi San, "South Korea: Death of a Young Worker Galvanizes a New Movement," *LaborNotes*, 2 January 2019, *labornotes.org*.

66   Kang Seung-woo, "Subcontractor operations criticized after young man's death," *The Korea Times*, 13 December 2018, *koreatimes.co.kr*.

67   Ibid.

68   Yi San, "South Korea."

69   Jung Hae-myoung, "Subcontractors' death not counted in gov't evaluation," *The Korea Times*, 17 December 2019, *koreatimes.co.kr*.

70   Yi San, "South Korea."

71   Kang Seung-woo, "Subcontractor operations."

72   Jung Hae-myoung, "Subcontractors' death not counted in gov't evaluation."

73   Jo He-rim, "Original contractors should be responsible for subcontractor accidents," *The Korea Herald*, 17 December 2018, *koreaherald.com*.

74   Jung Hae-myoung, "Subcontractors' death not counted in gov't evaluation."

75   Emphasis added. Yi San, "South Korea."

76   Jeong Eun-Joo, "How S. Korea has a low industrial accident rate, alongside the highest death rate," *Hankyoreh*, 27 June 2016, *english.hani.co.kr*.

77   Ibid.

78   "S. Korea's deadly conditions built on culture of cover-up," *Financial Times*, 5 December 2017, *ft.com*.

79   Ibid.

80   Ibid.

81   Ibid.

82   Ibid.

83   Jeong Eun-Joo, "How S. Korea has a low industrial accident rate, alongside the highest death rate."

84   Jo He-Rim, "Original Contractors."

85   Yi-San, "South Korea."

86   Nam Ji-Won and Jo Hyeong-Guk, "Lawmakers reach an agreement on the 'Kim Yong-gyun Bill' at the Last Minute," *The Kyunghyang Shinmun*, 28 December 2018, *english.khan.co.kr*.

87   Yi San, "South Korea."

88   Nam Ji-Won and Jo Hyeong-Guk, "Lawmakers."

89   Ibid.

90   Ibid.

91   Ibid.

92   Ibid.

93   Ibid.

Chapter Eight

The Big Picture: How Changing Values Impact Korea's Economy and Population

For hundreds of years, Korean societal values have been based on Confucian and Daoist traditions. As such, family values were cherished, and respect for elders was upheld above all else. In the past, Korea promoted itself as "the country of courteous people in the East," which translates as dongbangyeuijiguk (동방예의지국). Nowadays, it is still customary for people to bow with their heads to one another when they greet each other and to use a more formal Korean when speaking with elders.

Food Sharing Concept

Other notable values historically held by Koreans include generosity and sharing. The sharing of food with friends, neighbors and even strangers is widespread. This remains true even in modern-day Korea, with its amazing technology and infrastructure, competitive society, extensive use of makeup, plastic surgery and Botox, and omnipresent K-Pop. The concept of food sharing, which I discuss also in Chapter Two, is a touching and charming quality. It is a value that I admire deeply and one that will remain engraved in my heart for as long as I live. The number of times that I was invited to someone's home for a meal is too infinite to describe in this book. Suffice it to say that I felt honored to be asked to share a meal with various people. Also, I recall fondly being offered food by total strangers while traveling from one city to another using public transportation. It is common practice for buses to stop at rest stops for about 15 minutes for a comfort break. These rest stops, unlike those in the U.S. and other parts of the world that offer nothing more than restroom facilities and vending machines with sodas and junk food, are veritable vibrant malls that include full-service restaurants, coffee shops, music shops, and traditional Korean food mongers. During these breaks, because of the time limitation, most passengers, if they are going to purchase any food, gravitate toward items that can be enjoyed on the bus, such as roasted chestnuts. If I was traveling alone, it was not unusual for the person sitting next to me to offer me some of the food they had purchased.

On one occasion under different circumstances, I recall walking toward a Buddhist temple in a small town where I stopped to rest. Sitting next to me was a father and his two children. They were enjoying tangerines. After I sat down, the father half-peeled a tangerine and offered it to me. This was such a moving gesture that I could not imagine refusing the stranger's kindness. I observed a similar generosity or food-sharing behavior among the students enrolled at the American school where I taught.

Living so far away from home, I made an effort to maintain contact with my Korean friends who taught at the university level even though they lived in other cities. They became an important part of my experience in Korea, not only in terms of being able to become intimately familiar with the fabric of the Korean culture, but more importantly as a support network. In a sense, they became members of my extended family. We met regularly to share a meal even though we lived in separate cities. We would take turns visiting each other's city, usually on one-day trips. On one of those occasions when they visited me in Jeonju, they suggested that we have dinner in a restaurant on what they commonly referred to as "makgeolli/makkoli" street, so I could experience the food and accompanying raw rice wine called makgeolli/makkoli (막걸리), which is brewed to 6% to 8% alcohol by volume.[1] The food is served in small portions so as to enable the customers to taste as many dishes as possible. In the Spanish food vernacular, these dishes would probably be labeled "tapas." Makgeolli/makkoli was the alcoholic beverage of choice in Korea in the 1960s and 1970s. However, in the 1970s, it began to lose its appeal as younger generations turned to imported beverages such as beer. It is a fermented, unfiltered, milky-white, semi-sweet, lightly effervescent beverage served in bowls just like soup. Makgeolli/makkoli regained popularity among the younger generations in the 21st century on account of its health benefits and low alcohol content.[2]

As my friends and I were having dinner, I could not help but notice that I was the only non-Korean in a restaurant packed with people. This fact did not go unnoticed by other patrons, I am sure. The people sitting at the table next to ours were particularly curious about the type of dishes I preferred. As we continued to enjoy our meal, they became friendly and started to order dishes for us that they noticed I particularly enjoyed. I attempted to reciprocate their kindness, but they would not hear of it. I could sense that their effort to be friendly and kind was genuine. When I asked my friends whether this behavior was common in Korea, they explained that it was more typical in non-metropolitan areas than big cities like Seoul where the proliferation of Westerners had made their presence commonplace. They further clarified that it probably used to happen in Seoul a couple of decades earlier.

As I inquired about other food-sharing traditions, my friends related that generally speaking, when people move into a new neighborhood, particularly in rural areas, they make it a point to either prepare or purchase sweet rice cakes known as tteok (떡) and share them with their neighbors in their new community. Tteok is considered a celebratory food that is often shared on New Year's Day, weddings and birthdays. It "can range from rather elaborate versions with nuts and fruits down to the plain-flavored tteok used in home cooking."[3]

I was fortunate to experience many more food-sharing moments in Korea, too numerous to recount in this book; however, the one that probably stands out in my mind as an expression of kindness is one that occurred while I was bedridden for about five days with the flu. One late afternoon someone knocked on my door. Since my apartment was located in a secure area of the dorm that was accessible to residents only, I was particularly puzzled by the knock on my door. As I opened the door, I was surprised to see one of the school administrators who inquired about my condition as she handed me specially prepared, homemade chicken soup and side dishes in re-sealable containers. I was able to enjoy two servings of the delicious meal and it helped me regain my strength.

In all my travels in other parts of the world, I have never experienced such a genuine generosity in food sharing as I experienced in Korea. This tradition appears to be alive and well, especially in non-metropolitan areas. However, other longstanding traditions seem to be declining.

The Impact of Globalization

As we analyze the changes in values, traditions, customs and behavioral patterns that are taking place in Korea today, it is important to recognize the impact that globalization has had on cultures across continents. As a result, some of these elements are shifting or disappearing, others are being questioned, and still others are being imported and exported, then eventually adopted by other parts of the world. Because of the pronounced initial cultural differences, this trend is particularly palpable in the exchange between East and West.

For example, foods seem to be at the forefront of this cultural exchange. The American fast food concept, namely hamburgers and pizza, made its way into Eastern countries during the last twenty to forty-five years. McDonald's invasion of Eastern countries is a prime example of this exchange. The chart below shows the year that McDonald's opened its first restaurant in each of the Asian countries listed and the number of restaurant locations as of 2014.[4] The number of McDonald's locations in

Asian countries is an indication of the power of globalization in that it illustrates the proliferation of not only businesses but also traditions, practices, fads, customs, rituals, beliefs, and most importantly values from one country to another, and from one region of the globe to another thanks to television, movies, media, the internet, and access to unrestricted travel. Globalization is making us more alike rather than different from one another.

Figure 1: McDonald's Presence in Selected Asian Countries[5]

Country	First Location	Total Locations as of 2014
Japan	1971	3,300+
Hong Kong	1975	N/A
Singapore	1979	120+
Philippines	1981	400+
Malaysia	1982	N/A
Taiwan	1984	~397
Thailand	1986	~195
South Korea	1988	~300
China	1990	N/A
Indonesia	1991	~150
India	1996	300

Conversely, even though Chinese food had a head start in the United States as a result of the long history of Chinese immigration which began between 1848 and 1865 and coincided with both the discovery of gold in California and the start of the transcontinental railroad, Thai, Indian and Korean food has gained in popularity in many parts of the country. Similarly, in the West, more people are involved in Eastern-inspired meditation and yoga than ever before. The media has had a role in the cultural exchange we are witnessing. It is easy to see the influence of hip hop and Michael Jackson on K-Pop. Now, the K-Pop phenomenon has made its way into other parts of Asia and is gaining popularity in the U.S.

At a more profound level, there is no doubt that some of the evolution in values being experienced in countries around the world, particularly in Asia, and more specifically in South Korea, has been influenced in large part by the globalization process. Another portion of the evolution in values has been motivated by internal cultural changes instigated by country-specific conditions. The influence of Western values on Eastern societies may be more evident, and possibly more radical, because of the cultural shift that this evolution represents: Some of the values being adopted are diametrically opposed to existing traditional values. Some of the shifting values underway in Korea include the adoption of materialistic attitudes caused in part by the competitive aspect of the society and in part by influence from Western society, the emphasis on the physical appearance and the adoption of the efficiency concept, which is now firmly ingrained in the fabric of Korean society. Two value changes that are beginning to emerge are a shift from unity, conformity and consensus-building to an

343

individualistic model and the move from respect to disrespect for the elderly. The discussion below will focus on changing values rather than those that are already deeply embedded in the Korean culture, which are discussed in more detail in Chapters One and Three.

Family Values and Respect for Elders

Nowadays, family values are emphasized to a much lesser degree. Respect for elders is disappearing rapidly. Instead, youth and physical appearance are accentuated as witnessed by the emphasis on youth in the media as well as the extensive use of cosmetics, plastic surgery, and Botox. Wealth is one of the few commodities that keep the older generation in somewhat of a respectable societal position. However, the generational gap between the elderly and young people in their 20s and 30s is widening. Young Lee and I recognize that the challenges a generational gap represents are universal. However, the concept of respect for the elderly in Korea, specifically, is undergoing a radical 180-degree shift to disrespect for the elderly. Instead of referencing the traditional Korean phrase "respect the seniors" (경로), the phrase with the opposite meaning, "disrespect the seniors" (혐로) is often mentioned. The power struggle between the older generation, i.e., baby boomers, and the younger generation is even evident in popular Korean dramas. The growing gulf between the two generations appears to have three clear sources:

1. A sense that the older generation represents an economic burden to younger people, e.g., the higher cost of social services associated with a growing aging population

2. Political discord between the fervor of the older generation to support traditional values and the younger generation's rejection of the same

3. Youth's perception of the older generations as owning most of the individual wealth, which was amassed by heavy investments in real estate in somewhat of a speculative frenzy and which produced skyrocketing housing prices, particularly in large cities like Seoul, its surrounding areas, and Busan

Consequently, the younger generation sees itself as financially challenged by the older generation's aggressive investing, which had the net effect of making real estate unaffordable for the younger generation, given their salaries. Consequently, it is becoming more difficult for the younger generation to experience total financial independence without their parents' support. Many remain in their parents' home even after securing a job because of the exorbitant housing prices.

The other side of the coin concerning the perceived reasons for the generational gap between the older and younger generation is that it was the older generation who helped rebuild the country. The older generations are very aware of pulling Korea from the ashes after the Korean War through individual and collective sacrifices. Similarly, it was the older generation who helped to transition the country out of poverty through individual and collective sacrifices in the 1950s and 1960s and who helped to build Korea into the model economy that it is today.

In this tug of war between the two generations, it is important also to recognize the contribution of the younger generation to the transformation of the Korean culture, which is being exported to the rest of the world through K-Pop, soap operas, cosmetics, plastic surgery, and some of the most advanced technology. The technology coming out of Korea can compete in today's consumer-oriented society against all competitors including Apple, Ford, GE, GM, Google, Honda, Intel, Kenmore, Toyota, and Whirlpool. For better or worse, the Korean culture will never be the same. This cultural transformation is making significant contributions to the Korean economy as well.

As a personal observation, I recall experiencing a certain reverence for older adults and the elderly when I first began traveling around Korea in my mid-forties in the late 1990s. This respect for elders was evident in subtle ways. It was quite common for younger people to offer me their seat in the Seoul subway if I happened to board at a time when there were no seats available. It is true, however, that in those days I was one of a handful of Westerners visiting Korea. Nowadays, Westerners are more commonplace as the number of tourists has increased significantly, and so has the number of Western residents working mostly as educators in *hagwons* and international schools. However, I believe that age was a more critical factor than ethnicity in the Koreans' behavior toward me. In comparison, as I traveled in the Seoul subway during my latest stay as a gray-haired, 62-65-year-old man, no one except another senior citizen offered me his seat, which I politely declined. It is true, however, that now the Seoul metro, and perhaps others, has clearly identified seats for senior citizens, which I believe is different from 20-30 years ago. So, perhaps younger people do not feel compelled to give up their seat to the elderly because there are seats specifically designated for them.

Although the above example of the shift in the treatment of the elderly may appear mundane to the casual observer, evidence has been published recently in support of this observation. The National Human Rights Commission of Korea conducted a survey and published its findings in the 2018 "Report on Senior Human Rights."[6] Through the survey, the Commission found that 56% of the young people surveyed believed that senior citizens take jobs away from them. Another key finding indicates that young people believe that any increase in social services for seniors represents an additional burden on them. The report also showed that 81.9% of people in their 20s and 30s who participated in the survey responded "yes" to the statement: "The conflict between the younger generation and senior citizens is very serious."[7] Undoubtedly, the root of the conflict is complex and multifaceted, but it is natural for the younger people to feel the economic pinch associated with the increasing costs of social benefits for a growing aging population. There are indeed fewer actively working young people available to pay for these services. Unfortunately, the situation may be exacerbated in the future given the current low-fertility rate registered in Korea which is discussed later in this chapter.

The difference in political views between senior citizens and millennials may be a case of the older generations retaining traditional, age-old values and the questioning of those values by younger generations. Albeit subtle in many respects, the divide between these two entities may have become more pronounced and palpable in the recent past as different segments of the population declared stances on the impeachment of the first female president, Park Geun-hye. It was evident in the various demonstrations that took place throughout the country that senior citizens, for the most part, showed support for the former leader and reverence to her father, former President Park Chung-hee, who ruled Korea from 1963 until his assassination in 1979. Thus, her supporters identified with traditional values. Young people, generally speaking, stood on the opposite side of the scale: They supported impeachment. Also, as discussed elsewhere in this book, by adopting the term *Hell Joseon* in reference to Korea, some young people are voicing their rejection of some Korean values. They are notably rejecting the traditional formula for getting ahead socially and economically—through dedication, hard work, and sacrifice—as a result of their perception that the playing field is skewed in favor of the affluent. This topic is discussed in further detail later in this chapter.

Because of these differences, the older generation of senior citizens is increasingly perceived by young people as being conservative, inflexible, unwilling to or incapable of adapting to a new era with new ideas. As an example, the younger generation views the older generation as being technologically disadvantaged by lacking the capability to utilize computers and social media. Consequently, seniors realize that they are being left behind in some areas and fear further isolation and ostracizing. Thus, many are trying to gradually adjust to modern technology or at the very least, partially acquiesce to the demands of a new era. They are realistic enough to recognize that they cannot stop the wave of change by resisting it. Instead, some are trying to ride the wave. Senior citizens generally acknowledge the benefits of and sacrifices associated with the drive to become more efficient. They know that efficiency has moved the country forward in a relatively short period. Also, they have embraced the notion of maintaining an attractive physical appearance. Most senior citizens dye their hair black and use makeup; those who have the means to do so choose to wear stylish, youthful clothing. As far as the use of technology is concerned, some senior citizens make a concerted effort to update their skills by attending workshops or classes that teach them how to use computers, and social media. Many choose to stay socially active; they enroll in courses such as music, singing, drawing and traditional Korean dance to acquire new knowledge, fine-tune their skills, or merely to stay in shape. Some opt to attend church, participate in church-related activities, and share a meal with friends in their favorite restaurant. On weekends, some get together with friends to go hiking, which is a favorite Korean activity.

Despite these efforts by senior citizens, the divide between millennials and older generations remains vast, particularly when it comes to family values, individual sacrifice for the good of the whole, and respect for the elderly. Consequently, the older generation finds itself in a quandary. Should they adhere to the traditional values (e.g., emphasize the concept of individual sacrifice for the good of the whole; criticize the young people's option to postpone or avoid marriage; reject elective plastic surgery and Botox)? They realize that by keeping to traditional values, they are likely to grow the generational gap even further and become even more isolated and disrespected. Alternatively, should they accept the new values being espoused by the younger generation and provide support for them? Should they try to move with the times, close the generational gap, integrate into the country-wide decision-making processes and attempt to regain some of the lost respect? A third option may be to compromise. Perhaps elderly generations might accept some of the changes, but not others. Reversing the trend of changing from respecting to disrespecting elders is the responsibility of both parties. Both sides need to find a middle ground through an understanding of one another and respectful communication.

Emphasis on Materialism

Even though there are still plenty of television dramas that present historical perspectives and story lines involving *chaebols* and *gap* and *eul* relationships, the focus on materialism—youth, physical appearance, and luxury cars—is evident in Korean soap operas, which have been exported successfully to other Asian countries. It is true that these concepts are also prevalent in some American dramas; however, the difference lies in the pervasiveness and degree of intensity exhibited in Korean television dramas.

Some of the most popular Korean dramas that focus on materialism which have enjoyed success outside of Korea include the following: *Boys over Flowers* (2009), *Secret Garden* (2010), and *The Heirs* (2013). *Boys over Flowers* is a story about an average girl who finds herself attending a prestigious prep academy after saving a student's life.[8] *Secret Garden* is a Cinderella story between a stuntwoman and a high-end department store CEO.[9] *The Heirs* is yet another Cinderella story about a handsome heir of a conglomerate and the daughter of his family's housekeeper, an ordinary poor girl.[10] The role models in these dramas are good-looking young women and men who have shaped eyebrows, are in excellent physical condition, have undergone plastic surgery to acquire a chiseled look, and of course, wear makeup. Soap operas and K-Pop have both contributed enormously to the increase in the use of cosmetics in general. Korea has the distinction of being the eighth largest cosmetics market in the world.[11] Estimates indicate that the market size in 2016 was approximately $7.1 billion. Furthermore, the market expanded at an annual growth rate of 8.2% for the prior five years.

The surge in the use of cosmetics by men has been fueled by K-Pop idols who popularized an "effeminately masculine" or "beautiful male" aesthetic. Nowadays, it is common for Korean men, particularly millennials, to use cosmetics, and not just body and aftershave lotion and toner, but BB (blemish balm) cream and other cosmetic products:

> South Korea accounts for about 20% of the world market for men's cosmetics. This means annual sales of more than $1 million come courtesy of a mere 25 million men, and this figure will inflate by 50% over the next five years.[12]

The competitive nature of the society, in general, and the job market, in particular, appears to have influenced the rise in the use of cosmetics. In general, it is widely believed that skin appearance gives individuals an advantage in the job application process. Employers may have contributed indirectly to the concern with physical appearance, as most employers require job applicants to include a headshot on their résumé.

A cultural side note is in order here. In the United States, with a few exceptions, the practice of requiring job seekers to include a photograph with their job application is illegal. Two of those exceptions would be acting and modeling jobs for which the applicant's appearance is relevant to the prospective job. Several laws make requiring a photograph illegal, including "the Civil Rights Act of 1964 (Title VII), Age Discrimination in Employment Act of 1967… the Civil Service Reform Act of 1978, [and] the Americans With Disabilities Act of 1990.[13] It is important to note that all of these regulations were adopted in the U.S. in the latter part of the 20th century. The rationale behind these laws is to prevent discrimination in hiring and employment based on such factors as age, sex (including gender, gender identity, sexual orientation, and pregnancy), national origin, and disability. This difference between Korea and some Western countries, particularly the U.S., is subtle but important. In an earlier chapter, I referenced the ethnic and racial homogeneity of Korea versus the diversity of the United States. This factor, as well as the historical context of the U.S., has certainly contributed to the adoption of laws that protect the civil rights of individuals.

In Korea, cosmetic surgery and Botox are surgical parallels to an extensive use of cosmetics. Cosmetic surgery is quite commonplace these days in Korea, as it is throughout the world. Perhaps two of the most popular parts of the body that undergo cosmetic surgery in Korea, specifically, are the eyes and the nose.

The country's mentality around cosmetic surgery has undergone a significant transformation in recent years. As discussed in Chapter One, some Korean societal values today have their roots in Confucianism, particularly as it was practiced during the Joseon Era (ca. 1392-1910). Korean Confucianism espoused values and ethical practices including benevolence, politeness, diligence, obedience to superiors, wisdom, and goodness, which includes trustworthiness and honesty. Someone who adheres to these values and ethical practices would not alter their looks for practical reasons. Furthermore, having cosmetic surgery was historically considered shameful because essentially, those who had it done were trying to change the body that their ancestors/ parents gave to them. Under Confucianism, even cutting one's hair was considered disrespectful or disobedient to ancestors/ parents because the hair was considered a part of the body that individuals inherited from their ancestors/parents. In the infancy days of plastic surgery (mid-1950s-1960s), the older generations, baby boomers and older, considered the procedure dishonest or immoral, because through plastic surgery individuals change their appearance. It was also viewed as a sign of insincerity. Individuals who underwent plastic surgery were thought to be deceiving others. This deception consisted of deceiving others into believing that their looks were better than they actually were. In addition, there were guilt feelings on the part of individuals undergoing the procedure for disobeying or disrespecting their ancestors/parents.

Consequently, in the past, Koreans considered plastic surgery a taboo. Individuals who underwent cosmetic surgery, generally speaking, did not want it to become public knowledge. It was deemed to be shameful to admit that they had undergone this procedure because it showed that they were pretentious and highly concerned about their physical appearance.

For all intents and purposes, those beliefs are now considered passé. Nowadays, some Koreans have compelling reasons to undergo cosmetic surgery. Surgery provides them with yet another opportunity to invest in themselves and to gain an edge in a highly competitive environment. Koreans go under the knife to heighten their prospects in a job application process, a prospective marriage/ matchmaking, to underscore their socioeconomic status or merely to satisfy their desire to look better. Koreans who are wealthy enough to afford cosmetic surgery send a message consciously or unconsciously to the rest of their fellow countrywomen and men that they have money. Therefore, many are very open with their friends, family members, and acquaintances about undergoing the procedure. Plastic surgery has become less of a taboo and more of a status symbol.

Korea also exports its culture. Through television dramas and K-Pop, Korea is presenting its version of Hollywood to the rest of the world, particularly to Southeast Asian countries and China. As a result of the remarkable success of K-Pop and Korean soap operas, Korea has become a mecca for plastic surgery. Organized trips by medical tourism companies for people seeking plastic surgery are becoming more and more popular. One reason for this popularity, aside from the fact that Korean cosmetic surgery clinics are actively promoting themselves outside of Korea, is that cosmetic surgery in Korea, specifically in Gangnam of "Gangnam Style" fame, has developed a reputation for being very advanced as a result of the surgeons' reputation as being among the most accomplished in Asia.

As a result of this outstanding reputation, and with the help of the popularity of K-Pop and soap operas, people from Southeast Asia and China are flocking to Gangnam to have these procedures done. One of the reasons Koreans as well as foreigners are going to Gangnam to have plastic surgery performed is because Gangnam is where movie and television celebrities and K-Pop idols are having their plastic surgery performed. Also, Gangnam is where the best plastic surgeons and surgery clinics are located. Furthermore, Seoul's fashionable Gangnam district houses medical tourism companies that actively promote their services in other countries.

This effort appears to be well organized and to have the support of the Korean government. The website *Visit Medical Korea* offers medical tour packages in a wide variety of medical areas including traditional Korean medicine, stem cell treatment, knee joint stem cell treatment, artificial hip joint replacement, and of course plastic surgery and aesthetic. The website lists a total of 2,084 hospitals and 1,682 facilitators throughout the country. Facilitators are companies that provide medical tourism promotion and services, including consultation and hotel bookings. A spot check of the interpretation services available at these hospitals and facilitators include the following languages: Arabic, English, Chinese, Japanese, Mongolian, and Russian. The website indicates that its services are provided by the Korea Tourism Organization, a government entity.[14]

An example of the emphasis on materialism, as it relates to the competitive nature of Korean culture, is found in my personal experience with a parent's interest in her child's future success. This parent believed that taller people usually have greater success in life and their career. Therefore, she arranged for her child to receive growth hormones. During my experience teaching this student, he literally experienced growing pains and grew to be quite tall. By the time he was in the 10th grade, he was about six feet tall.

The Concept of Automation

The widespread use of automation in everyday Korean life is taken for granted by Koreans who profit from, and enjoy, the benefits of efficiency, convenience, and consumer savings that automation generates. Although automation is common in Korea, it may be quite subtle and unnoticeable for the average tourist. However, for a Westerner with the opportunity to immerse herself/himself in various aspects of the economy, the everyday lifestyle effects are striking. Some examples of effective technologies are discussed in Chapter Two. Those examples, and others, are reviewed here from an economic perspective. In today's Korean economy, automation relates to efficiencies associated with unemployment and other pervasive national issues.

Practical Automation that Improves Efficiency and Facilitates Better Customer Service

Traffic control dummies around construction sites: My extensive travels throughout the country enabled me to drive by various construction sites where traffic control dummies, instead of people, are used 24 hours a day to alert drivers to be extra cautious. Clearly, construction companies benefit by saving on personnel costs. Assuming that those savings are passed on to the project owners, they, too benefit financially.

Call buttons on restaurant tables: Call buttons are used universally in restaurants to provide efficient service for customers. The buttons enable diners to summon their server for any need. By using these call buttons, the client receives more prompt service; the servers are more efficient; and restaurant owners save money on personnel, thus making the restaurant more competitive. The savings are passed on to the customers, the ultimate beneficiary in this practice, in the form of lower food costs. As discussed later in this chapter, the proliferation of eateries is at the root of the competitieve environment in the restaurant business. Thus, restaurant owners need to utlize cost savings strategies to remain competitive and generate profits. Consequently, based on my experience, restaurant food prices in Korea are relatively inexpensive compared to some countries in the West.

Centralized self-service food-ordering system: These systems have been installed in food courts, at department stores, bus terminals, supermarkets, and rest stops where various fast-food restaurants are spatially close. The purpose of these systems is to make food ordering from multiple restaurants more efficient. These systems enable customers to first view the menu and food prices, place an order and pay their bill for any of the participating restaurants. Once customers place their order, they next proceed to the restaurant to pick up their food. By using these self-service food-ordering systems, restaurant owners save money on cashier personnel. Once again, the eventual beneficiary is the customer who enjoys lower food costs.

CCTV (closed-circuit television) cameras: CCTV cameras are ubiquitous in Korea. They are readily seen on streets as well as in and around buildings. CCTV is used for surveillance, grounds security, crime prevention and investigation, and parking enforcement. Consequently, police and security personnel costs are significantly reduced, if not eliminated entirely.

Speed monitoring system: Speed monitoring cameras are strategically located on city streets and highways. Through their use, street and highway patrol costs are reduced or eliminated.

Korean navigation systems: Korean drivers use navigation systems extensively. An added advantage of Korean navigation systems is the capability to alert drivers about the location of traffic/speed monitoring cameras. Given the emphasis on efficiency of the Korean culture, this information enables drivers to reduce their speed while their car is within the viewfinder range of the speed-monitoring cameras. Therefore, drivers might more easily comply with speed limits and avoid traffic citations.

Dash Cam Recorders: As described earlier, Korean drivers equip their car with a dash-cam recorder on the windshield that acts as a miniature "black box" in accident cases by recording all activity that takes place in front of the vehicle. The recordings are used to efficiently process claims adjustments in accident-related matters. By having the evidence readily available, claims adjusters save time on accident investigations, and customers enjoy a more convenient and efficient claims-filing procedure. Furthermore, litigation costs are reduced significantly thanks to the evidence provided by these cameras. Thereby, insurance companies save money on personnel by hiring fewer claims adjusters and customer service employees. As a result, insurance companies may pass the savings on to customers.

Client service machines in banks: Most bank branches utilize client service machines that issue sequential ticket numbers and direct clients to the appropriate bank teller based on the client's transaction needs and arrival time. This customer-service efficiency benefits clients directly and indirectly: Customers receive direct, quality customer service, and banks require fewer staffers to serve clientele.

Self-service machines in government offices: At government offices, customers who need essential services, such as obtaining proof of residency, utilize self-service machines to complete their transaction. By incorporating machines, government entities provide enhanced customer service and generate savings on personnel costs by hiring fewer office clerks. A comparable efficient use of technology in the United States is the self-check-out service available at some major chain supermarkets where customers who are inclined to use this service to avoid having to stand in long check-out lines can process the purchase transaction by scanning each of the items in their shopping cart, bagging their own groceries and using their debit or credit card to pay their bill.

Patient self-service machines in hospitals: As a Korean resident, I had the opportunity to visit both large hospitals and small clinics to receive medical attention over the course of my stay. The efficiency with which large numbers of patients' needs are met was most impressive. This efficiency is facilitated through the strategic use of technology. For example, I regularly visited a hospital which made use of patient self-service machines located in the lobby. These machines issue numbers for patient-processing purposes and direct patients to the appropriate window. They also pay for scheduled services, including doctor's visit and lab tests. Finally, machines even generate the patient's prescription after completing all services. Naturally, these self-service machines enable patients to enjoy prompt, efficient customer service and the hospital may pass on the savings generated by reduced personnel costs. Based on my observations, there is a proliferation of hospitals and clinics in Korea. Therefore, patients have many options. Consequently, medical clinics and hospitals are compelled to utilize technology to enhance efficiency and reduce costs on account of the fierce competition. Based on my experience, medical services in Korea are significantly less expensive than in the U.S.

Although Korea is a trend-setter in regards to the utilization of technology to enhance efficiency and provide better customer service, other countries are also making inroads in this regard. Hospitals in the U.S., for example, are also adopting technology to increase efficiency and provide better customer service to patients. Hospitals and other health care providers are now making apps available to patients so they can manage their health care by making doctor appointments, communicating with their doctors via email, tracking changes to their medical record such as blood test results, tracking the medications they are taking, and even paying their bills online. Clearly, by maximizing technology, health care providers reduce personnel costs.

Digitized systems in hospitals: In the previous Korean hospital scenario, once a patient completes the initial processing in the lobby area, they proceed to the designated hospital unit. Units employ a digitized system to manage patient intake and facilitate the processing of large numbers of patients. Once patients check in at the receptionist's desk, the automated system displays the patient's name and the order in which the doctor will see them. The technology enhances the efficiency of hospitals by processing patients in an orderly and timely manner. Patients feel satisfied because they benefit from efficient patient processing, which enables them to utilize their wait time effectively, as they know approximately when they will see the doctor. The system also helps nurses and doctors by informing them of the exact order of patients. From a financial perspective, through the effective use of technology, hospitals are able to save money by reducing the number of employees such as receptionists, thus decreasing administrative costs. Hospital savings translate into savings for patients as well in the form of lower medical costs. As aforementioned, by decreasing personnel costs and passing the savings on to patients, health care providers in Korea are able to deliver affordable health care services to patients, and survive the brutal competition in this field.

The purpose of including these automation examples is not to condemn Korea's implementation of efficiency into daily systems and institutions. Young Lee and I recognize that as societies advance technologically, automation is incorporated into everyday life. Similarly, advancements in technology facilitate efficiency in all sectors, which has the potential to affect enhanced customer service and cost reductions. However, it behooves policymakers to not only recognize the economic effects of intended and unintended consequences of maximizing efficiency, but also take into consideration these outcomes when making long-term projections and adopting economic policies that benefit all. The public has voiced complaints about job elimination caused by automation. However, once technological advancements are implemented successfully for automation purposes, it is practically impossible to take a step backward. Therefore, Young Lee and I pose a hypothetical question regarding the complaints about job elimination associated with automation: If it were possible to revert to a prior condition where automation and job losses did not exist, would the public be willing to relinquish the efficiency and monetary savings that automation has generated? From personal experience, it seems as if the public enjoys the direct and indirect benefits of automation, including efficiency, faster service, self-reliance, and lower prices, and accepts the inevitability of the job elimination that goes along with it.

Education

Korea has one of the highest literacy rates in the world. To support this statement, I will provide pertinent data from the National Center for Education Statistics (NCES), an entity within the U.S. Department of Education and the Institute of Education Sciences. These data are collected from OECD data provided by member nations. Per the NCES, in 2017, Korea distinguished itself by having the highest level of high school completion in the 25-34-year-old age group (those born between 1983 and 1992) among the 34 of the 36 OECD member nations that reported data in this category. While the average high school completion rate for OECD countries in this category was 85%, the high school completion rate for Korea was an astonishing 98%.[15] Not surprisingly, however, the high school completion rate for the 55 to 64-year-old age group was 64%.[16] These two statistics appear to reflect the emphasis that Korea has placed on education after the Korean War, especially since the 1980s. During this period, Korea also experienced the democratization of higher education, and an astonishing increase in the country's productivity as measured by GDP.

The Democratization of Higher Education

Among OECD nations, Korea has been uniquely successful at democratizing higher education. Consequently, in addition to having a high literacy rate, it also has one of the highest percentages of individuals with a post-secondary degree in the world. According to NCES, for 2017, Korea is third behind Canada and Japan among OECD countries in terms of the portion of the population 25-64 years old with any postsecondary degree at 48% or 11 percentage points higher than the OECD average.[17] In 2017, the OECD average among the 30 of the 36 member nations that provided data in this category was 37%. The percentage for Korea in this category doubled from 24% in 2000 to the aforementioned 48% in 2017 as a result of the democratization of higher education in Korea since the early 1980s. Only the small country of Ireland could match the astounding 24-point increase by Korea in this category in the same period.[18]

NCES further breaks down the postsecondary degree data presented above into two age categories: 25-34 and 55-64 years old. The data for Korea further underscores the enormous difference in accomplishment between the two generations and pinpoint the beginning of the democratization of higher education. Specifically, for 2017, the country holds the top spot among the 35 of the 36 OECD nations that submitted data on the percentage of the population who had attained any postsecondary degree with an amazing 70% in the 25-34 age group (those born between 1983 and 1992).[19] By contrast, the 55-64 age group (those born between 1953 and 1962) attained an expectedly dismal 21% in the same category.[20] The relatively unimpressive attainment of any postsecondary degree by the 55-64 age group is not surprising given that the people who make up this group were born in the years following the Korean War. No other country in the OECD comes close to matching the vast 48% differential between the two age groups. These data also provide further evidence of the amazing recovery after the Korean War and the central role that education played in the Miracle on the Han River.

The percentage of individuals aged 25-64 years old possessing a post-secondary degree is most likely destined to increase for the next few years, and it will undoubtedly continue to outpace the average of OECD nations by a wide margin. According to an article that appeared in *The Korea JoongAng Daily* on January 23, 2017, "69.8 percent of Korean high school graduates continued their studies at colleges as of last year [2016]. Even though the number of college-degree seekers has been declining in the country, the figure is still higher than the OECD average of 41 percent."[21] That almost 70% of Korean high school graduates transition to university is an amazing statistic; it is a testament to not only the fact that education is highly valued, but that it is viewed as the path to financial security, economic prosperity, and prestige.

This perception, along with the democratization of higher education and almost compulsive eagerness to earn a baccalaureate degree, has severe ramifications at various levels. One of these is the economic impact on employment/unemployment, not to mention individuals and families, given the amounts of money spent on private education from elementary through high school and beyond. *Hagwons,* along with private tutors, have become an industry in and of themselves. Parents see themselves having to spend a large portion of their income and/or savings to pay for their children's private education just to keep up with the neighbors, often having to go into debt to cover these costs. Another consequence is the level of stress that families and students experience. Parents feel the financial pinch and students experience sleep deprivation. Students generally remain under a great deal of pressure to meet not only the parents' but the family's expectations.

Of primary concern is the high number of cases associated with intentional harm that propelled it to be the leading cause of death among youth 9-24 years of age from 2007-2015. Critics may argue that the link between intentional harm and school-related stress has not been established through research. However, the potential correlation is difficult to ignore. Research has shown that 50% of Korean youths are dissatisfied with their lives. They have expressed shallow levels of happiness. They have identified school as the cause of stress. They spend very little time outdoors, and they spend very little time engaged in physical activity. Given these signs, experts are clamoring that the burden on youngsters be made lighter, that they be given more free time and activities in which to engage. These dismaying statistics beg the question: Are these statistics being treated seriously by Korean society?

Forced Exit from the Labor Force

One of the unintended consequences of the democratization of higher education is a high level of degree inflation. More students are graduating from university every year than the economy can absorb. Because of the large number of Koreans graduating from university on a yearly basis, there is a high level of unemployment and underemployment of highly-educated individuals. The overabundant labor supply makes it quite advantageous for employers to be financially efficient by refreshing their staff regularly to keep costs down. Therefore, it is common for people in their 40s and 50s to be pushed out of the labor force to make room for a younger, less costly, albeit less experienced labor force. Once again, economic efficiency is a factor. As a result of the degree inflation discussed above, job-related age discrimination is alive and well in Korea. However, given the practical nature of Koreans, it is not viewed as discrimination. Instead, Koreans consider this shift to be a direct result of the economic condition of the country, and thus a fact of life. Koreans know that their time as a part of the labor force is limited, so they prepare to make plans early on for this life transition that they know will take place sometime between their mid-40s and mid-50s. They know that during their 20s and 30s, they need to save money. Often, individuals who are pushed out of the labor force do not have sufficient savings for their retirement because of the expenses associated with their children's education. In some cases, after retirement, they still face educational expenses (e.g., the cost of *hagwons* or university tuition for their children). When individuals do not have sufficient savings and simultaneously find themselves jobless, they rely on the older generation to provide them with either a place to live and sometimes even sufficient money to start a small business.

Oversaturation of Small Businesses

Those who have access to financial resources, either theirs or their parents', or who can borrow money from a bank, often opt to launch a small business which does not require highly-specialized skills or even prior entrepreneurial experience. The most popular choices are coffee shops, convenience stores, pizza parlors and other food preparation and delivery businesses. However, the most common option is to open a fast-food restaurant or convenience store that is subject to franchising. The oversaturation of these businesses is evident, particularly when it comes to coffee shops, convenient stores, and restaurants. It is not unusual to find similar businesses in the same block competing for the same clientele. Consequently, the competition is brutal; working conditions are extremely demanding; in many cases, the income is less than minimum wage, given the long hours required to successfully operate small businesses. Also, the failure rate is quite high when owners lack small business management and entrepreneurship training.

OECD data reflect the situation for the entire country. They support the assertion that the percentage of self-employment in Korea is exceptionally high. According to 2018 OECD data, Korea's portion of self-employment is 25.1% of total employment. By contrast, the U.S.'s self-employment rate is 6.3%, and Japan's is 10.3%.[22] In October 2018, the number of small business owners in

Korea was estimated to be as high as 6.7 million, or approximately 26% of the economically active population.[23] The consistency in the high percentage of the economically active population that is self-employed is a testimony to the entrepreneurial spirit of the Korean people as well as the limited options available to individuals who are being nudged out of the labor force. These statistics may also be remnants of the days when Korea was still considered a developing country. Professor Ha-Joon Chang, who teaches economics at the University of Cambridge, asserts that "people are far more entrepreneurial in the developing countries than in the developed countries."[24] His assertion is based on data from an OECD study which shows that:

> in most developing countries 30 – 50 percent of the non-agricultural workforce is self-employed… In some of the poorest countries the ratio of people working as one-person entrepreneurs can be way above that… In contrast, only 12.8 percent of the non-agricultural workforce in developed countries is self-employed.[25]

The Korean Federation of Small and Medium-Sized Businesses conducted a survey of 700 small-business owners with less than five employees. They found that on average the small business owners work 10.9 hours per day, as the ability to hire part-time workers is limited.[26] On average, they take only three days off from work per month.[27] This reality underscores how hard self-employed small business owners have to work in order to make a living. As harsh as this situation is, it may resemble the life of small business owners in other parts of the world since running a small business is a 24/7, 365 days-per-year proposition. Even though the situation of small business owners is less than ideal, their options in Korea are limited.

Although it is impossible to confirm a causal relationship, high degree inflation seems to contribute to Korea's high unemployment rate. As aforementioned, this overabundance of overqualified candidates in the job market makes it financially efficient for company managers to replace workers in their 40s and 50s with younger, less costly, albeit less experienced employees in their 20s and 30s. In turn, this practice leaves a large number of unemployed middle-aged people with family responsibilities, some with pending loans used to pay for their children's private education. These people are looking for a way to make a living and possibly pay off those loans. Consequently, opening a small business is viewed as a quick and efficient solution for an individual's financial dilemma; however, the macroeconomic challenge remains unresolved and the high bankruptcy rate of small businesses is exacerbated.

Franchise companies make it easy for individuals with little or no small business management training to try their hand at entrepreneurship by providing the necessary services, products, and merchandise. Therefore, opening a small business by franchising is a simple and efficient, albeit risky, way of becoming a business owner. Ultimately, if the individual fails in their venture, it is the individual's financial burden, not the burden of the franchise corporation. This tension results in fierce competition amongst these small business owners, as well as a high bankruptcy rate. Many of these small business owners are forced to borrow money to support themselves and their families while they try to get the business off the ground. This predicament aggravates the family's financial situation.

Another reason why individuals may choose to generate some income by becoming small business owners after retirement is insufficient retirement savings. This insufficiency results from the parents' willingness to sacrifice everything, even their retirement savings, to support their children's private education costs. In the end, what appears to be a sure bet ends up being a long-term struggle for economic survival.

Conventional Expectations versus New Attitudes

In the recent past, young men were expected to be married by age 30 after graduating from university, completing their military service, and working for a few years. Young women were expected to be married by their late 20s. Nowadays, however, people remain single for a more extended period. Some remain single for a longer period to work and save enough money so they can successfully undertake the socially acceptable path. This path includes pursuing marriage at the appropriate age. However, members of the younger generation increasingly opt to remain single for a more extended period. In many cases, they choose to give up marriage altogether, on account of the financial commitment of having a family, raising children, and the fear of the inability to meet these expectations.

Fertility Rate

Private education costs are indeed associated with raising children and remain a source of consternation for prospective parents. The perception that these educational experiences are essential for students to stand a chance in the nation's competitive educational environment is universally accepted. Korean Statistical Information Service (KOSIS) data indicate that the fertility rate for the last ten years was as follows:

Figure 2: Fertility Rate 2008 - 2017[28]

Year	Fertility Rate
2008	1.19
2009	1.15
2010	1.23
2011	1.24
2012	1.30
2013	1.19
2014	1.21
2015	1.24
2016	1.17
2017	1.05

The fertility rate is not much higher even as far back as 1999. A similar phenomenon is also being experienced in other industrialized countries where fertility rates have been declining for years. Clearly, the persistently low-fertility rates are not high enough to replace the population. This trend is bound to have long-lasting repercussions.

Cultural and Economic Factors Contributing to Low Fertility Rate

More and more Korean young people are delaying, and in many cases, abandoning the idea of marriage entirely. This behavioral change appears to be a worldwide phenomenon, particularly in industrialized countries. In Korea, however, the prohibitive costs associated with raising a child, particularly the high cost of private education, contributes to these decisions to an unusual extent. An increasing number of young men view themselves as incapable of providing the standard of living that women expect for themselves and their children. Similarly, a growing number of young women feel incapable of meeting the social expectations placed on them. Traditionally, Korean women were expected to stay home to raise the children, take care of their husband and do the housework. Nowadays, Korean women are playing a more active role in the workplace; however, the social expectations are difficult to eradicate. Consequently, career women are finding it difficult to hold on to their career and meet the traditional social expectations, e.g., cooking, taking care of children, grocery shopping, and doing housework. Therefore, more and more career women are opting to remain single, or if they choose to marry, they may elect not to have children. Although these trends are pervasive in other industrialized cultures, Korea's cultural fascination with efficiency exacerbates these trends to a problematic extent.

Cultural, social and economic factors play a pivotal role in decisions associated with whether to marry or remain single or whether to have children. According to the Korean mentality, an ideal parent is one who can provide financial assistance to their children. This belief was confirmed through research conducted by Moon Moo-gyeong, head of international research and cooperation for the Korea Institute of Child Care and Education, who presented the results of a survey at the Childrearing Advancement Forum on December 13, 2016, and was reported by *The Hankyoreh* on January 1, 2017. According to the survey findings, "parents believe that financial ability is the most crucial requirement for being an ideal parent."[29] Furthermore, respondents consider themselves "inadequate as parents because of their perception that they are not providing enough financial assistance."[30] Therefore, it appears that some Korean couples view themselves as incapable of measuring up to these socio-cultural expectations and are opting not to have children rather than become parents at the risk of being unable to provide the necessary financial support for their children. Specifically, the survey cited above found that parents are spending "an average 24.8% of their household income on raising their children."[31] Furthermore, it was reported that according to the survey, "59.7% of parents feel pressured by these expenditures."[32]

Household Projections

For years, demographic projections about decreasing household size have anticipated what is already happening in Korea. Projections about households with children versus those without children, and one-person households, signal that the trend will continue through 2030 and beyond. According to a statistical analysis published by Statistics Korea in 2010, households with children were projected to undergo a significant reduction in the 20-year span from 2010 to 2030. Households with children were projected to decrease from 54.7% to 45.5% of total households.[33] In the meantime, households without children (including one-person households) were projected to increase from 36.7% to 45.9% of total households.[34] These trends will have a decided impact not just on the Korean economy but the society as a whole. Since almost half the time has elapsed since these projections were made, it behooves the Korean leadership to determine the accuracy of these projections and how prepared the country is for this eventuality.

Statistics Korea published the result of a similar demographic study in 2017. The two main differences between the 2010 and the 2017 study are as follows: The 2010 study compares 2010 and 2030 demographic projections, whereas the 2017 study matches 2015 demographic data with 2045 projections. The 2017 study also extracts the one-person household figures from the households-without-children numbers. In other words, all three demographic cohorts, including households of couples with children, couple-only households, and one-person households are presented separately.

The decided advantage of the 2017 study represents a double-edged sword. On the one hand, it provides projections further into the future than the 2010 study does. This advantage is particularly important for government leaders and others because it provides additional time to make the necessary plans to prepare for the future. On the other hand, human nature being what it is, is that key players may fall into the trap of complacency thinking that the year 2045 is a long way away and the urgency to engage in serious planning and take action may not be as critical. The 2017 study appears to confirm the trends that were anticipated back in 2010.[35] Specifically, households of couples with children are projected to decrease between 2015 and 2045. Conversely, couple-only households and one-person households are projected to increase in the same period.[36]

These projections have profound implications for the Korean economy and specifically, for families. Projecting what will happen in the future with a high degree of certainty is difficult. However, there is no denying that the demographic projections are beginning to materialize on university campuses. Therefore, it behooves government and academic leaders, policymakers, corporation CEOs (Chief Executive Officers) and CFOs (Chief Financial Officers), and economists to run computer models that yield possible scenarios. These scenarios will assist leaders to implement policies and set goals that will generate outcomes that produce sufficient jobs, promote economic growth, strengthen public safety, and help maintain social stability.

One likely scenario is that fewer working adults will be available to shoulder the responsibility of maintaining quality social services for a growing aging population. If these household projections materialize, and, as of the publication of this book all signs indicate that they will, unemployment might well level off. One variable that impacts unemployment is automation, which Koreans seem to embrace wholeheartedly. It is difficult to imagine a scenario whereby unemployment is not affected if innovation in technology and industry continue to advance. What will happen if business and industry continue to incorporate technology and automation into day-to-day operations in pursuit of enhanced customer service, higher efficiency levels and higher profit margins? Korea's track record seems to point to a continuation of similar practices. Will these practices exacerbate the existing high youth unemployment rate? Will they instigate social unrest or perhaps another wave of brain drain brought about by young people leaving the country in search of better job opportunities elsewhere? For the Korean economy to continue to thrive, major corporations must continue to innovate, generate sufficient jobs, and maintain or possibly increase export levels.

The efficiency generated through automation as well as technical and industrial innovation is already having an impact, not only in Korea, but in other advanced societies as well, for Korea does not have a monopoly on efficiency in all its forms. Efficiency is one of the foundations of capitalism. As a result, those of us who live in other capitalist countries benefit from efficiency and enjoy more leisure time than most Koreans do. The question is, "at what cost?" Korean style capitalism seems to have a more concentrated flavor like K-Pop and *kimchi* possibly as a result of the cultural values and idiosyncrasies, among them unity and harmony, conformity, consensus building, willingness to make individual and collective sacrifices for the good of the group, the emphasis on efficiency, and the *pali–pali* culture.

The Economic Squeeze

The Korean economy is being squeezed on both ends of the demographic spectrum, by both a low fertility rate and a fast aging population. According to Statistics Korea, the current and projected percentage of senior citizens aged 65 or over through the year 2050 are as follows.

Figure 3: Current and Projected Senior Citizens Aged 65 or Over[37]

Year	% of Population 65+
2017	13.8%
2018	14.3%
2020	15.6%
2030	24.5%
2040	32.8%
2050	38.1%

According to *Quartz Media*, the aging side of the double whammy situation (i.e., low fertility rate and an aging population) is described as follows:

With seniors on the verge of making up 14% of the population, Korea is on the cusp of becoming an "aged society"—a threshold that it reached much quicker than other developed countries. According to the National Statistics Office (pdf, p5), it took Japan 24 years to go from an "aging society" (defined as seniors making up 7% of the population) to an aged one— the number of over-65's stood at 34.6 million in Japan, or more than 27% of its population, according to figures released in 2016. It took Germany 40 years and France 115 years to make the same transition. Korea became an aging society just 17 years ago.[38]

Clearly, the current administration is cognizant of the economic impact of this precarious situation. The article goes on to quote a statement by the current president:

President Moon Jae-in said the country is facing a "national crisis," and that if the country doesn't do more in the next few years to encourage women to have more children, including child care, housing, and employment reforms, there would be "no way to repair the damage."[39]

Short- vs. Long-Term Solutions

The question remains: What are policy leaders, and the country as a whole, willing to do to confront this "national crisis," as the current Korean president terms this situation? Are they willing to approach these complex issues from a systemic or holistic perspective, or are they going to settle for short-term solutions? Is the nationalistic impetus going to resurface again, as it has in the past when the country faced difficult situations?

So far, it appears that quick fixes are the order of the day to stem the impact of the low-fertility rate and possibly reverse it. Some cities, for example, have implemented childbirth grants or one-time benefits to incentivize couples to have children and thus increase the fertility rate. Because cities award these grants, their dispersal varies depending on where the couples reside. For example, as of this writing, the Seoul government is allocating the equivalent of $300 grants for the first child and $1,000 for the second. The Busan government awards no grants for the first child, the equivalent of $500 for the second, and $1,500 for the third. These are all one-time grants that most couples rightly do not consider incentive enough to motivate them to have children, given the amount of money needed to raise them.

The government has attempted unsuccessfully to promote paternity leave, which is outlined by the Equal Employment and Work-Family Balance Assistance Act. This act allows employers to grant a child care leave for up to one-year per child under the age of eight. It is not uncommon for employers to be required to hire a replacement for the employee taking a childcare leave. For this and other reasons, the law presents severe challenges for small and mid-sized companies that do not have the resources of the large corporations. Korean workers are well-aware of these challenges. Therefore, although the law is quite generous concerning paid leave, Korean males are hesitant to utilize this benefit. They are often concerned that they may lose their job after returning from the child care leave, even though the law prohibits this result. Article 19 of the Equal Employment Opportunity and Work-Family Balance Assistance Act states:

(3) No employer shall dismiss, or take any other disadvantageous measure against, a worker on account of childcare leave, or dismiss the relevant worker during the period of childcare leave...

(4) After a worker completes childcare leave, the employer shall reinstate the relevant worker in the same work as before the leave, or any other work paying the same level of wages.[40]

According to an article that appeared in *Forbes* on August 25, 2015, only two percent of fathers in Korea take paternity leave.[41] The report also asserts that another reason for the lack of interest among Korean men to take advantage of this law is cultural: "Even though South Korea and Japan offer dads the most paid time off work, very few men avail of it due to cultural perceptions that raising a child is primarily the mother's task."[42] Yet another possible reason for the lack of interest in taking advantage of this option is the relatively low compensation. According to a chart provided by *Forbes*, the compensation that fathers who avail themselves of this childcare leave receive on average is 31% of the national earnings in 2014.

Figure 4: Where Fathers Receive the Most Paternity Leave[43]

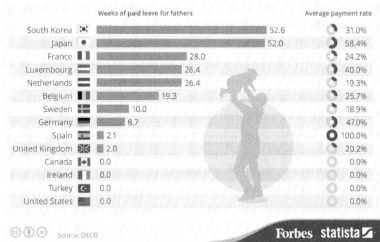

Where Fathers Receive The Most Paternity Leave

Weeks of paid leave and average payment related to national earnings in 2014

	Weeks of paid leave for fathers	Average payment rate
South Korea	52.6	31.0%
Japan	52.0	58.4%
France	28.0	24.2%
Luxembourg	26.4	40.0%
Netherlands	26.4	19.3%
Belgium	19.3	25.7%
Sweden	10.0	18.9%
Germany	8.7	47.0%
Spain	2.1	100.0%
United Kingdom	2.0	20.2%
Canada	0.0	0.0%
Ireland	0.0	0.0%
Turkey	0.0	0.0%
United States	0.0	0.0%

Source: OECD

Forbes statista

The Outlook for Higher Education in the Context of Demographic Projections

Available population data provides useful evidence for the future of higher education in Korea. The decrease in the 18-year old cohorts since 2000, along with the high youth unemployment rate, may indicate an increase in Korea's efficiency given that Korea's GDP has remained stable for the last few years. An article that appeared in the *Maeil Economy* published on June 18, 2018, cites some very sobering statistics from the Korean National Statistics Office.[44] Essentially, the 18-year-old cohorts have decreased since the year 2000 and are projected to continue to decline at least through the year 2040. The 18-year-old population is projected to decrease by a staggering 48% from 2000 to 2040.[45] This decline is clearly the product of the persistent low-fertility rate. The factors contributing to the low-fertility rate are discussed earlier in this chapter.

Figure 5: Actual and Projected 18-Year-Old Population[46]

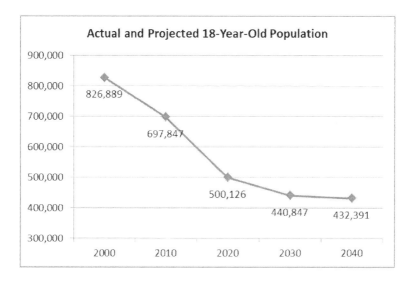

According to the article cited above, there are currently 197 four-year universities and 137 two-year vocational colleges. For 2019, the following freshmen quotas have been established by the two segments of higher education.

Figure 6: 2019 Freshmen Quotas; Four-Year Universities and Two-Year Vocational Colleges[47]

Higher Education Segment	Freshmen Quota
Four-year Universities	348,834
Two-year Vocational Colleges	206,207
Total Freshmen	**555,041**

The 18-year-old cohorts are decreasing in size on a year-to-year basis at a stunning pace. The article from the *Maeil Economy* compares the 2019 freshman quotas presented above to the 2021 quotas and goes on to analyze the actual impact of the projected decline in population just in a two-year period. The number of high school graduates for the 2020 school year is projected to be 456,000, or about 100,000 fewer students than the 2019 total freshmen quota cited above.[48] However, about 70,000 of the high school graduates for the 2020 school year are projected to be from vocational high schools; therefore, they are not expected to enter college or university in 2021. This implies that 170,000 fewer high school graduates are projected to start colleges and universities as freshmen in 2021.[49] Assuming that the 2021 quota is the same as for 2019, 30% or almost one-third of the college/university freshmen quota most likely will not materialize.

According to *Forbes*, this projected drop in the number of first-year college students will cause a financial hardship to the colleges and universities that will not be able to meet their quota. This drop translates to a reduction in funding which will negatively impact the programmatic quality of higher learning institutions as a result of the reduced financial support. This reduced support may impact local economies, as well.

The challenges caused by the long-standing low-fertility rate require Koreans at all levels including policymakers, university professors and administrators, national education leaders, economists, researchers, demographers, and citizens of any profession to put on their thinking caps and not only strategize how best to face these challenges, but develop a long-term plan to address them. Quick-fix solutions do not work in the long run; they seem to only prolong the pain and exacerbate the situation while giving the appearance that an effective solution is being implemented. As individuals with different backgrounds and expertise come together to face this difficult task, they must be cognizant that a nation is like an organism. They must take a holistic approach. Challenges of this magnitude cannot be solved if they are viewed in isolation.

Short-Term Solution to a Long-Term Challenge

A couples' decision to opt for one child is the rule, rather than the exception. This choice is evidenced by the long-standing low-fertility rate. Such a low birth rate appears to have a domino effect on the economy. With fewer younger people joining the workforce, thus reducing potential contributions to the cost of providing social services to an increasing number of retirees, the economy is being negatively impacted.

The effect of the low fertility rates is already being felt at the university level, where declining enrollments are not uncommon. Some universities are actively recruiting students from other Asian countries, primarily China, where university-aged students are found aplenty. Korean university faculties are concerned about the academic preparation of these international students. Faculties are troubled by the idea that these students are challenged because in most cases, if not all, they need to learn Korean before they can function effectively in an academic setting within the Korean higher education system. Without Korean language mastery, the academic achievement of these students is highly questionable. The overall concern for administrators is that the influx of academically unprepared international students may force faculty to water down the curriculum. International students also represent an added challenge to universities because they need to provide the necessary infrastructure for second-language acquisition, which includes Korean language classes to facilitate the learning for these students. Also, universities need to provide the appropriate support services to enable the adjustment of these students to their new environment.

The practice of admitting international students in more significant numbers to Korean universities is a relatively new concept. Therefore, its impact and unintended consequences on Korean universities may be felt for a long time to come. It appears that this practice of recruiting and admitting international students is yet again another efficiency-driven, quick-fix solution to a long-term challenge. Korean universities that are not as highly ranked have no choice. They either grow their student population, or they may face possible closure. Some universities, especially those in the lower tier category, also have the option of diversifying their curriculum to ensure that their graduates acquire the skillsets necessary to support business and industry. The question is: "Are they willing to do that?" This realistic and proactive action would certainly be considered viable in the United States.

Assuming a leveling-off of university-bound Korean students will occur, given the household projections cited above, universities will need to approach declining enrollments as a long-term challenge and thus generate long-term solutions. Universities that elect to identify recruitment of international students as a possible long-term solution need to recognize their moral obligation to develop or enhance the necessary infrastructure. This infrastructure includes student support services that exist while still upholding the academic integrity of the institution. If they wish to utilize this option to keep their doors open, they must ensure international student success and avoid negatively impacting the academic programs. Running two parallel but academically unequal programs would not only be impractical, costly, and unconscionable, but it would be a disservice to Korean students, international students, and the reputation of the institution. Building the necessary infrastructure may prove to be a costly proposition. Therefore, financial gains may not materialize for a while.

Hell Joseon

Some young people feel that the economic miracle of Korea does not apply to them. They feel angry, disenfranchised, and let down by a competitive system that claims to reward hard work and academic preparation which actually includes costly private education outside of the regular school curriculum. The private education cost that depleted their parents' life savings is one they cannot afford for their children, even if they dare to have any. This system was the very one that their parents had trusted to level the playing field for their children to have respectable careers, so that the children, in turn, could care for their parents in their golden years. For previous generations, hard work and academic preparation did provide an avenue to level the playing field for individuals from families with limited resources. However, some young people today feel that this is no longer true for the current generation. They feel both disappointed with the state of affairs and powerless vis-à-vis the prospect of having to give up the precious things in life that are valued by most human beings.

Today's generations of young Koreans goes by different names depending on the number of things they give up in life. The *Sampo* generation is made up of those who are forced to give up relationships, marriage, and children.[50] When giving up homeownership and social life are added to the list, they become the *Opo* generation.[51] It is not difficult to understand the young people's perception that homeownership in Korea is practically impossible for a working individual without financial assistance from parents or relatives. According to *Numbeo*, the property price index for Seoul in 2015 was 16.8 years.[52] In other words, given the median salary in Seoul, an individual would have to save their full salary for 16.8 years to afford an average-priced home. That figure appears to be trending upwards. *Numbeo* reported that the property price index for Seoul went up to 18.1 years based on the median salary in 2018.[53] Once dreams and hopes are added to the list of sacrifices, they become the *Chilpo* generation.[54]

For the younger generation, the list of things they must give up is so all-encompassing that they call themselves the *N-Po* generation, or those who must give up everything in life.[55]

The situation for this disenfranchised generation has become so hopeless that they use self-deprecating language to mock their situation. They hierarchize themselves as "clay spoon" (those who have nothing) as opposed to "golden spoon" (those who are privileged or born with everything they need) or even "silver spoon" (those who are born with some privileges, but not quite everything). To them, Korea represents a society where an individual's status is predetermined by her/his family's wealth or lack thereof. Therefore, if an individual is born into a family with limited resources, any sacrifices made by the individual or the family to improve their lot in life is of little or no consequence.

The situation for these young people has become so hopeless that they depict their lives in Korea as hellish and they use the term *Hell Joseon*, which alludes to the Joseon era, to refer to Korea.[56]

Many of these discouraged and desperate but adventurous young people have started a trend of creating a savings plan to emigrate to or obtain a working visa from another country, such as Australia, to start a new life. They hope to begin a life with a higher prospect of succeeding and maintaining at least some of their life dreams intact. Here is a case study from my personal experience: A university student saved money to leave Korea for Australia to be trained as a cook or chef. Before making his final decision to leave Korea, we gathered on a couple of occasions along with some of his closest friends. At these gatherings, we could sense his depression to the point where we were concerned about his safety. Luckily, he was a very mature young man and did not act impulsively. Eventually, he made peace with his decision to leave Korea in search of a brighter future and regained his sense of humor and thirst for life. Once he made his decision, he invited us to attend a farewell gathering with his friends where we all contributed financially according to our own means to help him make his daring journey come true. He left Korea in pursuit of his dream to become a chef, find a more solid financial situation, and to lead a life with less competition and stress. Subsequently, his girlfriend joined him in Australia, where they still live after almost five years. He is working as a cook, learning to become a chef and enjoying life more than he would have had he stayed in his native Korea. He is now in the process of applying for Australian residency.

I was fortunate enough to keep in touch with him via text messaging. I told him that I was writing this book about Korea and asked if he would be willing to answer a few questions about his experience in Australia that could be included in the book. He agreed. Below are some of the thoughts he shared about his choice to leave Korea:

> i feel very lucky to work in the kitchen where [I am] support[ed by a] good staff and [we] work as a team. I already achieved more than i expected. [B]eing a good chef is what i want for now.

> [If I had stayed in Korea,] I think i might [be] work[ing] as an office worker. In korea... My body would be comfy and relax, but mentally i don't think i [would have] stop[ped] searching for something that makes me happy.

> I decided to [keep] working [in Australia]... no need to keep searching for something related to my future.[57]

The feeling I perceive from reading his comments is a sense of relief. Being away from Korea enabled him not only to pursue his dream of becoming a chef without the social stigma of working in a service industry rather than in an office as a white collar worker, but it also relieved him from the stress caused by concerns about future employment. Based on my experience, this is not an isolated case. Other young Koreans are looking to pursue their dream elsewhere.

What will happen to Korea as a result of this exodus of young, energetic, entrepreneurial young people who are emigrating or moving temporarily to other countries in search of a better life?

Young people leaving Korea in search of a better future elsewhere present both a significant challenge to and an opportunity for the country. This phenomenon is not new to Korea. In the 1960s and 1970s the exodus of middle-class families and young people to the United States and other Western countries became a brain-drain concern. Later, this concern dissipated somewhat. Eventually some well-educated, English-fluent, second-and-third generation Koreans born in the West, mostly scientists and engineers, returned to Korea and contributed to the country's globalization efforts.

In spite of the unprecedented economic success of Korea since the end of the Korean War, it is evident that the country's economy has experienced some challenges in recent years. Part of the problem, especially during and after the financial crisis in the U.S., was caused by the slowdown in the economy. Decreasing exports, a slowdown in the Chinese economy, and the decline in the price of oil all contribute to this cause. Since Korea must import all its oil, one would think that the low oil price would benefit the economy. However, since Korea is an exporting nation of high-tech machines, automobiles and such, oil-producing countries had less money to import goods from Korea.

Gross Domestic Product and Per Capita Income

According to the World Bank, the GDP growth and per capita income for each of the last four years was as follows:

Figure 7: GDP Growth and Per Capita Income[58]

Year	GDP Growth	GDP Per Capita
2014	3.3%	$27,811
2015	2.8%	$27,105
2016	2.9%	$27,608
2017	3.1%	$29,743
2018	2.7%	$31,363

The Korean Finance Minister at the time projected that the economy would reach 3.1% growth in 2016, something many Koreans doubted.[59] In retrospect, it is evident that the economy did not reach the government target. For 2018, the government projected a GDP growth of 3.2%, which did not materialize. Even if the projected growth had been achieved, it is doubtful that this growth would have been enough to produce the number of jobs needed to accommodate the number of university graduates on an annual basis.

Youth Unemployment

Even though the national GDP is respectable, youth unemployment is considered high: "Youth unemployment in South Korea hit a record 9.8 percent in 2017, almost three times the national rate of 3.7 percent and worse than the 4 percent youth unemployment rate in Japan and 8.1 percent in the United States."[60] A large percentage of young people with a bachelor's degree hold irregular jobs that can barely pay the cost of a matchbox-style apartment, some groceries, and the cost of street fast food, with highly questionable nutritional value. These young people are working at irregular jobs often associated with minimum wage, or full-time jobs with part-time pay, and no fringe benefits.

The Moon government has expressed concern about the high youth unemployment, and as of this writing, his administration is planning to propose a supplementary budget to boost business subsidies. Per *The Segye Times*, March 21, 2018, the purpose of the subsidy is to close the large gap between the entry-level salary at large companies (~$35,000 or 38 million Korean won) and small/mid-sized companies (~$23,000 or 25 million Korean won) on a temporary basis. The emphasis here is on **temporary** for the next three to five years. *The Seyge Times* also reports that many people believe that this subsidy will not help to solve the fundamental problems associated with high youth unemployment. A similar, previously-implemented, unemployment subsidy program also failed. People have expressed concerns in social media about the proposed subsidies. Many predict the program will fail for the following reasons:

1. Several factors seem to indicate that working conditions are better in large companies than in small/mid-sized companies.

   a. People claim that work hours are longer in small/
       mid-sized companies than in large companies.

   b. Smaller companies occasionally cannot pay
       employee salaries on time.

   c. Smaller companies tend to hire temporary workers or
       contract workers usually for a maximum of two years.
       These individuals have reason to be severely anxious
       about their future after the initial two years.

   d. Many young people would not settle for a salary-
       matching situation.

2. Workers have expressed a concern that the three- to
    five-year subsidy is a stopgap measure with potentially
    negative impacts in the long run. They are concerned that
    the gap in both salary and working conditions between
    small to mid-sized companies and large companies will
    be wider after the subsidy expires. Consequently, their
    purchasing power and quality of life will be negatively
    impacted. Young people are particularly apprehensive
    that they would be placing their future at risk for a small
    temporary subsidy.

Back to the Roots

Given the high rates of urbanization experienced from the
1960s-early 1990s discussed in Chapter Six, it is not surprising to
find that the farm population underwent a similarly astounding
decrease between the late 1960s and the early 21st century: "The
combined number of South Koreans [living] on farms plunged to
2.84 million in 2013 from 14.4 million in 1970."[61]

In recent years, however, a small but significant trend has begun to emerge. Because of the amazing urbanization pace that has been pervasive since the 1960s, and the lifestyle challenges that come with it such as overburdened infrastructure, traffic congestion, housing shortages, exorbitant housing costs, environmental factors, air pollution, and the faster life pace of the big cities, some families are choosing to return to rural life. These families are in search of a slower life pace, close contact with nature and a much less competitive environment. The article from *Yonhap News* cited above states that in 2015, "a total of 11,959 households living in the countryside came from big cities…"[62] This figure represents an 11.2% increase over the 10,758 households the prior year.

Albeit small, this migration trend towards rural life, together with the exodus of young people, and the *Hell Joseon* sentiment all represent an indictment of some of the values that Koreans adopted as a nation and that were instrumental in achieving the miracle on the Han River. Having tasted economic and technological success, these contrarian waves are most likely not sufficiently powerful enough to change Korea's path. However, could they be warning signs to the rest of the country that something is amiss? Could they be a wake-up call to remind everyone that the pendulum has swung too far in one direction? Could they be a call to the citizenry that it is time to become more humanistic and take better care of each other, prevent future catastrophes, and reduce the widening gap between the haves and have-nots?

Endnotes

1   Adam H. Callaghan, "Should you be drinking makgeolli?", *Eater*, 20 February 2017, *www.eater.com*.

2   "Makgeolli," *Wikipedia*, accessed 12 October 2019, *www.wikipedia.org*.

3   "Tteok," Trifood, accessed 2 November 2019, *www.trifood.com*.

4   Michelle Yen, "First McDonalds Location in Asia," *Getchee*, 20 February 2014, *blog.getchee.com*.

5   Ibid.

6   "Growing Hate toward Elders: "Good Reasons to Hate Elders" vs. "Still Need to Respect Elders," trans. Young Lee, *World Daily* 18 September 2019.

7   Ibid.

8   *Boys Over Flowers*, dir. Jeon Ke-Sang, *Netflix*, accessed 23 August 2019, *netflix.com*.

9   "Secret Garden (2010)," *MyDramaList*, accessed 10 October 2019, *mydramalist.com*.

10   "The Heirs," *MyDramaList*, accessed 10 October 2019, *mydramalist.com*.

11   "Cosmetics," *export.gov*, accessed 10 October 2019, *2016.export.gov*.

12   Ibid.

13   Wanda Thibodeaux, "Is there a law against asking for a photo with a job application?", *BizFluent*, last accessed 2 November 2019, *bizfluent.com*.

14   "Hospitals," *Visit Medical Korea*, accessed 21 August 2019, *english.visitmedicalkorea.com*.

15   "International Educational Attainment, *NCES National*

Center for Education Statistics, last updated May 2020, *nces.ed.gov*.

16   Ibid.

17   Ibid.

18   Ibid.

19   Ibid.

20   Ibid.

21   Kim Young-Nam, "Enrollment in Vocational Schools Surges," *Korea JoongAng Daily*, 23 January 2017, *koreajoongangdaily.joins.com*.

22   "Self-employment rate," *OECD Data*, last accessed 2 November 2019, data.oecd.org.

23   Heo In-Hoe, "6.7 Million Small Business Owners Angry about High Rent and Minimum Wage Regulation," trans. Young Lee, *JoongAng Magazine* no. 11, 17 October 2018.

24   Ha-Joon Chang, *23 Things They Don't Tell You About Capitalism*, New York: Bloomsbury Press, 2010.

25   Ibid.

26   Park Sung-Jin, "Small Business Owners Work 11 Hours a Day and Take 3 Days off Per Month," trans. Young Lee, *Yonhap News*, accessed 21 August 2019, *naver.me*.

27   Ibid.

28   "Major indicators of Korea," *Korean Statistical Information Service*, accessed 2 November 2019, *kosis.kr*.

29   Hwangbo Yon, "Parents spending roughly a quarter of their income on raising kids," *Hankoryeh*, 1 January 2017, *english.hani.co.kr*.

30   Ibid.

31   Ibid.

32   Ibid.

33   *Statistics Korea*, accessed 10 October 2019, *kostat.go.kr*.

34   Ibid.

35   "Household Projections for Korea, 2015-2045," *Statistics Korea*, accessed 10 October 2019, *kostat.go.kr*.

36   Ibid.

37   *Statistics Korea*.

38   Isabella Steger, "South Korea is Aging Faster than Any Other Developed Country," *Quartz*, 31 August 2017, *qz.com*.

39   Ibid.

40   "Equal Employment Opportunity and Work-Family Balance Assistance Act," *Korea Law Translation Center*, accessed 10 October 2019, *elaw.klri.re.kr*.

41   Niall MacCarthy, "Where do Fathers Receive the Most Paternity Leave," *Forbes*, 25 August 2015, *forbes.com*.

42   Ibid.

43   Ibid.

44   Kim Hyo-Hye, "60 4-year Universities May Not Receive any Students in 2020," trans. Young Lee, *Maeil Economy*, 18 June 2018, *news.naver.com*.

45   Ibid.

46   Ibid.

47   Ibid.

48   Ibid.

49   Ibid.

50   "The Young and Sick: 'Opo' to 'Chilpo,' The 'Give-Up' Generation," *Korea BANG*, accessed 22 August 2018, *koreabang.com*.

51   Ibid.

52   "Cost of Living," *Numbeo*, accessed 10 October 2019, *numbeo.com*.

53   Ibid.

54   "The Young and Sick," *Korea BANG*.

55   Ibid.

56   Ibid.

57   Anonymous, personal interview by John Gonzalez, text message, 8 September 2019.

58   *The World Bank*, accessed 24 August 2018, *data.worldbank.org*.

59   Donald Kirk, "What is 'Korean Miracle'? 'Hell Joseon Is More Like it As Economy Flounders," *Forbes*, 27 February 2016, *forbes.com*.

60   *Reuters*, last accessed 10 October 2019, *reuters.com*.

61   "More S. Koreans go back to rural life in 2015," *Yonhap News Agency*, 30 June 2016, *m-en.yna.co.kr*.

62   Ibid.

Afterword

Since the end of the Korean War, the distinct characteristics of the hard-working, entrepreneurial, goal-oriented, practical, and sacrificial Korean people have contributed enormously to the nation's macroeconomic and technological advancements. Equally important for the miracle on the Han River was the tremendous value Koreans place on education and efficiency. They recognize both education and efficiency as the keys to success for individuals in the country's highly competitive environment. As alluded to earlier, education is one of the pillars of the Korean culture. Thus, it is emphasized from elementary to graduate school. Also, efficiency is similarly embedded into the fabric of the culture starting at an early age in education and from business to the top levels of the socioeconomic and political strata. The latter is evidenced by the public expectancy of 3% annual growth in GDP. This expectancy is based on the country's actual annual GDP growth for the last few years. Since 2013, Korea's economic growth has hovered consistently between 2.7 % and 3.3%.[1] Because the success of a presidency is largely determined by this annual metric during the single five-year term, the emphasis is placed on short-term rather than long-term goals. This expectation exemplifies Korea's obsession with quick results.

Some Koreans I have spoken with feel that it is time to revisit the question of the one-term presidential term and consider adopting a two-term limit. If this change was enacted, it would enable a sitting president to set both short and long-term goals for the nation. The attitudes of other Koreans about this shift run the gamut from hesitant to skeptical. The latter group, the skeptics, are concerned that implementing a two-term limit might open the door to a possible dictatorship. The memory of dictatorial rule brings back memories of years past, particularly for baby boomers. Furthermore, Koreans seem to have an understandable, instinctual aversion to dictatorships given the constant threat from the north in addition to their own past history. This concern is valid and deserves to be respected. It is clearly up to the Korean people to decide whether they will keep the current format and maintain the focus on short-term goals. Otherwise, they could adopt a two-term limit which would provide continuity in national policies and change the national attention from short to long-term goals with appropriate intermediary measurable objectives. This fundamental change at the national level, if implemented, would require a paradigm shift throughout the rest of society. This shift would require less of an emphasis on quick results and more on solid, long-range goals.

In essence, the one-term limit resonates with the concept of efficiency. If, on the one hand, a president implements policies that promote a strong economy and contribute to a "successful" regime, the mission will be accomplished. If, on the other hand, the president's policies are viewed by the general public as ineffective in maintaining a strong 3% annual GDP or higher, the administration is considered unsuccessful. In such a case, the pain is endured for only one term. Afterwards, a new person can have the opportunity to change course and lead the country to more prosperous times.

The Role of Education

As discussed earlier, the competitive nature of Korean society has resulted in a Korean emphasis on education, and specifically private education, to a higher degree than in other countries. The promotion of education as an efficient formula or a panacea for future financial well-being has turned Korea into a country with not only one of the highest literacy rates, but also one of the highest percentages of an educated population in the world. The nation has embraced the concept that education is an escape from poverty and a way to maintain or improve one's socioeconomic status.

The belief that education is the key to success, and the fervor with which Koreans pursue higher education degrees, has created a period of degree inflation. Currently, Korea is experiencing an oversaturation of individuals possessing undergraduate and postgraduate degrees. As aforementioned, traditionally a Bachelor of Arts or Sciences degree from a reputable university opened the door to the "dream job" with a concomitant higher salary and job security at one of the conglomerates or *chaebols*. However, the present-day job trajectory in Korea is very different than it was for baby boomers. A bachelor's degree from a top-tier university no longer guarantees an ideal job. Therefore, young Koreans are frustrated at the inability of the government and large corporations to create well-paying permanent jobs in sufficient numbers to accommodate the number of students graduating from universities on an annual basis. The insufficient number of desirable permanent jobs in government and at major corporations has contributed enormously to the competitive nature of the Korean society. It is important to clarify that in this case, the designation of "permanent" jobs excludes contingent full-time jobs that are allowed for a maximum period of two-years. Several factors have contributed to Korea's emphasis on efficiency in the workplace. These are reflected in the extensive use of contingent workers to minimize labor costs, as well as the 1997 Asian Financial Crisis, known among Koreans as the IMF Crisis, globalization, which requires corporations to survive in a competitive global market, and the reliance of the Korean economy on exports, which forces Korean companies to be lean to compete successfully against other global manufacturers.[2]

The job market has become so competitive that even some students from top-tier universities struggle to secure a job at a large corporation. The rude awakening of the job market causes some young people to refer to present-day Korea as *Hell Joseon*. This term essentially rejects the aspects of Korean society that makes it difficult for some young people to find opportunity and happiness, such as the competition, the financial sacrifice, the unfulfilled promise of education as a panacea for financial success, and the high youth unemployment.

Korean families, as well as children, pay a very high price for academic achievement in an extremely competitive environment. Families make economic sacrifices and students endure a stressful environment, as the aforementioned survey results show. This high-stress environment, in turn, may contribute to an unusually high suicide rate among youth aged 9-24.

The Domino Effect of the High Cost of Private Education

As stated earlier, families spend as much as one-quarter of their family income on private education for their children. Other families dip into family savings and even borrow money. The high-profile role of education in Korean culture, and the large sums of money spent by parents on private tutoring makes education intertwined with the Korean economy to an unusual extent. Even though some young people view education as an unfulfilled promise, as evidenced by the epithet *Hell Joseon*, and given the difficulty students encounter in securing a position at large corporations, the predictable pursuit for a bachelor's degree, and the extended university stays has kept some smaller third-tier universities afloat.

The high cost of real estate as well as the high cost of private education discourages many young couples from having children. Consequently, Korea is experiencing a persistent low fertility rate that began before the turn of the century. This rate, in turn, generates fewer children per generation and thus, lower enrollments in second and third-tier universities. Some of these institutions gravitate toward the recruitment of international students to fill empty seats and to receive government funding. Although effective as a stop-gap measure, this strategy seems to create other significant, unforeseen academic challenges. There is now a need for universities to provide international students with additional time and support to acquire the Korean language in order to function in an academic environment. The economic challenge of low university enrollments is a direct byproduct of low fertility rates. Low fertility rates continue to decline. As a result, the government has no choice but to consider some of the less-successful, smaller public universities as potential targets for closure.

Lifelong Impact of Test Preparation Strategies

The reliance on test results for the sake of theoretical fairness and efficiency underscores the cutthroat and competitive aspect of the Korean culture. Both conglomerates and universities rely almost exclusively upon test results to make what would be life-changing offers. This overemphasis on testing fuels a costly, universally-utilized private education industry in Korea. Privately-funded education providers, specifically those that specialize in test preparation, rely primarily on strategies that focus exclusively on short-term memory gains. Rote memorization, repetition, and test practice are practiced at the expense of creativity, independent thinking, and self-expression.

The efficiency strategies learned for problem solving in a test preparation environment seem to carry over to everyday life. A heightened emphasis on efficiency reveals the general public's inability to successfully identify and solve the systemic and recurring root cause/s of accidents, in general. Both man-made and industrial accidents, therefore, are usually resolved in an efficient manner with little regard to systemic issues. To expediently return to business as usual, corporations and government entities fail to address or acknowledge contributing fundamental factors to these problematic accidents when the issues first surface. Eventually, they address these vital systemic concerns after a pattern develops and officials are under pressure from the public. In the meantime, innocent lives are lost unnecessarily.

Accidents

It goes without saying that accidents happen even in the most highly advanced societies. However, Korea has had more than its fair share of tragic accidents. When "accidents" occur frequently, one must consider to what extent they are true "accidents," and not a result of cultural imperatives. The point here is not that accidents occur only in Korea, but that recurring behavioral patterns, including those of the general public, have contributed enormously to some of these accidents. These behavioral patterns appear to be deeply rooted in societal attitudes.

To their credit, when major accidents do occur, Koreans demonstrate their resiliency and ability to rally behind a national cause. As a nation, they steadfastly face difficult situations, such as the *Sewol* ferry tragedy and the Jecheon hospital fire. In these and other instances, the government has mobilized resources to assist the victims and their families. In addition to the plaintiffs who filed a lawsuit seeking damages from the government and Cheonghaejin Marine in relation to the *Sewol* ferry disaster, some newspaper reporters and editors insist that there were missteps in the rescue operation of the *Sewol*.[3] Even so, the fact remains that the rescue operation for the *Sewol* appears to be significantly more palpable than for the *Sohae* two decades earlier. This is an indication that some progress is being made in terms of rescue-

and-recovery operations. Needless to say, this progress in the nation's rescue-and-recovery operations is of little consolation to the families of the 304 victims of the *Sewol* ferry tragedy.

I discussed earlier the concrete components of the post-accident knee-jerk reaction by the general public following the initial shock and period of mourning. Suffice it to say that to a Western observer, like myself, who subscribes to a Western moral human imperative of individual safety which promotes life under any circumstance and rejects unnecessary death for any reason, including for the good of the country, the Korean public must more closely examine the root causes of these accidents. If the end goal for Korea is to avoid a repeat of those incidents, it seems that the public's post-accident reaction misses a demand for an analysis of the role that societal attitudes play, an acknowledgment of the complicity of the public, and a concrete plan to avoid similar accidents in the future.

What seems to be lacking, once the investigation is complete, is the implementation of fundamental and sustainable attitudinal changes. These fundamental changes would include the adoption of stiff penalties for lawbreakers, a commitment by the general public to internalize the rationale behind public safety regulations and abiding by existing or newly adopted safety statutes in order to avoid or minimize the probability of repeating similar accidents. I am not saying that a heart-felt apology to society at large, and particularly to the victims' families as well as prosecution of wrongdoers are not important; they are. What I suggest is that profound fundamental attitudinal changes are required for

Korean society if Koreans do decide that individual human lives are more valuable than general economic gain. If wrongdoers are prosecuted and punished, but a flawed system that allows for the public's complicity driven by shortsightedness and an emphasis on cutting corners for the sake of convenience or short-term financial gains remain in place, the probability is high that further infractions, and consequently future individual accidents, will occur. Put another way, Korean society emphasizes quick and easy fixes for the sake of getting back to business as usual. These fixes only underscore the society's emphasis on efficiency instead of systemic analysis of the contributing factors behind these incidents, which an appreciation of individual human life requires. It is no wonder that some Koreans are asking publicly: Haven't we learned from all these accidents?

The repeating patterns and similarities in the accidents identified in this book should come as no surprise to Koreans. News outlets have published a number of opinion articles following major events comparing the conditions and identifying the similarities between the latest incident and any number of previous accidents. The frustration, impatience, anger, despair and a sense of impotence in view of the repeat patterns come through these articles loud and clear. Yet in the end, the authors and editors manage to muster a ray of hope that things can change provided that the general public's attitude changes. It is important to note that Korea's psyche was understandably affected after the sinking of the *Sewol* ferry, not only because of the tragedy but because a string of deadly accidents followed in the same year. The two quotes below from opinion articles illustrate my point.

The following excerpt is from an opinion article published following a string of accidents after the *Sewol* ferry tragedy and a fire at Hyosarang Hospital on May 28, 2014, comparing it to another hospital fire that happened four years before. The article also acts as a premonition of hospital accidents that have happened since the date the article was published:

> The latest hospital fire is reminiscent of a fire that blazed through an elderly nursing center in Pohang, North Gyeongsang Province, four years ago, when 10 people were killed mostly from smoke inhalation. It's pathetic that we learned nothing from that deadly incident…
>
> There is no denying a possible recurrence of similar calamities in them, given that hospitals and nursing homes for the elderly have mushroomed over the past decade in accordance with the country's rapid population aging.
>
> The recurring disasters are a reminder that there are no safe places in Korea, but that's why we should double efforts to try to ensure safety in public facilities.[4]

Finally, in the opinion article quoted below, the author briefly describes accidents that took place on May 2, May 26 and May 28, 2014 following the sinking of the *Sewol* ferry. He concludes:

Those [accident] cases reveal that nothing has changed since the Sewol tragedy. Our society is business as usual, as if the shipwreck never happened. We still stick to our old habits.[5]

Furthermore, the writer of the opinion piece reports that Kim Geo-sung, Chairperson of Transparency International Korea, who was present at a roundtable discussion organized by *The Korea Times*, said:

stressed that the nation should focus on long-term remedies to rebuild society by restoring values that respect human lives.[6]

Finally, the author concludes with a sober remark about the litany of accidents in the country and the need for societal change:

I am extremely sorry to say that Korea still has a long way to go before becoming a safe place to live. We have to take a first step, however small it may be, to break out of our old habits and change ourselves to cure the ills of our society.[7]

I am optimistic that Koreans eventually will take the necessary steps to raise the level of consciousness of the entire nation to advance public safety and human life to as prominent a level as, or higher than financial returns. It is part of the human evolution. The adoption of the "Kim Yong-kyun Bill" is a small step in the right direction. However, it is up to the Korean people to decide whether to honor "Hong-ik In-gan" [홍익인간], the unofficial motto of Korea and a founding principle of the nation, meaning "to broadly benefit humanity/devotion to human welfare"[8] or "to strive for the wellbeing of humankind."[9]

Consciousness Raising

Some Koreans, particularly academics, are beginning to point to the absence of a systemic approach to deal effectively with public safety. They also ask about approaches to confront Koreans' attitude regarding public safety, and the need to change it. As an example of this nascent consciousness-raising, an article titled "Safety Before Money – People have to change in order for the country/government to change" appearing in the *Seoul Times* on April 16, 2018, quotes Professor Kim Dae Gun, Public Administration Science at Gangwon University:

> Accident awareness and response have improved. However, the regulatory and systemic aspects have not kept pace with said progress. Legislators are very deliberate at passing new, stricter safety regulations. For Korea to evolve as a safe country, Koreans' awareness and attitude toward public safety need to evolve. Such a change among Koreans can influence legislators to pass the necessary safety and enforcement regulations. Safety enforcement through regulation will help to change the Korean people's behavior.[10]

It is encouraging to see this emerging consciousness-raising. I agree wholeheartedly with professor Kim Dae Gun's opinion that stricter safety regulations and enforcement policies need to be adopted and that the people's mindset vis-à-vis public safety must change. These changes are needed for Korea to evolve and claim its rightful place among the highly developed countries of the world, not just economically and technologically, but in the area of public safety as well. I recognize that stricter regulations and enforcement alone will not eliminate all future accidents. A populace fully cognizant of the rationale for, as well as the need to abide by safety regulations, must be part of the formula to reduce the number of accidents significantly.

Following the fire in Jecheon, an opinion article written by Lee Jae-min, Professor of Law at Seoul National University, underscores the need for people to change their attitude vis-à-vis yet another issue related to public safety. Professor Lee terms this disturbing public nuisance "random parking" or "liberal parking," which has been identified as a major obstacle for firefighting personnel when responding to fire emergencies. In some cases, illegal parking has been a contributor to fatalities in large structure fires. Therefore, although the topic of random or liberal parking may appear mundane to people from other developed countries, its impact on Korea's psyche cannot be underestimated:

> Belatedly, everyone now realizes just how dangerous a threat this problem [random or liberal parking] poses. We have learned that in the deadly blaze in Jecheon City in December [2017], 20-plus cars were lined up

along the alleys and passages, only to block the access of fire trucks and delay rescue operations. As what happened there may repeat itself elsewhere in major cities in the country, the public now perceives it as an important social safety issue.

In response, relevant laws have been recently amended to provide firefighters on the field with more discretion and authority in emergency situations: Illegally parked cars can be pushed out of the way, towed or even destroyed, when necessary, without... concern over associated liability and compensation problems. An appropriate amendment, indeed.

There are other regulatory changes that need to be done. Penalties should be made effective and more strictly enforced. Requirement for proof of parking space should be imposed on constructors of at least certain sizes of buildings and facilities. Perhaps, restaurants that do not have their own parking spaces should be required to show how they will handle their customers' cars before they run valet parking booths. Right now, [restaurant] owners make money because of increased customers, valet parking operators also make money if they park as many cars as possible, and customers benefit as well because they can forget about their cars after [they arrive] at a restaurant. The price for these gains and benefits is being paid by all of us.

Most importantly, the public attitude should change. Random parking or liberal parking, whatever you may call, is not an inevitable or condoned practice in Seoul. It has now become a serious social safety issue.[11]

Here, Lee identifies the relationship between the Korean love affair with personal convenience and short-term financial gains and the propensity for breaking the rules and inconveniencing their fellow Koreans to achieve their goals. Furthermore, Professor Lee's urgent call for social change provides a breath of fresh air in a country that has endured innumerable human tragedies resulting from the acceptance of sacrifice of a minority for the benefit of the majority, as well as from the suffocating insistence on perpetuating deeply-rooted behavior and refusing to accept change that will benefit most citizens. Articles such as the one cited above show that there are elements that are beginning to contribute to the consciousness-raising process of the masses. According to a code of ethics which values individual human lives, it behooves Korea to have individuals who demonstrate the courage to sensitize the general public about the importance of upholding safety standards and adhering to regulations even in areas as mundane as parking.

As stated earlier, following industrial accidents and other cases, the emphasis has been on punishing the person/s responsible instead of reviewing the incident from a systems perspective. By viewing the incident from the perspective of a systemic flaw, one might better determine where the system failed and where the system is vulnerable to compliance violations. The country may be able to implement lasting changes if review systems emphasize both prosecution of wrongdoers and correction of the system. Thus, these corrections will ensure that appropriate and current safety rules and stiff fines are in place and strictly enforced to discourage future violations. These measures would send a clear message to the general public about the primordial importance of public safety and zero tolerance for violators. Furthermore, they would go a long way toward discouraging individuals from continuing to fixate solely on convenience and efficiency for the sake of quick financial profits with little regard to public safety.

Is the Country Ready for Profound Change?

The government cannot legislate attitudinal change. The desire for change must come from the general public. Only the people can instigate meaningful strides toward adopting a culture that values public safety, recognizes the intent of, and supports the strict enforcement of safety regulations.

Ensuring public safety will require the implementation of a multi-prong strategic plan that includes at least four steps:

1. Promoting a paradigm shift on the part of the general public. Choosing to uphold public safety and recognize that an attitudinal change toward public safety is in everyone's best interest. Acknowledging that an emphasis on public safety will take time and come with a hefty price tag in the form of personal inconveniences

416

and higher prices for goods and services. Committing to balancing the quest for short-term financial gains while upholding public safety.

2. Undoing years of cost-cutting measures by inspecting existing buildings for questionable construction practices by reinforcing, retrofitting structures or addressing safety concerns and demolishing and rebuilding them when safety issues cannot be resolved any other way.

3. Ensuring that safety inspections are conducted in a thorough and timely manner by adequately trained individuals, making sure that safety regulations are current. Acknowledging that implementing detailed and honest reviews of processes and systems are costly and time-consuming, but in the long run, these reviews produce more sustainable and lasting results than the current finger-pointing and quick-fix solutions.

4. Conducting a thorough review of the contractor-subcontractor relationship and its impact on the economy as well as on public safety. Passing new and or updating existing laws to regulate contractor-subcontractor relationships to prevent the "outsourcing of dangers," retain control of and promote industrial risk management, and ensure the protection of irregular workers in the form of safety training and risk containment. Also, conducting a thorough analysis of the impact of the Occupational Safety and Health Act amendment, commonly referred to as the "Kim Yong-kyun Bill," in honor of the subcontractor employee who was killed at the KOWEPO Thermal Power Plant in Taean.

Implementing a cultural shift of this magnitude will not come quickly, easily or without financial repercussions. However, in the long run, the country will be better off. Korea may assume its place among the elite nations of the world, and more importantly, innocent lives will be spared.

Positive Signs

In spite of the litany of recent man-made and industrial accidents, some encouraging signs indicate that progress toward establishing a higher level of consciousness of individual suffering is taking place. Government officials, legislators, and the public appear to be taking significant steps towards procedures which reduce death tolls in accidents of any origin. Specifically, as a result of public pressure, government officials and legislators are taking tougher measures and adopting legislation that protects the rights of contingent labor and upholds public safety. For example, the Seoul metropolitan government adopted the amendment to the Framework Act on Fire-Fighting Services. The amendment, which went into effect on June 27, 2018, and was implemented on August 10, 2018, gives authority to local police and fire departments to deal more proactively and decisively with violators by increasing fines and enabling fire departments to act more resolutely in firefighting situations.

The December 27, 2018 passage of the amendment to the Occupational Safety and Health Act, also known as the "Kim Yong-kyun Bill," is yet another example of the forward movement in legislating the protection of contingent labor and upholding general public safety.

Furthermore, government officials appear to be taking collective public safety more seriously. Unlike the actions surrounding the June 1995 Sampoong Department Store building collapse, which were driven by corruption and greed, on December 12, 2018, the Gangnam District Office had the courage to order the evacuation and closure of the 15-story Daejong Building due to reports that the building had shown signs of "structural defects."[12]

Goal Setting with Measurable Achievables

In January 2018, the former Deputy Prime Minister for Economic Affairs, Kim Dong Yeon, announced his plan for economic and technological development. This plan contained concrete goals with measurable achievables. These goals included a 3% GDP annual growth and $32,000 GNI per capita. Additionally, he proposed the implementation of an autonomous bus system in Seoul by 2020 and the utilization of 3,700 drones in public services, including mail delivery, police services, and firefighting by 2021.[13] Even though these goals may not be applicable anymore because the Deputy Prime Minister for Economic Affairs has since been replaced, by making these targets public at the time, the government made them official national goals. By doing so, they enlisted the participation of the general public.

By contrast, safety-related government pronouncements appear to be somewhat general in nature and lack concrete metrics. The language generally includes: "We want to make Korea a safe place," or, "We want to ensure that these accidents do not happen again," or, "we will ensure that safety regulations are obeyed." It is unclear what the definition of "safe" is for the Korean government. Does safety mean 10%, 15%, or 20% fewer accidents per year? Or one less accident per year? How are government officials going to ensure that the public obeys safety regulations? Are strict and stiff fines for violators going to be imposed? Are existing penalties going to be enforced? Are current sanctions going to be increased so that they truly become a deterrent for would-be violators? In summary, it is unclear how these lofty, general goals will be achieved or what steps will be taken to ensure that these objectives are met. As opposed to the economic goals Kim Dong Yeon referred to, specific, concrete metrics have not been presented for public safety goals to ensure that the success or failure of the public safety goals can be measured.

The difference between the specific economic goals stated by the former Deputy Prime Minister for Economic Affairs, Kim Dong Yeon, and the lofty, general goals pertaining to public safety expressed by public officials after man-made or industrial accidents is striking. When objective criteria or concrete metrics are stated, government officials, executive officials at large corporations and small company owners can be held accountable for reaching or failing to reach the stated goals. If the goals are not met, individuals in leadership positions will be compelled to explain why the goals were not achieved.

However, when vague goals are established without concrete metrics and without stipulating who will be responsible for meeting them, it is challenging to hold anyone accountable for them. In the latter case, the vague goals become empty promises. These promises might either save face, appease a nation or both. In the case of shoddy construction that is prone to accidents or the rapid spread of fire, and buildings that do not meet safety regulations, would it not make sense to be transparent and tell the public, for example, how many buildings will be inspected each year to determine whether they meet safety standards? Moreover, once those inspections are done, wouldn't it make sense to be transparent and share with the public what percentage of the buildings fail to meet safety standards? How many of those buildings must be demolished and rebuilt following strict safety regulations? Wouldn't it make sense to be transparent and publish the number of building owners who were fined, and for how much money, because they were found in violation of safety regulations, such as remodeling a part of the building without obtaining the proper approval or permits, failing to procure the appropriate building inspection, allowing the blocking of emergency exits, allowing illegal parking that blocks access by emergency equipment, or illegally deactivating fire sprinkler systems? If these solutions do not make sense for reasons of national security or otherwise, they might be explicitly stated, as well.

Changing social paradigms that are deeply rooted in the fabric of a nation and undoing years of building construction that fails to meet safety standards will take time and money. However, the effort and financial investment in this regard will demonstrate a serious commitment to public safety. It will signal a new era for Korea, one where everyone, including government, corporation and small company officials as well as the general public will have to sacrifice some short-term financial gains in exchange for public safety.

Action Speaks Louder than Words

Public safety must be one of the core values of major corporations which provide services or make products that touch the lives of many people. Regardless of industry, these corporations influence every sector of business from pharmaceutical companies to airlines, power plants, and railroads. However, it is not enough for corporations to adopt lofty core values that emphasize public safety if they do not back their words with actions and sufficient funding. Corporations can quickly lose the public's trust if they place efficiency or financial profits over public safety. More importantly, putting lives of people at risk, whether they be customers, patients, passengers, or workers, for the sake of efficiency or financial profits, is unconscionable.

Korail, the state-owned national rail operator has adopted safety as a component of one of its core values. At the time of this writing, these values are expressed on the official Korail website as follows: "Core Values: Safety First, Customer Satisfaction, Change and Challenge…We prioritize safety over work performance.[14]

However, the public has questioned the company's commitment to safety. Despite this commitment, a significant number of accidents associated with trains, particularly high-speed KTX trains, and subways have happened. For a period of three weeks in November and December of 2018, a total of 10 accidents occurred culminating with the derailment of the Seoul-bound KTX from Gangneung.[15] These accidents left 15 people injured. Reports indicate that the high-speed train was traveling at 103 kilometers per hour. Reportedly, experts expressed concerns that the derailment could have "caused serious casualties."[16] These casualties would have occurred had the train been traveling faster or if it had been "moving through a curved section."[17] *The Korea Times* reported that "according to Korail records, there [were] more than 660 mechanical failures on its trains between 2013 and July [2018]."[18]

Train accidents represent more than mechanical failures. Reportedly, these accidents also reflect a reduction in Korail's maintenance budget. According to *The Korea Times*:

> Despite the increasing number of train failures each year, Korail cut its hiring budget for rail maintenance and repair workers by around 10 billion won ($8.9 million) from 2015 to 2017. Its records show it operated with 205 fewer repair personnel than recommended to keep almost 10,000 kilometers of railroad in working condition.

> The spending cuts, at the risk of passenger safety, are expected to continue. Korail recorded an operating loss of more than 500 billion won [~$445.1 million] [in 2017].[19]

Three factors regarding the number of increasing mechanical failures and the subsequent operating losses have reportedly forced Korail to significantly reduce its maintenance budget: First, based on the number of mechanical failures, it appears that Korail has failed to live up to its public commitment to safety, which it claims on its website. Second, the public has raised questions about political appointments to key positions at Korail and other public corporations. The media has questioned whether the leadership appointed to run the company is equipped with the necessary experience and expertise in rail safety. Specifically, an opinion article appearing in *The Korea Times* on December 14, 2018 explicitly questions the appointments of non-experts to highly sensitive positions dealing with public safety. The article cites as an example the resignation under fire of the former Korail CEO, Oh Young-sik, who "offered to resign after a strong backlash against his lack of expertise in trains and public transportation."[20] Furthermore, the article goes on to strongly criticize other appointments to posts linked to public safety:

It seems hardly a day goes by without a safety-related problem. President Moon Jae-in has often mentioned the Sewol ferry sinking to highlight his emphasis on public safety. But even after all the controversy over the appointment of the former Korail leader, Moon appointed another non-expert to lead the Korea Airport Corporation this week.

The latest series of accidents, coupled with incomprehensible appointments to public corporations that are closely linked to people's lives, lead many to believe that this administration is not very serious about doing things better than its predecessors to ensure public safety.[21]

Third, given the company's mechanical failure record and its massive operating losses, is it time for the government to acknowledge that the current business model is not working? Is it time to try something different? Insanity, as per Einstein and others, is doing the same thing over and over and expecting a different outcome. If government leaders truly want different results from Korail, they need the fortitude to do something different and try something new.

A New Paradigm

Some Koreans would argue in favor of being faithful to the formula that brought the country from the poverty level at the end of the Korean War to having a guaranteed seat among the G-20 nations. That formula, they will argue, includes an emphasis on efficiency and short-term financial gains. However, the country's economic and technological advancements have placed the nation at a very different level, one based on a rock-solid foundation, which enables the citizenry to forge the country's future and take advantage of forward momentum rather than fearing the loss of ground to competing countries. This privileged position has gained Korea the respect and admiration of friends and foes alike. The time has come for policymakers, business leaders, and most importantly the general public, to establish a new paradigm that includes a focus on long-range goals with measurable objectives at designated intervals, a citizenry with a mindset that understands the rationale behind safety regulations and balances short-term financial gains with public safety, government leaders with the necessary stamina to pass stringent safety regulations and the fortitude to enforce them rigorously, and business leaders and policymakers willing to play a proactive role in public safety with a willingness to work with academicians and others to analyze public safety matters using a systemic approach.

Korea's Public Face

Anyone who watched the opening ceremony of the PyeongChang 2018 Winter Olympics witnessed a carefully choreographed and technologically-saturated event which included the use of over 1,200 drones and lots of beautiful faces, some probably artificially chiseled, except for the children who were naturally beautiful as most children are. This event served to showcase to the world a polished image of Korea with historical and symbolic overtones. Without a doubt, all countries that host these types of events do their utmost to present a polished image to the world. Therefore, Korea is no exception. However, I wonder if Koreans who have been touched by any one of the recent tragedies, and even Koreans in general, as proud as they are and should be about their country's economic and technological advancements, could identify with the glossy image of Korea presented to the world during the opening ceremony? An informal and non-scientific survey of some of my Korean friends tells me that as proud as many Koreans felt about hosting the 2018 Winter Olympics, some in fact did not identify with the opening ceremony. This exercise in public relations is no different from the habit that Koreans have at the micro-level of checking their image on publicly located mirrors, be it in an elevator or a building lobby, to ensure that they look their best to the world, their skin is glowing, and every hair is in place, whether or not it reflects actuality.

Behind the Public Façade, the Perfect Storm

Unsurprisingly, the country's stellar economic and technological trajectory has been accompanied by growing pains, challenges and tragic catastrophes. Other developed or developing countries that have matured from an agrarian stage, through the Industrial Revolution, and eventually through to the Information Age, have also encountered similar growing pains. One such challenge for Korea was what became known as the IMF crisis (ca. 1997~2001) during which the country rallied to overcome an economic crisis by accepting harsh austerity measures, liberalizing its trade, restructuring its corporate governance and paying off a historically unprecedented IMF bailout loan three years earlier than expected. Today, even though the Korean economy ranks as the 12th largest in the world, according to the IMF and The World Bank, the country is facing some tough macroeconomic challenges. Some might even say that these challenges may be signaling the ripe conditions for a perfect storm, looming on the horizon. Some of these challenges include the following:

- » a long-standing low-fertility rate
- » limited immigration which fails to offset the economic impact of a low-fertility rate
- » an increasingly aging population that requires additional spending on social services
- » a widening of the gap between the haves and have-nots
- » real estate market prices that have gone through the roof fueled by pervasively low-interest rates, which may promote speculative investments in real estate, particularly in big cities like Seoul and Busan, and make other investments less attractive
- » a high rate of self-employed which makes up a high percentage of the economically active population
- » a high bankruptcy rate of small mom-and-pop businesses
- » record high youth unemployment
- » a high rate of "intentional harm" as the primary cause of death among youth 9-24 years of age.

It is true that several capitalist economies, including the United States, are experiencing similar conditions such as a persistently low fertility rate, an increasing aging population, a widening of the gap between the haves and have-nots, high real estate prices, and low-interest rates. However, some of prevailing conditions, including a high rate of self-employed, do not exist in the U.S. and other developed countries. Another advantage in countries like the U.S. is that historically, immigration has offset the economic impact of a low-fertility rate. The fertility rate as measured by total births per woman in the U.S. was less than 2.0 from 1973 through 1988 and again from 2010 through 2017.[22] Other countries besides Korea, like Japan, have faced or are facing similar conditions caused by comparable circumstances, including a low fertility rate, a growing aging population, limited immigration which fails to counterbalance the economic impact of a persistently low fertility rate, and skyrocketing real estate prices. However, Korea also has some unique cultural aspects that may be exacerbating the perfect storm outlook.

Several reasons lead Young Lee and I to believe that Korea's potential perfect storm forecast may be more pronounced than in other capitalist countries. Some of the differences between Korea and other capitalist countries appear to be culturally driven, such as immigration policies. Korea makes immigration difficult and that is one of the reasons why the nation has remained homogenous. As aforementioned, other capitalist countries, like the U.S., have been historically more open to immigration, which has helped to counterbalance the economic impact of a low-fertility rate. Young Lee and I are not suggesting that liberalizing immigration is the answer for Korea, for it may exacerbate not only the high youth unemployment rate, but unemployment in general.

The proliferation and high cost of private education is yet another condition which is particularly pronounced in Korea. This condition contributes to parents' relatively limited retirement savings. Because of the unique emphasis on private education and the persistently low-interest rates, their investment is usually concentrated on home ownership. Consequently, if real estate prices decrease significantly, the impact on the parents' net worth will be much more severe. Also, cost efficiency, a high degree of competition in the job market, and limited jobs all make it possible for employers to push Koreans into "retirement" from their mid-40s-50s. These forced "retirees" have very few options outside of becoming entrepreneurs and self-employed often without much training in entrepreneurship and business management. As mentioned earlier, at 26%, Korea has one of the highest percentages of small business owners among developed nations. This is very different from other capitalist countries where the percentage of small business ownership hovers below 12% of the economically active population and often stays in the single digits. The brutal competition among small businesses also causes a high bankruptcy rate. Given Korea's relatively small economy compared to other capitalist countries, a high bankruptcy rate in this segment of business and industry has a more sizable impact on the economy.

Directly related to the problem of high youth unemployment are two factors: First, the democratization of higher education has caused an enormous degree inflation challenge by graduating more young people with a bachelor's degree on an annual basis than the economy can absorb. The degree inflation, however, extends beyond the baccalaureates. The competitive environment in the job market has prompted individuals wishing to gain an edge in the job market to pursue post graduate degrees in higher numbers than the economy needs. These actions have exacerbated the overwhelming degree inflation challenge, and they have propelled the competition for jobs to an even higher level. Second, the economic imbalance caused by the concentration of wealth and resources in the conglomerates or *chaebols* has also contributed to high youth unemployment. When the economy slows down, the major corporations, as well as mid-sized companies, naturally cut back on their hiring. It follows that any hikes in unemployment are applied demographically and youth employment tends to be the first to be impacted.

The pervasively low interest rates present yet other potential macroeconomic problems, aside from the general public's tendency to look for risky investments that generate higher returns. One such option is real estate. Rampant speculative investments often cause real estate ownership to become difficult to afford for a large portion of the population and can end badly by creating economic bubbles and hurting investors as well as hurting the overall economy. Typically, ultra-low interest rates also may contribute to capital flight. However, any changes in interest rates need to be approached cautiously, keeping in mind the possible negative impact on the already high bankruptcy rate of small mom-and-pop businesses that may have outstanding loans. Consideration also needs to be given to the potential adverse effects on existing mortgages which may have been generated by a speculative frenzy and by families willing to sacrifice everything, even to borrow money, to afford their children the best possible private education.

For these reasons, Young Lee and I feel that Korea has a more concentrated flavor of capitalism, and therefore, a more challenging perfect storm may be looming in the horizon than other developed nations under similar circumstances. The economic adversities appear more daunting given the unique cultural factors. These challenges combined may be signaling the perfect storm for the Korean government and business leaders, as well as the public, to face together. However, it is essential to recognize that these issues will require long-term rather than the short-term solutions that the general population has historically favored and tolerated. The emphasis on efficiency that permeates throughout the culture, which is reinforced through a private education that focuses on test preparation, may be prompting some people to pin the blame for the present state of affairs on the current administration. This reaction is not much different from the general public's attitude in the aftermath of a major accident which seeks to find a scapegoat, identify the key culprits as well as the persons in charge; punish them and get back to business as usual as soon as possible.

Some people are becoming impatient with the current administration's tendency to propose what is viewed as short-term, Band-Aid solutions to systemic challenges. Short-term solutions gloss over the fact that many of these problems have been developing for many years, even before the current administration took office. Societal attitudes fueled these problems and behavioral patterns that reflect the competitive nature of the nation and the emphasis on efficiency.

Happiness Indicators

It is most interesting to note that while South Korea has become more prosperous as a country in terms of GDP and GNI per capita, and Korean people seem to be placing a higher emphasis on materialism, efficiency, and short-term financial gains, Korea's ranking in the *World Happiness Report* dropped significantly from 41st in 2012 to 57th in 2017. Then in 2018, it increased slightly to 54th out of 156 countries reporting.

According to the report: "The overall rankings of country happiness are based on the pooled results from Gallup World Poll surveys from 2015-2017, and show both change and stability."[23] The survey results are organized by country. Therefore, the comparison of Korea's happiness ranking from 2012 to 2017 and 2018 provides an indication of how Koreans themselves view their level of happiness based on the survey results from those two years. In other words, based on the drop in the rankings, the survey results tell us that Koreans feel that they were less happy in 2017 and 2018 than they were in 2012.

The 2017 report identifies the six variables that support well-being. They are as follows:

> GDP per capita, healthy years of life expectancy, social support (as measured by having someone to count on in times of trouble), trust (as measured by a perceived absence of corruption in government and business), perceived freedom to make life decisions,

and generosity (as measured by recent donations). The top ten countries rank highly on all six of these factors.[24]

Since Korea is doing so well in so many areas, yet their happiness level decreased from 2012 to 2017, two of the variables deserve some attention: trust, as measured by a perceived absence of corruption in government and business, and GNI per capita, formerly referred to as GDP per capita.

Regarding trust as measured by a perceived absence of corruption in government and business, this particular measure of happiness should provide food for thought and reflection for politicians, business leaders and the general public, particularly in view of the country's recent history at the top level of government. It is up to the entire Korean nation to determine whether the country has the fortitude to eradicate this cancer or continue to live with it.

Focusing on GNI per capita, Korea seems to be doing well based on the latest government statistics. However, what is the quality of the growth achieved? The *World Happiness Report 2017* cited above underscores the importance of emphasizing both happiness and GNI per capita. The head of the UN Development Program is quoted in the report as speaking against what she referred to as "the tyranny of GDP", instead:

> …arguing that what matters is the quality of growth[:] 'Paying more attention to happiness should be part

of our efforts to achieve both human and sustainable development.'[25]

The *World Happiness Report* ranking is extremely significant and should be taken seriously because human beings by nature strive to be happy. Furthermore, happiness is a metric that can be used to determine human progress. The Korean people's pursuit of happiness is reflected in their actions and their culture. For instance, parents want their children to be happy, so they do everything in their power to ensure their children receive the best education possible. They know that doing so will increase their children's chances of success in a competitive environment. If successful, their children will afford their own children the best education possible. They too will be happy, and the cycle will repeat. However, when the old formula to success and happiness becomes less and less reliable despite the sacrifices and effort put forth by parents and children alike, it follows that people will express a lower level of happiness.

Sustainable Development Solutions Network has published the report annually since 2012. According to the 2017 iteration of the report:

> [It was published]…in support of the UN High Level Meeting on happiness and well-being. Since then we have come a long way. Happiness is increasingly considered the proper measure of social progress and the goal of public policy.[26]

So, I ask: Is happiness one of the goals of public policy in Korea?

This substantial drop by Korea in the *World Happiness Report* rankings appears to coincide with another potential happiness indicator that I have discussed in this book and which seems to be a sign of distress: the use of the term *Hell Joseon* by disenchanted and possibly disenfranchised young people. As discussed earlier, this seems to be their way of expressing their apparent rejection of the current state of affairs, including high youth unemployment, as well as the competitive nature of Korean society in general, and the unmet promise of the traditional, well-established path to "success," which includes a high dose of costly private education and sacrifice. This unhappiness among millennials about the state of affairs seems to be a call for change. Some may argue that this condition only applies to a small subset of the Korean population; however, in a free society, societal change often originates not with the masses behind a cause, but with a cadre of citizens who voice their discontent with an injustice caused by a societal condition. Their voices then sensitize others who are also impacted or who may sympathize with the cause, and finally the voices grow louder and the larger society pays heed to the calls for change.

Another segment of the population that appears to be negatively impacted by the nation's extremely competitive economic environment is composed of individuals who are part of the workforce but who are compelled to retire early from their mid-40s-50s. They are particularly financially vulnerable if they are parents and had to dip into their retirement savings to afford costly private education and university tuition for their children. At that age, they are still productive citizens with family obligations; however, society is forcing them out of the workforce. Therefore, if they wish to remain productive, self-sufficient citizens, they have no choice but to take an economic risk by joining the self-employed ranks with little to no training in business management. Even though this segment of the population is not using the term *Hell Joseon*, the stress level of their situation is understandable.

Korea's ranking descent in the *World Happiness Report* appears to triangulate with the country's relatively high suicide rate. According to the World Health Rankings, based on 2017 World Health Organization data, the 16,078 suicide deaths in Korea represented 6.56% of total deaths: "The age adjusted Death Rate is 24.21 per 100,000 of population ranks South Korea #10 in the world."[27] These two indicators, as well as the high rate of intentional harm which has been identified as the primary cause of death among youth 9-24 years of age, and the dissatisfaction with Korea's current conditions as expressed by youth through the *Hell Joseon* reference, should raise a red flag among policymakers and the public in general.[28] These factors, amongst others, are far from trivial, particularly for a country that has the 4th largest economy in Asia and the 12th largest economy in the world. Is this the price the people have to pay for achieving economic success? Do the ends justify the means? At what point does the balance tip to the side of being humane and genuinely caring for one another as fellow human beings, versus being efficient for the sake of achieving economic prosperity that falls short of achieving true happiness?

Given Korea's stellar trajectory since the end of the Korean War, it would not be surprising to find that people from other countries, such as China and Vietnam, may be looking to Korea as a model to follow in pursuit of economic and technological success. One cannot underestimate the power of movies, television, and the media. As we have seen, nowadays, Korea is exporting its modern, high-tech culture through the glossy images, finely sculpted faces, and extravagant glamour in soap operas, movies, K-Pop, and worldwide sports events. Before embarking on a similar path, it would behoove other developing countries that wish to emulate Korea to consider the price Koreans, adults as well as children, have had to pay in the process of achieving economic and technological accomplishments on the international stage. In the 1950s, 1960s, and 1970s, while Korea was recovering from the ravages of the Korean War, Japan was playing a leading role economically and technologically among Asian countries. Now, it is Korea's turn. The country that replaces Korea in this enviable position would benefit greatly from studying not only the successes but also the areas where Korea has fallen short of the mark. Equally important would be an examination of the culturally as well as capitalist-driven behavioral trends that propelled the country's success, such as the emphasis on efficiency and short-term financial gains at all costs: even public safety.

Endnotes

1   "GDP Growth (annual %) – Korea, rep.," The World Bank, accessed 22 June 2019, *data.worldbank.org.*

2   "Irregular Workers," trans. Young Lee, *Wikipedia.com*, accessed 23 October 2019, *ko.wikipedia.org.*

3   Park Yoon-Bae, "Old Habits Die Hard," *The Korea Times*, 4 June 2014, *koreatimes.co.kr.*

4   "Recurring Disasters," *The Korea Times*, accessed 1 September 2019, *koreatimes.co.kr.*

5   Park Yoon-Bae, "Old Habits."

6   Ibid.

7   Ibid.

8   "Hongik Ingan," *Wikipedia*, accessed 1 September 2019, *Wikipedia.com.*

9   Robert W. Compton, *Transforming East Asian Domestic and International Politics: The Impact of Economy and Globalization*, New York: Ashgate Publishing, 2012, p. 109.

10   Lee Jung-Soo, "Safety before money – People have to change in order for the country/government to change," *The Seoul Times*, trans. Young Lee, 16 April 2018, *theseoultimes.com.*

11   Lee Jae-Min, "Liberal Parking Not Condoned Practice," *The Korea Herald*, accessed 23 October 2019, *koreaherald.com.*

12   The District Office ordered an emergency safety inspection of the structure and "determined that the building's safety was at level E, the lowest in its safety measuring index." "Incessant Safety Failures," *The Korea Times*, accessed 31 March 2019, *koreatimes.co.kr.*

13   "Korean Government Policy Briefing for 4th Industrial

Revolution and Innovative Growth," *Naver*, trans. Young Lee, 24 January 2018, *n.news.naver.com*.

14   "Mission and Vision," *Korail*, accessed 23 October 2019, *info.korail.com*.

15   Lee Suh-Yoon, "Korail Under Fire After Yet Another Accident," *The Korea Times*, accessed 23 October 2019, *koreatimes.co.kr*.

16   Ibid.

17   Ibid.

18   Ibid.

19   Ibid.

20   "Incessant Safety Failures."

21   Ibid.

22   "Fertility Rate, Total (births per woman)," *The World Bank*, accessed 23 October 2019, *data.worldbank.org*.

23   J. Helliwell, R. Layard, & J. Sachs, *World Happiness Report 2018*, New York: Sustainable Development Solutions Network, 2018.

24   J. Helliwell, R. Layard, & J. Sachs, *World Happiness Report 2017*, New York: Sustainable Development Solutions Network, 2017.

25   Ibid.

26   Ibid.

27   "South Korea: Suicide," *World Health Rankings*, accessed 23 October 2019, *worldlifeexpectancy.com*.

28   Ibid.

Acknowledgments

It is a pleasure to acknowledge the dedication, support, and expertise of our editor, Marguerite Happe. Her incisive questions, keen observations, and insightful comments contributed enormously to the final product.

Made in the USA
San Bernardino, CA
03 February 2020

63712391R00246